Economy and Ritual

Max Planck Studies in Anthropology and Economy
Series editors:
Stephen Gudeman, *University of Minnesota*
Chris Hann, *Max Planck Institute for Social Anthropology (Halle)*

Definitions of economy and society, and their proper relationship to each other, have been the perennial concerns of social philosophers. In the early decades of the twenty-first century these became and remain matters of urgent political debate. At the forefront of this series are the approaches to these connections by anthropologists, whose explorations of the local ideas and institutions underpinning social and economic relations illuminate large fields ignored in other disciplines.

Volume 1
Economy and Ritual:
Studies of Postsocialist Transformations
Edited by Stephen Gudeman and Chris Hann

Volume 2
Oikos and Market:
Explorations in Self-Sufficiency after Socialism
Edited by Stephen Gudeman and Chris Hann

Volume 3
When Things Become Property:
Land Reform, Authority and Value in Postsocialist Europe and Asia
Edited by Thomas Sikor, Stefan Dorondel, Johannes Stahl and Phuc Xuan To

Economy and Ritual

Studies of Postsocialist Transformations

Edited by

STEPHEN GUDEMAN AND CHRIS HANN

berghahn
NEW YORK · OXFORD
www.berghahnbooks.com

First edition published in 2015 by
Berghahn Books
www.berghahnbooks.com

Library of Congress Cataloging-in-Publication Data

Economy and ritual : studies of postsocialist transformations / edited by Stephen
Gudeman and Chris Hann.
    pages cm. — (Max Planck studies in anthropology and economy ; volume 1)
    Includes bibliographical references and index.
    ISBN 978-1-78238-569-1 (hardback) — ISBN 978-1-78533-519-8 (paperback) —
ISBN 978-1-78238-570-7 (ebook)
    1. Economic anthropology—Europe, Eastern—Case studies. 2. Economic
anthropology—Former Soviet republics—Case studies. 3. Rites and ceremonies—
Economic aspects—Europe, Eastern—Case studies. 4. Rites and ceremonies—
Economic aspects—Former Soviet republics—Case studies. 5. Post-communism—
Social aspects—Europe, Eastern—Case studies. 6. Post-communism—Social
aspects—Former Soviet republics—Case studies. 7. Europe, Eastern—Social life and
customs—Case studies. 8. Former Soviet republics—Social life and customs—Case
studies. I. Gudeman, Stephen, editor of compilation. II. Hann, C. M., 1953– editor of
compilation.
    GN585.E852E46 2015
    306.3—dc23
                                                                    2014033538

British Library Cataloguing in Publication Data

A catalogue record for this book is available from the British Library

ISBN: 978-1-78238-569-1 hardback
ISBN 978-1-78533-519-8 paperback
ISBN: 978-1-78238-570-7 ebook

Contents

Illustrations

Acknowledgments

This book is the product of a postdoctoral research group which we led between 2009 and 2012 at the Max Planck Institute for Social Anthropology. We are grateful to numerous visitors to Halle during this period. Comments and suggestions from Aliki Angelidou, James Carrier, Gerald Creed, and Mihály Sárkány have been particularly helpful. Ildikó Bellér-Hann and Roxane Gudeman accompanied the project in myriad ways, forcing us to rethink the concept of the academic house economy. We are particularly indebted to Anke Meyer for her organizational assistance in every phase of our work, and for her expert assistance in preparing the final manuscript.

Map of Field Sites for Economy and Ritual Group
Source: Max Planck Institute for Social Anthropology Halle/Saale, Germany.
Cartography: Jutta Turner.
Base maps: http://www.lib.utexas.edu/maps/europe/easterneurope.jpg; http://www.lib.utexas.edu/maps/commonwealth/kyrgyzstan_pol_05.jpg; accessed 19 April 2012.

Introduction

Ritual, Economy, and the Institutions of the Base

Stephen Gudeman and Chris Hann

From pig-sticking to displaying barrels of wine, from large private weddings to modest community festivities, and from helping kin dry tobacco leaves to offering a sheep's head in honor of a senior male, the rituals explored in this volume all have to do with economy. This is our puzzle and theme. What is the connection of economy and ritual, and what does it tell us about the changing postsocialist regions in which the members of our group worked?

The Economy and Ritual group consisted of six anthropologists who worked together at the Max Planck Institute for Social Anthropology in Halle, Germany, during 2009–2012. After developing the theoretical background and agreeing on the main contours of the comparative agenda, each researcher carried out an extended study in a different area. During this field research we convened in Macedonia to share initial findings and to finalize a common questionnaire. Later, the researchers returned to the Institute to write up their results. Some returned to the field again later to fill in gaps. The questionnaire we used and other details about the research are presented in the Appendix.

All six researchers held Ph.D.'s and had extensive knowledge of the change from socialist to market economies in one or more countries. Several opted to work in a country that they already knew well, either because it was their native country or because they had carried out research there previously. Some returned to a small community that was already well known to them. We emphasized rural situations (in the one exception, the Macedonian town of Prilep, the focus was on recent immigrants who maintained close links to the countryside) in order to take maximum advantage of anthropology's traditional strength in conducting holistic ethnography of established, "face to face" communities. Despite their experience and prior knowledge, none of the researchers had previously focused on ritual in relation to economy. We emphasized the need to keep in mind links to other settlements and the larger histories of regions and nations, not only the world-historical significance of socialism but also *longue durée* histories of political economy and of religion. However, our main focus was on the micro level—on house and community economy in relation to ritual. The results, as the reader will find, are not strictly comparable in a statistical, correlational sense. This was to be expected, given the great diversity in postsocialist conditions. The comparative process has led us to challenge any simple division between secular and religious rituals or between ritual and economy. The shift from socialism to market economy is not illuminated by the teleology of modernity and economic development.

Economy and Ritual Viewed Broadly

For most economists, ritual and economy have little to do with one another in the contemporary world. Economy is treated historically as a realm of struggle, of material production on which ritual actions are a drain, a cultural barrier to efficiency. Numerous modernization theorists since Max Weber tell us that the rise of instrumental thinking and bureaucracies overcome and eradicate ritualistic practices. According to evolutionary schemes in anthropology since Edward Tylor and James Frazer, magico-religious thought declines with the advance of technologies of production and storage. A Nobel laureate in economics has recently proclaimed that magic and religion are nonrational solutions to economic uncertainty, which in his opinion can only be reduced by changing the institutional framework of economy to make it more rational (North 2005: 15–18, 59). From the opposite direction, anthropologists have made significant advances in studies of ritual by considering it separately from instrumental practices: ritual, they suggest, is first and foremost *performative*; it does and says something, usually with the help of tangible objects, but disconnected from mundane economic concerns and causalities (Leach 2000). Given these perspectives, our question about the relation between economy and ritual is problematic if not anachronistic: it has been answered. With the onset of modernity, as epitomized by economic development, connections between ritual and economy are severed.

But with a moment's reflection we can see that the separation is incomplete. Most rituals require the deployment of some material resources, in some cases minimal but in others extremely costly. One might expect elements of an economizing attitude to enter into the planning and even the execution of the ritual (what is the minimum number of expensive fireworks that must be set off in order that the participants go home satisfied?). The relationship is no less complicated within the domain of economy. Much of our behavior as consumers is public and highly ritualized, e.g., when we watch sporting events in a stadium. If ritual is defined in terms of the cultural standardization of a habitual activity, then we engage in a simple secular ritual every time we pick up a knife and fork, quite irrespective of whether we have given the meal a religious meaning by the uttering of a grace. Clearly a great deal of production and distribution consists of highly routinized encounters between persons, and between persons and things. Perhaps some lucky individuals are able to cultivate a zen attitude and apply it to lend all their activities the quality of a ritual. An observer might insist on classifying them as exploited proletarians or *lumpen*-intelligentsia, but if a human being draws no subjective distinction between labor and "leisure," we might conclude that he or she has successfully ritualized both.

We conventionally use economy and ritual as ideal types, the former associated with the short-term maximization of utility and the latter with something deeper, the accumulated long-term values of a society (cf. Parry and Bloch 1989). In following these conventions, we must be alert not only to the multiple ways in which each type is modified empirically, but to changing causal links between the two in concrete situations. For example, students in business schools are not taught to eradicate everything that smacks of ritual from the production process of a capitalist firm. Instead they learn of the virtues of organizing costly "away days" to boost team spirit in the enterprise and its subunits. Rituals did not vanish from the City of London with the "big bang" financial reforms of Margaret Thatcher: traditional "old school tie" patterns of sociality in the Home Counties may have weakened, but new forms of the cocktail party and international conferencing proliferated in their place. Cementing trust through rituals may be especially significant in the financial sector, but comparable practices can be identified in many nooks and crannies of capitalist industrial production and consumption, from obligatory politeness formulas to staff uniforms, from advertising slogans to retail sales campaigns at Thanksgiving. However, from the salesperson's manipulation of a fashionable brand to the propagation by sophisticated managers and consultants of a distinctive corporate culture, the uses made of ritual in these examples are subordinated to the logic of efficiency and profit maximization. If an enlightened transnational corporation diverts funds to support some traditional ritual in a country where it is active, and the local managers participate in those rituals, this too is good for image and ultimately for shareholder value. But the incidence of ritual in economy cannot always be reduced to a logic of this kind. We are also interested in cases where there is no adaptive fit, where rituals persist (or are newly devised) not in order to maximize individual satisfaction or to improve the functioning of households or firms in a domain called economy, but in order to express something of value to a larger collectivity known as society.

Anthropologists have analyzed the relationship between economy and ritual in societies very different from those of contemporary capitalism, but early efforts in this direction were not followed up as specialization set in within the discipline. The vast literatures on ritual phenomena and economic phenomena make little reference to each other, because *we* categorize them as separate domains. Evolutionists such as Frazer (1909) argued that magical beliefs and ritual taboos had an adaptive logic that facilitated the "growth of institutions" such as private property. However, sociologist Robert Bellah (drawing on historian Johan Huizinga) has recently suggested that ritual has its origins in "serious play," where humans cooperate in a "relaxed field," free of immediate economic pressures (Bellah 2011). In this account, ritual (together with myth and the later emergence of Gods and religion as we know it) is opposed to work and to selective pressures (at least at the primary level). However, the causalities remain unclear. Bellah notes that the elaborate rituals of tribal societies require considerable material resources, implying a need for storage facilities. Ethnographers have commonly argued that ritual is the key instrument in mobilizing large work parties to construct such facilities in the first place.

This debate has not advanced significantly in the last hundred years. Karl Bücher, Max Weber's contemporary in the junior generation of the German Historical School, showed how the performance of work depended on what he called "rhythm," exemplified by singing together to carry out tasks that were difficult or simply tedious (see Spittler 2008). One of Bronisław Malinowski's earliest contributions to anthropology was to extend Bücher's argument to magic and ritual for the case of Australian Aborigines (Malinowski 1992 [1912]). He returned to the theme repeatedly and the main subject of his last monograph on the Trobriand Islanders was once again "the relation between purely economic, rationally founded and technically effective work on the one hand, and magic on the other " (1935: xx). Malinowski continued his Preface to that work with the ringing assertion that "No human beings, at whatever stage of culture, completely eliminate spiritual preoccupations from their economic concerns" (ibid.). It has become almost commonplace to suggest that capitalist consumption opens up a world of enchantment analogous to that of magic and traditional forms of religion. But Malinowski was writing about *production,* and his invitation to question the very notion of the "purely economic" has even wider validity, even though his own answers remained somewhat muddled to the end.

A decade before these formulations by Malinowski, Marcel Mauss had concluded his famous study of *The Gift* by suggesting that the rituals associated with reciprocal giving might still play an important role in our own economies, even though these were dominated by markets and contract (Mauss 1990 [1924]). Karl Bücher had in fact made this argument even earlier (Bücher 1922). Later ethnographers found that embryonic entrepreneurs calculated how to take advantage of differing spheres of value and distort traditional modes of hospitality and feasting for their own commercial benefit (Barth 1967). But despite these and other voices, even in the subfield of economic anthropology the tacit assumption has been the modernist one stated above: economy and ritual have little or nothing to do with each other. We know from our mass media that certain rituals celebrated domestically, notably Christmas, have a massive impact on GDP, as do major public spectacles such as the Olympic Games. The tourist industry has long known that the rituals of others, staged and unstaged, can be very good for business. But how exactly are we to theorize the force of the "purely economic" in relation to actions that defy this calibration, the products of everyday sociality as well as deeper "spiritual preoccupations"? Is this relationship necessarily different in a complex contemporary economy, in comparison with a "tribal economy" such as that of the Trobriands? If so, is it constant across all industrial economies or might it differ in the variants we label capitalist and socialist? For example, what differences might we expect to find if we examine the relation between ritual and economy with reference to the Moscow Olympics of 1980 and the Los Angeles Olympics of 1984, each boycotted by the other side in the era of the Cold War?

The end of socialist planning and its replacement by capitalist market economies provided a unique opportunity to investigate the confluence of economy and ritual. Earlier studies by Gerald Creed (2002) in Bulgaria and Cynthia Werner (1999) in Kazakhstan were both concerned with feasting and hospitality. Werner found that such activity had increased with the end of socialism and the advent of markets. With the help of her informants, she interpreted this upsurge in terms of the need to strengthen social relations and trust in circumstances of increasing uncertainty. This was a return to forms of mutual indebtedness characteristic of the presocialist era but suppressed in the decades of collective farming. Creed, by contrast, found that hospitality rituals were undermined by the market relations that had come to dominate in postsocialist Bulgaria. The declining economic conditions, reduced state support, and loss of remunerative jobs left no funds available to sustain the ritual hospitality. While Werner stressed that investing in relationships was both a risk-aversion device for the community and at the same time a good "business" strategy for elites, in postsocialist Bulgaria it was not possible to fall back on earlier forms of community mutuality. Whereas Werner finds that behavior in a significant domain of ritual is ultimately subordinate to an economic logic, Creed suggests in a later publication that ritual (in this case the performances of folk mummers) can be a domain for resisting this logic and protesting against the broader phenomenon of postsocialist "cultural dispossession" (Creed 2011).

The differences between these scholars may derive from the timing of their observations, or they may have been due to enduring differences between the particular locations studied (but not necessarily between the wider regions), or to the different anthropological perspectives of the two authors. One of the starting impulses for our project was to investigate the apparent discrepancy in their accounts in a novel, comparative way. Building on an earlier model of "economy's tension," the dialectic between market and community (Gudeman 2008), we approach ritual in terms of notions of house economy and human sociality in order to offer an alternative, heterodox perspective on economic life. Before we describe these key points of theory and introduce our collective project and its six case studies, let us look a little more closely at the many referents of ritual.

Ritual and Sociality

In the social sciences and humanities, rituals have been differently defined and viewed but rarely considered in relation to economy. We use the concept of ritual in a particular way because of this focus. All of our case studies are oriented to local economies of the house and community in the context of the larger historical and contemporary economies of which they are a part. Before relating how we view ritual, it may be useful to note other applications of the term, some of which overlap ours.

Ritual refers to a sequence of actions that we share with others as in a marriage or death ceremony, or a greeting, such as shaking hands and kissing on both cheeks. Similarly, ritual can mean a personal, repeated action or even a habit, as in a ritual performed on arising or going to bed. Some people have customs that they perform unfailingly, such as opening a door in a certain way, knocking on wood, or wishing good health to someone who sneezes. Habits can be seen as "economical" ways of acting: by eating the same food at breakfast or lunch, or wearing the same style of clothes, we spend less time deciding what to consume or wear, although the line between "compulsive repetition" as ritual and "rational repetition" as acts of economizing can be thin. Do we economize with such rituals? Are they an instance of "satisficing"? (Simon 1956) Or are they manifestations of deeper biological and/or emotional drivers?

By ritual we often refer to an expressive or symbolic aspect of life, such as praying to a divinity, pledging allegiance to a nation, or swearing fealty to a leader. Such rituals are not causal or mechanistic practices but acts of commitment. Some of these rituals have reflexive effects, as in a consoling prayer or a joyous wedding that lifts the spirits. In relation to economy, these rituals may "assist" practices, such as prayers for help with a harvest, pleas to a saint to cure an illness or animal, or appeals that working with certain machines or chemicals should not prove harmful. Evolutionists such as Frazer and Bücher and functionalists like Malinowski emphasized effects of this kind, arguing that such assistance was indispensable to persuade people to work at all and conducive to raising productivity.

In relation to material economy, a ritual may cost time and wealth. For example, as prosperity increases, so may the size of a ritual as a form of display or thanks, as in weddings and birthdays. As wealth falls, ceremonial expenditures may decline. Are rituals involving ample expenditure—the extreme case being the Northwest coast potlatch—cost efficient in some fashion or irrational demands? Costly rituals are found in several of our studies and it is by no means obvious what they accomplish. Ritual in this expressive sense can still be a domain in which economic struggles and conflicting explanations of the world are played out. The soul can be sold to the devil for riches; spirits may possess humans who transgress standard practices or are forced into unaccustomed behavior. Ritual practices may express separation from or resistance to a market economy. In our cases, rituals may represent a reaffirmation of the connectedness of socialism vis-à-vis the divisive individualism of market economy.

Modern markets themselves can be studied from the perspective of ritual. In some markets participants must go through a rite of passage to enter and participate. The New York Stock Exchange is opened each day by the pounding of a gavel, and it is closed by ringing a bell. Trades take place only during this sacred time, except for after-hours trading; and traders must purchase a "seat" to participate. We do not directly find these rituals of entry and exit in our cases, but participation itself can be ritualized. In most markets everything is brought to the measuring rod of money, and those who participate must practice calculative reason. This requires a change of mentality on entering a market, equivalent in reverse to that required when entering a religious sanctuary or ritual.

The process of linking means to ends, and of ends to means, is the central act in markets and might be seen as a ritual for some of those involved. It is the opposite of enchantment in the Weberian sense of a world made by nonrational processes, but the instrumental linking of means to ends can have a ritualistic aspect when it involves compulsion and enchantment. Commercial and financial practices may be undertaken as complete, sufficient, and satisfying acts in themselves.

For us rituals are related to economy through the social connections they make and break. Rituals express, reiterate, and sustain social ties. They can make and recognize commitments to others or sever them, as in rites of passage. Rituals are often essential for extending sociability, as in gestures of friendliness, hospitality, and words of kindness; and they can revivify or recuperate connections as in special gatherings. Rituals also can hide social ties and personal interests by veiling them as something else; and they may mystify wants and desires by presenting them as what they are not.

Rituals are no less fundamental to institutions, which as we shall elaborate are fundamental to economy. Institutions are made up of social connections, as epitomized by the house and the community. The state and the church are more encompassing institutions. Our case studies are not concerned with state holidays or church services but more intimate gatherings at the local level may be informed by these larger institutions. Some rituals may not be considered religious by the participants, but if pressed they may recognize a religious back cloth. Uncovering this entanglement of interpersonal sociability and the role of institutions is a central focus for us. In doing so, we resist a simple division of religious and secular rituals, and of ritual from economy. These separations are not those of the people in the house and communities studied, and for this reason alone it is important to question these categories.

Economy Comparatively

The six economies studied in our project were all postsocialist. What is this condition? The many answers given by scholars have been strongly colored by their political perspective on socialism itself. Ernest Gellner, for example, considered central planning to be a key element of a monist project continuing the traditions of Byzantine Caesaro-Papism. For him socialism was the antithesis of the modern (Gellner 1994). This lack of modernity was demonstrated by the efforts, overwhelmingly unsuccessful, that socialist states made to promote both public and private rituals to legitimate their power. Socialist economies were caught up in an elaborate ritual performance that contrasted with the "reality" of the world dominated by market capitalism. We find this dichotomy much too simple and offer instead a view grounded in the social and economic changes that took place in people's lives under socialist rule, and in their assessments of that era after it had come to an end and they were obliged to encounter capitalist markets. We are not arguing that there were no differences between the centrally planned economies of the Soviet bloc and Western market economies, but we should not mistake the models of each for the reality. A focus on the relationship between economy and ritual can help us to a better understanding of how these competing systems actually differed in practice.

During the Cold War, many Western universities offered courses in Comparative Economic Systems. Teachers of such courses pointed to the varieties of capitalism, such as the difference between the United States and Japan, but the dramatic chasm was that which separated capitalist from socialist economies. Such courses are now less fashionable.[1] Today, two decades after the disintegration of the Soviet bloc, we are more aware of the diversity that characterized the socialist camp. One of our field sites is in Macedonia, formerly part of the Socialist Federal Republic of Yugoslavia, which maintained a nonaligned stance throughout the Cold War. Yet even Yugoslavia, with its distinctive system of self-management and absence of collective farms, remained clearly socialist in its main contours, notably the social ownership and control of the most important productive enterprises. The Hungarian, Romanian, and Bulgarian variants of central planning were also unequivocally socialist by this criterion, although they differed greatly from each other. The Moldavian and Kyrgyz republics of the Soviet Union had yet different histories but nonetheless shared many common features of that federation. The family resemblances of socialism in our six cases are clear.

Unlike capitalism, the origins of which have always been highly contested, it is superficially quite easy to trace the genealogy of socialism: to writings of Karl Marx and Friedrich Engels in the nineteenth century, in which they developed their critique of alienation and exploitative class relations in the new capitalist industrial society. They supplemented this analysis with an evolutionist "historical materialism" that began and concluded with communism. Their critique of the economics of their age, however, offered few clues for the economic management of communist states in the twentieth century. The states of the Soviet bloc and Yugoslavia all claimed to be socialist, and disavowed having reached the higher stage of communism. Central planning was motivated ultimately by an emphasis on the community pole of Gudeman's dialectic of market and community. It was encapsulated in the slogan "from each according to his ability, to each according to his need." The extent to which socialists implemented the second component of this shibboleth is demonstrated by the evidence in this volume for the persistence of state redistribution at the micro level. Both components of the mantra reflect enduring impulses of community, as vividly demonstrated in Monica Vasile's discussion in this volume of how wealthy wedding guests in Transylvania are cajoled into making more generous gifts as part of the "community endowment" of the newlyweds.

Administrative redistribution controlled by the state is by no means the whole story of the socialist period. Economic policies in Eastern Europe were shaped less by Marxist doctrines than by the overriding goal to industrialize backward agrarian societies as rapidly as possible, at a time when

Europe was divided by an "iron curtain." As Johanna Bockman has recently shown, it was increasingly recognized by the planners themselves that the mechanism of the market and techniques of Western "neoclassical" economics were indispensable for ensuring efficient outcomes (Bockman 2011). In the pure world of economic models, successful accomplishment of the plan should be mathematically identical with market equilibria. In practice, many socialist economists drew on transnational developments in their discipline to critique "over-centralization" and promote less hierarchical models. Hungary and Yugoslavia evolved particularly distinctive forms of "market socialism." The market form of integration was less well developed in the other countries covered in this collection but was never entirely absent. For example, the collective farm markets of the Soviet Union allowed villagers to sell the produce grown on their private plots at prices higher than those paid to the collective by the planners through the procurement system.

Socialism thus combined redistributive planning with elements of market mechanisms and this combination left significant space for individual or household economy, including the development of reciprocal and solidary links between social actors. The cases studied in this volume combine this socialist legacy with an enduring legacy of rurality. In some ways it was easier to implement communist ideals in village communities than it was in the city. The collective farm (Russian: kolkhoz) was a "total institution" charged with organizing the local farm economy and transforming it according to communist ideals. It is instructive to compare the workings and accomplishments of this institution with the "modernization" of rural societies in other parts of the world, for example with regard to rates of rural exodus and patterns of social as well as geographical mobility. Anthropologists were slow to turn their attention to Europe, however; socialist Eastern Europe could not be adequately investigated until research access improved, which in several states did not happen until the 1990s after socialist regimes had collapsed. In many regions it has only now become possible to look back on the socialist decades (several generations in the case of the former Soviet Union) and assess the full impact of socialist ideals and institutions. To stick with the example of wedding rituals: the pattern identified by Vasile in a forest community in postsocialist Romania bears similarities to what earlier ethnographers of the Mediterranean have documented, when communities previously oriented toward subsistence and survival gain access to new sources of wealth and accumulation. This suggests common patterns of development, largely independent of particular institutional forms.[2]

While acknowledging commonalities, we are suspicious of a universal telos of modernization. The economic institutions of central planning obviously made a difference locally, despite all the intrasocialist variation. In addition to the space afforded at the local level by institutions such as the kolkhoz markets, the implementation of socialism was profoundly economistic in the sense that the highest priority was attached to meeting ever-inflated production targets. Lenin's embracing of "Taylorism" was as fervent as that of any contemporary capitalist. The abuses of norm-setting were endemic to all planned economies. They were most extreme in the Gulag system and persisted after its elimination in the 1950s. When levels of violence were reduced, the scope for rational calculation increased. Within the institutions of central planning, it was rational for farm leaders to negotiate plan figures with their superiors with the goal of maximizing the resources at their disposal and creating more room to maneuver for their members (Creed 1998; Humphrey 1983; Verdery 1996). Economists have no difficulty in understanding this kind of behavior; they can model the behavior of those who offer and accept bribes in capitalist and socialist systems alike. Some might insist on the irrationality of the planning institutions but claim that individual decision makers behave as rational maximizers within that deplorable framework (as does a Trobriand Islander when cultivating more yams than he can possibly consume, the ensuing surplus being disposed of in the form of gifts to affines, gifts that will in large part eventually be left to rot). Other observers might detect similarities between the plan negotiations of socialist farm managers with ministerial officials and price negotiations between capitalist farmers and their trusted agribusiness agents, although in both cases the "economic" negotiations take on a ritual aspect. Both are likely to be lubricated by alcohol, albeit different types and brands.

This brings us back promptly to ritual, the other key term of this volume. We have already noted how the scope of ritual in modern capitalist economies is defined to exclude the economy, and spectacular ritual events organized by the holders of power are the exception that proves the rule. At the level of the enterprise, support for the sports club or for the senior managers to visit the opera after the annual general meeting can be documented in yearly reports and incorporated into the accounts. The separation between the world of work and that of leisure is supposed to be sharp. One-party socialist regimes blurred these boundaries through a more visible and encompassing ritualization.

This salience of ritual, both public and private, was clearly related to the difficulty many socialist states experienced in satisfying the consumer wants of their populations. The "market socialism" of Hungary after 1968 was a partial exception to this misery, but the shops of Romania, Poland, and much of the Soviet Union remained poorly supplied in the 1980s, even in terms of material "necessities." This led to large "second" or "underground" economies, and more or less elaborate discourses and rituals surrounding "questionable" transactions, for which *blat* became the generic name in Russia (Ledeneva 1998). Governments that could not find legitimation in the markets were almost obliged to compensate in the realm of ritual. Within the domain of economy more narrowly construed, they invested in rituals to boost production, such as those of "socialist competition" and the "communist Saturday," which meant working voluntarily without additional pay. The sphere of consumption was heavily ritualized, for example in the conscious promulgation of new wedding practices. The Soviet Union attempted to create new ritual calendars for the state, and even to intervene in the life-cycle rituals of families (Binns 1979, 1980; Lane 1981). Between the state and the family, resources were also invested at levels such as that of the collective farm and the ubiquitous socialist institution of the Culture House, which was generally supported financially by the farm as well as the local state administration (Donahoe and Habeck 2011). The extraordinary high turnout achieved for noncompetitive elections at every level can be considered another form of ritual in a socialist system aptly characterized by Lane (for the case of the USSR) as a distinctive variant of political religion.

The effects of this socialist ritualization were pervasive. With the exception of small numbers of dissidents, by the last decades of the Soviet Union few questioned the system (Yurchak 2006). For example, compared with the meetings of a Western trade union, where the outcome of a debate over a strike proposal is indeterminate, the meetings of socialist trade unions at every level had a more formal quality, in the sense that the outcomes were generally known in advance and the speechmaking more formulaic. Yet even here the differences are not always black and white. Ritual infiltrates even the most democratic political organs, and the most perfect socialist choreography does not always proceed according to the script. It takes good fieldwork to capture the latter through careful analysis of "backstage" reactions and the informal, "subaltern" expression of what cannot be expressed openly and formally.

This volume is not concerned with ritual at the exalted level of the state, or with political ritual at other levels, but engages primarily with the level of the locality and the house. The focus upon house has many antecedents. Classical work by the Russian agrarian economist Alexander Chayanov (1987) has shown how the "family-labor farm" follows an economic logic that is quite different from that of a capitalist enterprise. These insights have inspired much later work in economic anthropology (Sahlins 1972) and peasant studies (Shanin 1990). Other strands of research in anthropology and history have prioritized the relationship between household and family, the composition of the domestic (residential) group and the intergenerational transfer of property (Goody 1976; Laslett 1972). While some have approached the "house society" culturally (Carsten and Hugh-Jones 1995), others have analyzed how households articulate with changes in global political economy, specifically the rise of capitalism (Smith et al. 1985). All of these strands have shaped our comparative project. Of particular importance for the Ritual and Economy group is the way in which house economy has been theorized in opposition to the corporation in previous work of Gudeman (e.g., Gudeman and Rivera 1990). The house is built on the sociality of its members around its hearth. This principle of solidarity is older than the principle of market exchange, with which it necessarily has to engage more and more intensively in the course of capitalist penetration. The novelty of our case studies lies in the socialist and postsocialist context; we investigate the impact of these transformations on the models and practices of the house economy.

Concerning ritual, the main diagnostic is in principle the same regardless of the level of analysis: ritual is understood as a domain of marked behavior that cannot be reduced to the pragmatic criteria of a short-term logic of economizing, not even where its effects seem clearly conducive to efficacy in this domain. For all the emphasis on meeting plan targets and other indications of economism, many socialist economic institutions allowed surprising scope for rituals that evidently did not augment production, whose effects were the opposite of the Stakhanovite campaigns. Labor discipline was in practice modified in ways that Western managers would hardly countenance, for example through the custom of celebrating name days and birthdays at the workplace (Dunn 2004). In this volume, Miladina Monova explains how the socialist tobacco Kombinat in Prilep, Macedonia, allowed even its key workers to take extended leave when they needed to harvest their private tobacco fields. In the former East Germany, socialist brigades were required to participate in campaigns and accept propaganda disseminated from above; but even in urban contexts, many became a lively forum of sociality for their members, who kept very much the same company outside their formal working hours. Political convictions generally played little or no role (Müller 2007).

In addition to the ritualization observable inside socialist institutions, many other rituals persisted in the intimate confines of family and community. Despite the repression of religion in favor of scientific atheism, several of our researchers found that the feast days of local Christian saints were celebrated with great enthusiasm and expense under socialism. This took place first and foremost at the level of the household. It is now recognized that stereotyped images of the extended family household or *zadruga* in Southeast Europe have been exaggerated; far from being primordial throughout the Balkans, it came to prominence relatively recently in particular historical circumstances, which varied considerably from region to region (Todorova 1989). After allowing for some myth-making concerning this particular form (to which foreign scholars contributed substantially), it remains the case that celebrations of the *slava* were the central celebration in which the household constituted itself as both an economic and a ritual unit (see especially Monova's chapter in this volume).

Despite the imposition of collectivization, we found that secular rituals of the old independent peasantry such as pig-sticking continued to flourish and even to increase in scope (see Vidacs's contribution to this volume). Despite governmental condemnation of wasteful expenditure, in many regions the amounts spent on hospitality and weddings soared in the last, relatively prosperous years of socialism. No doubt much of this house-based activity was motivated by considerations that an economist could quickly grasp and begin to model: if one's neighbor has organized a lavish wedding party, then I must do the same in order to maintain my reputation. Economists can also understand how such expenditures resolve a collective problem: the community endowment is in effect a form of revolving credit association. Rituals are thus present in both socialism and capitalism. But the scope of ritual may have been greater under socialism, for two reasons. First, as noted above, for their legitimation purposes the new regimes promoted political ritualization through new socialist ceremonies in all domains of social life, from orchestrated parades on Mayday to the celebrations that underpinned the sociality of the brigade. Some of this ritual was alienating to those whose participation was required. Second, socialist economic life remained less "disembedded" from citizens' life-worlds than the outcomes of the "great transformation" wrought by capitalism. In spite of revolutionary pretensions, socialism in many places came to allow for deeper continuities with the past, and for the efflorescence of older forms of religion and community and the values and solidarities that they express.[3]

Much of this—not everything—changed very quickly following the encounter with capitalist markets after 1990. How significant are the path-dependencies between the socialist and presocialist periods? Are the communities documented in this volume still undergoing a protracted transition, such that we should be wary of drawing any general conclusions? Or do both the socialist and postsocialist "windows," because of the emphatic nature of their respective ideologies, afford insight into the more general, even universal character of the tension between community and market identified by Gudeman? What does the radical shift of recent years tell us about the relationship between economy and ritual?

Opponents of socialism represent it as a monstrous intervention in a natural economic order, a "constructed rationality," which, in the terms of Hayek (1944), leads ineluctably to both economic breakdown and political "serfdom." Those who uphold the superiority of the "free market" and pro-vide the intellectual justification for the neoliberalism of recent decades allege that socialism has been tested and found wanting.[4] Some insist that all the dislocation of the present is due not to the new markets but rather to the legacy of the socialist interlude and, in particular, the propagation of beliefs and values contrary to those of the free market. Not only did social-ism fail to promote modernity for its citizens: according to the conservative critique, by failing to deal with "moral hazards" through the rigorous spec-ification of property rights, it undermined the chances of ever reaching the condition of modernity. Large populations, according to this point of view, have been erroneously led to believe that there is an alternative to a world based on the primacy of the market.

These debates are not new. When Friedrich Hayek was formulating his passionate defense of the free market, Karl Polanyi had only recently pub-lished his own devastating indictment of laissez-faire, as model and as reality. Polanyi showed in *The Great Transformation* (1944) that the heyday of liberalism in the nineteenth century was made possible only through the interventions of states, above all the British (the tight synthesis of state and market throughout history was also a key theme of Karl Bücher). Ac-cording to this critique, the self-regulating market was a contradiction. The pursuit of this "utopia" destroyed the fabric of society and inevitably stim-ulated reactions, some of them benign, such as a trades union movement to defend the interests of workers, and some of them reactionary, such as populist or jingoist movements that targeted scapegoats. We view the so-cialist movement in its entirety as the most powerful crystallization of this reaction to the rise of market capitalism. For most of the twentieth century, most of the Eurasian landmass was governed by Marxist-Leninist-Maoist regimes (Hann 2006). They have now disappeared. With the exception of North Korea, even those East Asian states that still claim to be socialist have abandoned the old models of central planning and political religion. In their place, we find everywhere much greater reliance on market mech-anisms. In assessing their impact, we must recall Polanyi's message that these markets can never be truly self-regulating or "free." Rather than fol-low the apologists of neoliberalism back into the ideological wars of the last two centuries, in this volume we ask on the basis of meticulous case studies whether the convulsions of the last two decades have contributed to mov-ing the dialectic in the human economy forward a few inches. Or has it now become even harder than before to acknowledge that some activities are valued by humans for intrinsic reasons that cannot be reduced to a calculus based on efficiency or fitness?

Comparative methods have a long history in anthropology. Compara-tive projects within and between "culture areas" were common until the middle of the twentieth century, as was the more general theorization of comparison. For a variety of reasons, some sensible and some not so sensible, this tradition withered. Perhaps it was the turn to history and away from social science, perhaps it was the rigors of mastering growing amounts of ethnography, perhaps it was the (postmodern) realization that anthropologists were not objective viewers and did not hold a privileged (scientific) perspective, or perhaps comparison did not yield the hoped for results, but this form of analysis and illumination largely disappeared. We aim to counter that trend, for we think that our large "culture area," which stretches from the Balkans through Eastern Europe to the center of Asia and is home to differing postsocialist experiences and differing encounters with market life, offers fertile terrain for the comparative endeavor. Our studies may be most accessible to those already familiar with the historical and contemporary commonalities of this region; but we hope also to reach wider audiences and inspire readers to extend the comparisons beyond the boundaries of an Area Studies community.

Economy Institutionally

Our perspective on economy is social, cultural, and comparative, and it is institutionalist. We are not New Institutionalists in the sense of that school within economics whose adherents look at organizations from the perspective of rational actors and (in many cases, including the work of Douglass North) evolutionary fitness. In anthropology the word "institution" is no longer common. A century ago, Frazer and Malinowski were concerned with developing an institutional approach, but their grasp of economy was weak. We are economic institutionalists in the sense of Karl Polanyi and, in an earlier generation, Karl Bücher and Thorstein Veblen. Proceeding from a substantive concern with material livelihood, in each study area the researchers break down the monolith "economy" into institutional domains. They distinguish the house economy from material life in community, and both from the domains of commerce and finance. All found the house to be a central site of economic practices in their field locations, and the varying house economies within communities became one baseline for comparison.

Of course we needed to take account of the larger systems of which the house and local communities were a part, especially the demise of socialism. For example, the continuation of state support through pensions, welfare, and small grants was important to villagers, nowhere more so than in the Hungarian materials presented by Bea Vidacs. In Macedonia, as described by Miladina Monova, a failing tobacco enterprise employed persons willing to take insecure, poorly paid jobs because they offered the possibility of receiving a pension. Pensions and other state entitlements were also important supports in the Bulgarian villages described by Detelina Tocheva, where many family members had found more or less permanent employment outside the village.

National and international trade flows also influenced the communities studied by our group. For example, in the Apuseni Mountains of Romania studied by Monica Vasile, villagers have profited from opportunities in the lumber sector. Larger state and private enterprises offered some employment in many rural areas, though seldom sufficient to support a family. Cash cropping, as Nathan Light reports for bean-growing villagers in Kyrgyzstan who draw little benefit these days from state redistribution, is also encountered. But overall we can state that the impact of commercial markets in these rural areas was not as important as in other sectors of the national economy.

We might classify economies on an institutionalist scale from low market to high market. Malinowski's Trobrianders could be considered "low market." Truly small communities, such as lineages and feudal manors, exemplify economies articulated by social relationships, although these economies are never isolated from external relations. In contrast, high market contexts, with anonymous contracts, unaffected by cronyism, insider knowledge, price-fixing, and copying (as in bubbles), may be fewer than we imagine, although some financial markets, grain markets, and natural resource markets offer approximations. Pictured as a scale, the postsocialist economies about which we write mostly fall around the midpoint. Most were also nearer the "low market" pole under socialism, although Vidacs's Hungarian village has in some respects moved in the opposite direction. The "house economy" is necessarily constituted to a high degree through social relationships and commitments rather than contracts, although we emphasize that they are by no means self-sufficient.[5]

Looking outward from the house, we explore how this sphere of economy articulates both with communities and commercial markets. International markets for tobacco (Monova), beans (Light), wine (Cash), and timber (Vasile) had more impacts on these local economies than nonmarket forces such as NGO initiatives or foreign philanthropy. More broadly, financial markets with interest bearing loans, and metafinancial tools such as structured investment vehicles, fall outside our study because their local impact is negligible. Light notes that "interest rates" calculated in progeny on animals loaned in a Kyrgyz village are very similar to interest rates charged on local monetary loans, but he interprets this in a "reverse" way as evidence of the subordination of narrowly economic criteria to social relations. We do observe, however, that while financial institutions may not be visible in the villages studied and did not directly affect loaning and "investments" in them, financial markets have had a "trickle-down" effect, for example through their impact on government supports and grants, employment opportunities and tourism, possibilities for securing loans from the European Union and elsewhere for local investment, and on wages. Invisible but influential, these larger economic institutions and markets have affected our regions, causing many to become more reliant on their house economies and state entitlements than before.

In each case, the researcher looked at the flows of material life: how people live, what they produce and how, what they eat, and how wealth is conceived and kept. As part of our institutional approach, studying and understanding transactions was a central focus, especially in relation to rituals. These relationships included sharing, reciprocity, barter, measured exchanges (such as sharing according to the amounts invested), and market trade. We took account of the historical and contemporary links between the rural areas and larger towns, cities and government structures, and of policies in other states and at the supranational level that affected the field sites, especially within the European Union. For example, the demand for Macedonian tobacco fell dramatically after the collapse of socialism due to EU restrictions on its import, while the production of wine after socialism in Moldova dropped with the curtailing of imports by Russia and Ukraine.

All this might be termed the structural dimension of our institutional approach. As the researchers became more familiar with their areas, they gave increased attention to local discourses about economy and the concepts and words, or cultural models, that people use to express and orient their material lives. This is the hermeneutic dimension of our institutionalism. The method of hermeneutics is conventionally associated with fields such as religion and ritual, but for us it is no less central to the study of economy; indeed it is the best way to appreciate the mutual embedding of economy and ritual. It may be helpful to distinguish multiple levels of hermeneutics. As argued above, ritual was conspicuous under socialism, which provided a common language rooted in the classics of Marx, Engels, and Lenin that filtered down to be expressed in every issue of every newspaper and at every general meeting of every collective farm. However, beneath the general exegetical principles, socialism was everywhere inflected to a significant degree by national discourses ("with Bulgarian characteristics"). Finally, the hermeneutic study of economy also requires an engagement with regional and local life-worlds. The case studies in this volume explore both the hermeneutic and the structural dimensions of economy at these multiple levels.

This institutional and cultural approach opens up key zones of ambiguity in the meanings and effects of rituals at the house and community levels of economy. Ritual in relation to economy, and economy in relation to ritual, together have multiple effects. At times, ritual is a mode of economy, and at other moments economy becomes part of a ritual. Rituals may support or legitimate economic practices through the sociability they bring and by substituting for them. In almost all our cases rituals fill gaps in sociality between houses as the older socialist institutions have disappeared. But ritual can also be a façade or mystification of sociality that does not exist. Rituals, as Werner (1999) and Creed (2002, 2011) observe, draw on material resources sometimes with profit, sometimes at a loss and sometimes to attract economic connections and exchanges. Rituals in all cases help express house identity and resilience. However, they can also express economic power and inferiority. They frequently mystify community identity and cohesion, sometimes with barely concealed nostalgia.

It is hard to avoid using the words "ritual" and "economy" as if they were discrete ideas, practices, and institutions. On the ground, however, people do not define their activities in this manner. It may be only in high market situations that ritual and economy are separated, especially as the market realm becomes abstracted or "disembedded," although disembedding can never be complete. One conclusion to emerge from the small-scale studies in this volume is that this conceptual separation in "modernity" (and in the disciplines that study it) is a result of our own categories and reflections on economy at a particular moment in world history.

The Studies

The six regions on which we focus have been unevenly integrated into market life. Five of them are villages and the sixth is a small town surrounded by rural life. All have suffered twice economically: first from the demise of socialism and the slow "advance" of new forms of market life, and second from the global crisis that erupted just as we began our fieldwork. As the six areas are located at the margins of developed market economies, the effects of the great crash may have been less significant than elsewhere, but this insulation only speaks to the often precarious material life of these communities.

In chapter 1, Jennifer Cash tells about economic and ritual ambiguity in a village of southeast Moldova. During the socialist period a principal form of livelihood was growing grapes and making wine for export to other parts of the Soviet Union. This trade no longer exists, and the privatization of collective farms has left village households with surplus wine and little cash. Across the presocialist, socialist, and postsocialist periods, wine produced by village houses has symbolized their independence. Together with bread, wine forms the base of the house economy. Serving wine to visitors is a ritual of hospitality, and serving it to workers in the fields is sometimes part of a larger exchange of noncommoditized labor. However, wine also flows into the domain of the market. In the recent past, it was a commodity within the socialist system; in the postsocialist period it now accompanies the payment in cash made by houses to hired day labor, and sometimes it is the sole means of payment. Wine payments, however, raise moral concerns and the houses that pay for their help in wine often express the wish that these workers would accept food instead. Do wine payments merely exploit the alcohol dependency of workers? Or, is there a more subtle relationship between ritual and economy reflected in the ongoing negotiation between a house and its workers over whether payment will be made in cash, food, or wine?

Wine offered can indicate a social connection, it can signify hospitality, equality, and a gift economy, or it can point to a market-like transaction. There are continuities between the use of wine as a house ritual of sociality and as a payment for work. Workers who request only wine wish to be respected by those who hire them and in village society, but the request itself indicates that the worker lacks his own wine—the very substance that symbolizes and engenders respect among men who share it. Why do some people "work for wine" when most houses that run short of wine acquire it through barter or purchase, displaying it as their own? Do wine payments ritually restore respect to the poor, or do they mystify the reproduction of social inequality and marginalization?

In chapter 2 Nathan Light describes the decay of infrastructure in the community of Beshbulak in Kyrgyzstan after the collapse of socialism, including the collective farms, and public support for many local institutions. Cash cropping, especially of beans, has helped provide an economic basis for the village, but as in socialist times and before, the main focus of economic life is animal breeding. With the demise of socialism and the connections made through its institutions, as well as the lifting of Soviet constraints on ritual practices, the raising and use of animals at rituals has increasingly helped to make social connections, and the frequency of rituals for different occasions has increased. The house, which bears some physical resemblances to a yurt, especially in the way it is used during rituals, remains the center of material and social life. Much of ritual life, focused around multiple rites of passage from birth through marriage to death, has to do with the household and the connections it makes. Even more than was the case under socialism, marriages have become important moments for social rearrangements, and kin outside the house have become more prominent in providing help and material support.

With the slow rise of market activities, animals remain the symbolic if not the sole material thread of the economy. Most households do not sell many of the animals they raise. They are a social currency that connects houses. Ritual occasions with their provision of meat attract visitors from far and wide, so making and reinforcing alliances. At bridewealth celebrations, often held long after the wedding itself, large numbers of animals pass from the groom's side to the bride's. Although the bridewealth is supposed to consist of animals, in their absence money may be provided; however, this money has to be represented as if secured through the sale of animals, rather than derived from cash cropping. Animals are thus valued as wealth, for their ritual uses, for their place in making sociality, for their ability to reproduce and multiply, for their products, and for their symbolic representation of an autonomous, self-sufficient house. In some ways they replace money, but as Light observes, the rate of interest for borrowing an animal is now far higher than external rates of interest for borrowing money. The animal rate of interest dominates, for it seems to pull up the cost of money loans in the community.

Animals in this area of Kyrgyzstan are rather like wine in Moldova, for they are the symbolic if not the actual backbone of economy. The Kyrgyz put a high premium on large-scale events and human skill in exchanging large animals, while in Moldova skill is expressed in the production and sharing of valued wine. In both we find a contrast between a ritualized economy and the commercial economy that dominates outside the community. The ritual transactions are either separated from (as in Kyrgyzstan) or used to mystify (as in Moldova) market relations; in both cases the villagers have much freedom in their interpretations.

A striking contrast to this form of relationship between economy and ritual is presented by Bea Vidacs in her study from Eastern Hungary (chapter 3). Like most of the other settings, this village has suffered economically since the end of socialism. In earlier decades, households maintained gardens for growing crops, raised animals, and engaged in labor exchanges. Unlike many other collective farm members, those studied by Vidacs did not cultivate a plot on collective land, but instead received maize from the collective to feed their animals. In return, some of the house animals were sold through the farm, where a large number of villagers worked. With the end of this socialist symbiosis, the infrastructure of the village has declined, jobs in the village have become scarce, younger people have left to pursue education, and many people now subsist by combining a pension with welfare and workfare provided by the village. The land was privatized, but most people rent their plots to one of two large farm enterprises.

With the decline of resources and community enterprises, as well as low productivity of house farms, what has happened to ritual life? Pig-sticking, an important practice in traditional household economy, has declined, while a communal ritual modeled on this practice now attracts the participation of outsiders. In the past, this work required the aid of at least one other house, but it was primarily an arduous house activity that helped support the family through the winter. With only a few ritual elements, such as sending fresh meat products to kin, neighbors, and friends, this was an important, material event in the house economy; pig-sticking was practiced before the socialist era and only late during socialism were freezers introduced that helped pave the way for a change. Pig-keeping has since diminished, and people now buy meat for consumption, because it takes less time and does not require arduous dirty work.

Beginning in 2007, pig-killing was cultivated as a ritual at the village level. It is the central event of a community festival that draws on the contributions of village houses, associations and clubs as well as the local state. Involving the slaughter of several pigs, with at least one done by traditional methods, all the pig products are cooked for the festival and enjoyed by the participants, for a money price. The event draws visitors and attention and may return some money, if only because the labor of mounting it is unpaid. But what is this shift from household practice to community ritual all about? Vidacs explains that the event is differently interpreted by insiders and by outsiders, and that insiders differ in their views concerning the way it creates sociality or expresses power. Either way its persuasiveness comes from presenting an act of household economy as if house economies still existed, as if the village were a solidary unit, and as if its economy were still viable. This transformation of an arduous household economic practice to a festive village ritual is an obvious mystification of the rather bleak reality of material life in the village today.

As in Moldova and Kyrgyzstan, serving food or drink and eating together is an important part of the Hungarian ritual. The three rituals all have a material base. In every case ritual is redolent of house values, such as hospitality, inclusion and friendly relations. But the ritual in Hungary has shifted to the community level as the viability of the house economy has diminished in the new economy; it seems that sentiments of connecting to others can only be kept alive through the invention of a new ritual.

Detelina Tocheva studied the village of Belan, high in the southern Rhodope Mountains of Bulgaria. Her study highlights a different aspect of the economy-ritual relation, and the way villagers are coping with significant changes in their lives. From well before the beginning of the last century, most of the people of this area lived from sheep flocks as owners, shepherds, or associated craftspeople. After the Second World War and political revolution, flocks were collectivized. They remained so until 1992, though villagers were allowed to hold small numbers of animals privately. During socialism villagers took wage-labor jobs at collective farms and other new organizations inside and outside the village. They combined this income with house provisioning of field crops, supplemented by the milk and meat of their privately held sheep and cows. The *kurban* ritual that Tocheva describes is a sacrifice, observed by both Muslims and Christians, with celebrations at houses as well as the church and mosque. When socialism ended, all the collective assets were sold, many to buyers from outside the village. Today, the house is the principal economic unit. It survives through a combination of activities and sources: wages, pensions, and a few salaries in local administration. Some houses host tourists, especially in the summer months. Almost all undertake some small-scale farming, usually in a house plot, and keep animals.

In the summer sheep are kept in a cooperative—not a collective—herd. They are milked together, with the daily yield going to one or another house. The amount is carefully calculated, so that each participating household in the rotation receives the share that is its due according to the quantity of milk its animals contribute to the flock's total yield. The method used to determine a share is traditional, but the reasoning is familiar and modern. Everyone receives a share based on calculation of the proportionate contribution: return is mathematically correlated with input. Due to the rotation, the milk available is sufficient for one household to convert into yogurt and cheese. Some of the flock's milk is rendered to the shepherd, and some is contributed each year to the village *kurban.*

In contrast to the calculative reason employed in managing the flock, the contribution to the central ritual event of the village is a collective donation. The ecumenical *kurban* ritual is valued for itself and for the prosperity and protection it offers. Animals are sacrificed and their meat is cooked and served for free to anyone who attends. Food must be eaten on-site and in the company of others. The entire affair is rather low-key as people arrive from within and from without the village, and then eat and leave. This ritual, first performed in 1992, is an adaptation of a presocialist collective ritual performed in spring "for the sheep." As in Vidacs's Hungarian village, commensality at the village level is emphasized, but in this case the ritual depends not on associations and the local state but entirely on donations (mostly in cash) and help from villagers who are members of households.

The *kurban* ritual in the remote mountains of Bulgaria plays out what is patently not the case in everyday practices. It creates the semblance of equality in all spheres of life, acknowledges the shared need for prosperity and well-being, expresses full openness to outsiders, and relies on household commitment and volition for its success. These values are expressed through material goods (ewe's milk and mutton) that were once the basis of the local house economy. The ritual is a new affirmation of community in radically changed economic conditions. A competitive, individualistic economy of households is transformed to a ritual economy of sociability. Through the ritual a part of the local economy is "re-embedded" in society (to adapt Polanyi's expression). The secret of the *kurban* ritual does not lie in organized religion (for both Christians and Muslims participate) but it nonetheless has transformative effects on everyday material practices. Is it going too far to view it as an expression of resistance to the fragmenting impact of markets? The changing economy has affected sociality, but economic practices are now turned to sociality in an attempt to renew precious community cohesion.

Focusing on weddings in a study of another upland region recently integrated into the European Union, Monica Vasile takes us in chapter 5 to a village in the Apuseni Mountains of western Romania. Considered part of a poor, even "backward," area through socialist times, the community she studied has experienced a remarkable spurt in wealth. The economy improved in the 1980s and then underwent a veritable boom when market relations became possible, for the village could now draw on a bountiful resource: timber. Its house economies depend primarily on felling trees, milling the wood at home, and sending the lumber to urban areas where it is sold to satisfy market demands spurred by a building boom. This village, despite its traditionally marginal position, is now highly integrated into the national market economy and is no less vulnerable to global economic conditions than our other field sites. Just as the boom at the turn of this century lifted the economy and spirits of the community, so economic times in the wake of the worldwide crash were becoming more difficult as Vasile finished her fieldwork.

The relation of this house economy to ritual has remained the same "underneath" but dramatically changed on the surface. Weddings traditionally served to endow a couple with some of the wealth necessary to make a new household economy. As most people were poor, weddings involved relatives, neighbors, and friends who could provide small sums of money for the event. Newlyweds borrowed money for the wedding feast but received more in contributions than its cost. The result was a communal endowment. Under the guise of a ritual, the money was presented as a gift but was also the counterpart to the investment in the feast by the couple, paid for with borrowed money that was repaid after the contributions. The number of wedding guests and the costs and returns of a wedding have now exploded, perhaps 100-fold. The pattern, however, is the same. The conjugal fund is rather like a rotating credit fund, except that couples are paid first and then have to repay (give to others) for the rest of their lives. The sanctions for its continuance are both social and semi-religious, as demonstrated in the exhortations used. Through the ritual, money loans are transformed to monetary gifts that are used to pay back the money borrowed and yield a surplus that provides the foundation for a house. Ritual transforms economic relations to sociability and back.

Yet, as Vasile shows, this ritually invoked economic practice contains within it a tension between the sociality of house members and sociality between houses. If the support for a wedding is not the same for all members of a family, house sociability suffers. Compared to the rituals examined in previous chapters the wedding ritual in the Apuseni mountains has been more heavily economized if not financialized. This ritual is at once embedded and disembedded from society, which manifests the tension that comes into view with the transition from socialism to market economy.

Securing funds has become a perpetual problem in the town of Prilep in Macedonia, as described by Miladina Monova in chapter 6. The tobacco factory, which was the major employer during socialism, has shrunk in size and the payment of wages is intermittent. Houses are the principal units for organizing material life. Many now raise tobacco in nearby fields for sale to the factory, and some of this work is accomplished through family assistance in the harvesting and stringing (or drying) of the leaves: sociability is turned to economy. Ritual life is vibrant. The number of days celebrated since the end of the socialist period has expanded enormously. Even if the amounts expended for a particular ritual have not, overall expenditure has. Many rituals are centered on the house, and others require house participation. We encounter an apparent paradox. The town economy has tumbled, employment is increasingly insecure, tobacco growing is supported by government subsidies, and this support may disappear due to lack of money and European Union pressure. Why do people take time from work and money from scarce resources to participate in an active ritual life? As Monova shows, through ritual life people make and remake social connections, which in turn are information sources, pathways to work, potential sources of loans, and ways to find help. Ritual life, through the sociality it makes, provides a kind of "safety net" that the market system needs. It offers the flexible support that flexible capitalism apparently requires. Ironically, and perhaps against expectations, ritual life is strengthened—not as a flight to beliefs and an escape from economic reality—but as a stabilizing force and buffer for the house in uncertain conditions. Declining economic circumstances lead to a rise in rituality and sociality, which in turn become ties of economy.

Monova draws out this change by turning to what she terms the "tobacco growing configuration" and the "*slava* feasting configuration." Both are founded around the house and they overlap. One is a practical work group, the other is a ritual configuration that perdures, for a *slava* celebrates the patron saint of a house and can be passed from father to son. The two are not simply separated as the profane to the sacred, for *slavas*, if now smaller, have multiplied in number and can be expensive to offer; the more prosperous houses are expected to offer larger ones.

Unlike the Hungarian case in which a house practice became the model for a community ritual in face of economic collapse, and unlike the Bulgarian example in which the *kurban* ritual helps bring together a disparate collection of households, in Prilep communal *slavas* have diminished in favor of more frequent and smaller house *slavas*. It is precisely the house economy with its many tendrils on which people have come to depend, rather than the shrinking tobacco factory that dominated the local economy in socialist times. Yet, ritual life in Prilep is vibrant almost to the extent that it takes away from productive endeavors. The *slava* ritual asserts a world of equality and mutuality as opposed to the unequal world of tobacco growing, But membership of the two assemblages overlaps, and ties through *slava* can help secure favors or part-time work in the larger economy. The two intermesh; the shorter-term ties of the practical material side of life are transformed through ritual to sociability, establishing a precarious balance (or perhaps a continuous tension) in an increasingly uncertain economic situation.

Transformation and Its Aftershocks

The ideas and realities of social transformation that we engage with in this book are by no means specific to the postsocialist countries. Let us recall that American economists first experimented with shock therapy to counter inflation in Chile, before applying essentially the same prescriptions to Eastern Europe. Government subsidies had to be withdrawn, price controls lifted, and the market allowed to operate. Even if the implementation seldom came anywhere near to approaching this blueprint, this theory influenced policies in the postsocialist states, partly through the pressure exerted by supranational entities. Joseph Stiglitz (1993), an expert on imperfect information in markets, argued that a structure for the transition had to be put in place. Like many others, he urged that a stable system of property rights needed to be established in law and enforced (to counter cronyism); social supports or "safety nets" should be in put in place to ease the shift in employment from government to private enterprises. In effect Stiglitz, a Nobel laureate economist in the mainstream of the profession, was arguing against a neoliberal or market fundamentalist position, by insisting that markets require an appropriate institutional structure for their operation.

We agree with Stiglitz concerning the importance of social institutions as part of economy, but observe that the 10,000-meter view of most economists still misses the importance of bottom-up institutions and fails to appreciate the enormity of what happens when local relationships are demolished. In the course of its professionalization, economics has become mathematically and statistically more sophisticated, but it has lost the connections it formerly possessed to concrete worlds of work, commerce, and consumption. Markets depend on social relationships, at all levels, and thus social relationships are part of economy. Our six team members have focused on the increased importance of the house and local community relations following the eradication of socialist institutions. At the community level and beyond, many mechanisms of economic and social support collapsed, but the house remained resilient as the final buffer, "safety net," or building block of sociality. During socialism it had been an important component of economy, in a more or less symbiotic relationship with the collective organizations. With the collapse of socialism, households suffered, and through the 1990s and beyond they faced greater risks and uncertainty. In some cases, notably that of the Kyrgyz as studied by Light, new institutions of market (cash cropping) and community (based on both kin and neighborhood) emerged to replace those of the socialist farms. Little of this was "stabilizing" (as it should have been according to the neoliberal discourse). In many rural locations the results included not only unemployment but also worsening alcohol addiction, heightened mortality rates, and a decline in general health as social and health services shrank.

Our studies of the intimate links between economy and ritual must be set against this back cloth. In all six cases, economy exists through sociality, starting with the sociability of the house, on which most people are even more dependent than before. This local sociality, from which larger institutions start and on which they must depend, sustains material life that by means of ritual becomes human connections. We reach this conclusion through comparative research that is based on an institutional perspective, with both structural and hermeneutic dimensions, applied at multiple levels between the house and the global economy. Thus, we offer these studies as a fresh contribution to illuminate the economy-ritual nexus, as a return to the comparative method that we think enriches both anthropology and economics, and as an anthropological critique of the dominant economic paradigms of the postsocialist moment in world history.

Notes

1. They have been partially replaced by courses such as "Varieties of Capitalism," but the number of varieties recognized tends to be small, e.g., a "liberal" Anglo-Saxon variant and a "corporatist" continental alternative.

2. A similar pattern of inflation of wedding gifts was described by Mihály Sárkány (1983) in the last decades of Hungarian socialism; see also Vidacs, this volume.
3. The metaphor is an allusion to the substantivist tradition in economic anthropology, and in particular, to Karl Polanyi's argument that the free market destroyed the connectedness (embeddedness) accomplished by other "forms of integration." See further discussion below, Polanyi 1944, and Hann and Hart 2009.
4. This is the position to which Hungarian economist János Kornai has gravitated over a long career, which began in the era of Stalinist central planning and continued throughout the decades of market reform in that country. Kornai eventually concluded that piecemeal reform was an illusion without more radical market freedoms underpinned by strong private property rights. See Kornai 2008.
5. We explore this theme in greater detail in a separate volume with the same authorial team: see Gudeman and Hann, forthcoming.

References

Barth, Fredrik. 1967. "Economic Spheres in Darfur." In *Themes in Economic Anthropology*, ed. Raymond Firth, 149–174. London: Tavistock.

Bellah, Robert. 2011. *Religion in Human Evolution: From the Paleolithic to the Axial Age.* Cambridge, MA: Harvard University Press.

Binns, Christopher. 1979. "The Changing Face of Power: Revolution and Accommodation in the Development of the Soviet Ceremonial System." Part I. *Man* 14, no. 4: 585–606.

———. 1980. "The Changing Face of Power: Revolution and Accommodation in the Development of the Soviet Ceremonial System." Part II. *Man* 15, no. 1: 170–187.

Bockman, Johanna. 2011. *Markets in the Name of Socialism: The Left-Wing Origins of Neoliberalism.* Stanford: Stanford University Press.

Bücher, Karl. 1922. *Die Entstehung der Volkswirtschaft: Vorträge und Aufsätze, Sammlung 1 und 2.* Tübingen: Laupp.

Carsten, Janet, and Stephen Hugh-Jones, eds. 1995. *About the House: Lévi-Strauss and Beyond.* Cambridge: Cambridge University Press.

Chayanov, Alexander. 1987. *The Theory of Peasant Economy.* Manchester: Manchester University Press.

Creed, Gerald. 1998. *Domesticating Revolution: From Socialist Reform to Ambivalent Transition in a Bulgarian Village.* University Park: Pennsylvania State University Press.

———. 2002. "Economic Crisis and Ritual Decline in Eastern Europe." In *Postsocialism: Ideals, Ideologies and Practices in Eurasia,* ed. Chris Hann, 57–73. London: Routledge.

———. 2011. *Masquerade and Postsocialism: Ritual and Cultural Dispossession in Bulgaria.* Bloomington: Indiana University Press.

Donahoe, Brian, and Joachim O. Habeck, eds. 2011. *Reconstructing the House of Culture: Community, Self, and the Makings of Culture in Russia and Beyond.* New York: Berghahn Books.

Dunn, Elizabeth. 2004. *Privatizing Poland: Baby Food, Big Business, and the Remaking of Labor.* Ithaca, NY: Cornell University Press.

Frazer, James. 1909. *Psyche's Task: A Discourse Concerning the Influence of Superstition of the Growth of Institutions.* London: Macmillan.

Gellner, Ernest. 1994. *Conditions of Liberty: Civil Society and its Rivals.* London: Hamish Hamilton.

Goody, Jack. 1976. *Production and Reproduction.* Cambridge: Cambridge University Press.

Gudeman, Stephen. 2008. *Economy's Tension: The Dialectics of Community and Market.* New York: Berghahn Books.

Gudeman, Stephen, and Alberto Rivera. 1990. *Conversations in Colombia.* Cambridge: Cambridge University Press.

Gudeman, Stephen, and Chris Hann, eds. Forthcoming. *Oikos and Market: Explorations of Self-Sufficiency after Socialism.* New York: Berghahn Books.

Hann, Chris. 2006. *"Not the Horse We Wanted!" Postsocialism, Neoliberalism, and Eurasia.* Münster: Lit.

Hann, Chris, and Keith Hart, eds. 2009. *Market and Society: The Great Transformation Revisited.* Cambridge: Cambridge University Press.

Hayek, Friedrich A. 1944. *The Road to Serfdom.* London: Routledge.

Humphrey, Caroline. 1983. *Karl Marx Collective: Economy, Society and Religion in a Siberian Collective Farm.* Cambridge: Cambridge University Press.

Kornai, János. 2008. *From Socialism to Capitalism.* Budapest: Central European University Press.

Lane, Christel. 1981. *The Rites of Rulers: Ritual in Industrial Society—The Soviet Case.* Cambridge: Cambridge University Press.

Laslett, Peter, ed. 1972. *Household and Family in Past Time.* Cambridge: Cambridge University Press.

Leach, Edmund. 2000. "The Aesthetic Frills—Ritual." In *The Essential Edmund Leach,* ed. Stephen Hugh-Jones and James Laidlaw, Vol. 1, 153–209. New Haven: Yale University Press.

Ledeneva, Alena V. 1998. *Russia's Economy of Favours: Blat, Networking, and Informal Exchange.* Cambridge: Cambridge University Press.

Malinowski, Bronisław. 1992 [1912]. "The Economic Aspects of the Intichiuma Ceremonies." In *The Early Writings of Bronisław Malinowski,* ed. Robert Thornton and Peter Skalník, 209–227. Cambridge: Cambridge University Press.

———. 1935. *Coral Gardens and Their Magic: A Study of the Methods of Tilling the Soil and of Agricultural Rites in the Trobriand Islands.* London: Allen & Unwin.

Mauss, Marcel. 1990 [1924]. *The Gift: The Form and Reason for Exchange in Archaic Societies.* New York: Norton.

Müller, Birgit. 2007. *Disenchantment with Market Economics: East Germans and Western Capitalism.* New York: Berghahn Books.

North, Douglass. 2005. *Institutions, Institutional Change and Economic Performance.* Cambridge: Cambridge University Press.

Parry, Jonathan, and Maurice Bloch. 1989. "Introduction: Money and the Morality of Exchange." In *Money and the Morality of Exchange,* ed. Jonathan Parry and Maurice Bloch, 1–32. Cambridge: Cambridge University Press.

Polanyi, Karl. 2001 [1944]. *The Great Transformation: The Political and Economic Origins of Our Times.* Boston, MA: Beacon.

Sahlins, Marshall. 1972. *Stone Age Economics.* London: Tavistock.

Sárkány, Mihály. 1983. "A lakodalom funkciójának megváltozása falun." *Ethnographia* 94: 279–285.

Shanin, Teodor. 1990. *Defining Peasants: Essays Concerning Rural Societies, Expolary Economies, and Learning from them in the Contemporary World.* Oxford: Blackwell.

Simon, Herbert. 1956. "Rational Choice and the Structure of the Environment." *Psychological Review* 63, no. 2: 129–136.

Smith, Joan, Immanuel Wallerstein, and Hans-Dieter Evers, eds. 1984. *Households and the World Economy.* London: Sage.

Spittler, Gerd. 2008. *Founders of the Anthropology of Work: German Social Scientists of the 19th and Early 20th Centuries and the First Ethnographers.* Berlin: Lit.

Stiglitz, Joseph E. 1993. *Globalization and Its Discontents.* New York: Norton.

Verdery, Katherine. 1996. *What Was Socialism and What Comes Next?* Princeton, NJ: Princeton University Press.

Todorova, Maria. 1989. "Myth-making in European Family History: The Zadruga Revisited." *East European Politics and Societies* 4, no. 1: 30–76

Werner, Cynthia A. 1999. "The Dynamics of Feasting and Gift Exchange in Rural Kazakstan." In *Contemporary Kazaks: Cultural and Social Perspectives,* ed. Ingvar Svanberg, 47–72. Richmond, Surrey: Curzon.

Yurchak, Alexei. 2006. *Everything Was Forever Until It Was No More: The Last Soviet Generation.* Princeton, NJ: Princeton University Press.

1

Economy as Ritual

The Problems of Paying in Wine

JENNIFER CASH

Although "ritual" is sometimes defined only by reference to its structure or form as a "performance of more or less invariant sequences of formal acts and utterances not encoded by the performers" (Rappaport 1992), most uses of the term within anthropology and ritual studies continue to be influenced by earlier approaches (e.g., Turner 1969) and reference events and practices that also interrupt, punctuate, or transform a larger flow of sequenced activities. From this perspective, ritual is normally assumed to be extraordinary, even though it is not independent of the everyday mundane concerns of politics, economy, or social hierarchy. Rituals reinforce power imbalances even as they provide the opportunity for critique and inversion (cf. Alonso 1990); they mystify, hide, and deceive (Lukes 1975); and their transformative powers are better understood by some participants than others, even if no one ever fully grasps their total effect or potential (Bell 1992). It could be said that the domain of ritual is penetrated by, and sometimes indistinguishable from, the domain of economy, where calculation, self-interest, and personal gain frequently overshadow considerations of community, mutuality, or the collective good. But could it also be said that the domain of economy, as the domain of the ordinary, is sometimes indistinguishable from the domain of ritual? Can ritual be so mundane and all-pervasive that it constitutes economy?

In this chapter, I reconsider the fundamental distinction between the ordinary and extraordinary, or between economy and ritual, by looking at the ways in which "economy" in the sense of making a living, provisioning a household, and organizing household help is undertaken in and through ritual in rural Moldova. Rituals may sometimes operate according to economic logic, but the patterned behaviors of economy could also be described as rituals because they convey their own meaning, making a reality in the moment of performance. Economies, too, incorporate ideological visions of what social life might be like, and actual transactions are often shaped, at least in part, as efforts to bring that world into being, if only temporarily.

My focus is on the payment of day labor in wine in rural Moldova. While it is clearly a rational transaction that pertains to the domain of economy, I shall demonstrate that this type of payment draws its social meaning from the wider spectrum of rituals and in so doing becomes a ritual itself that helps to constitute the locally specific form of house economy and its tensions (Gudeman 2008). The problem, for nearly all village households, is how to balance the forms and relations of dependency in ways that make one's household appear to be independent, respectable, and equal to others. Paying day laborers in wine is a particularly useful way for households to be able to hire the help they need (rather than exchanging labor), dispense with a surplus agricultural product that they cannot sell, and divert scarce cash to other purposes. It is also a practice that makes it impossible to deny social difference, inequality, and actual relations of interdependence. I do not conceptualize the work relation itself as a ritual (consisting of the negotiation of the terms of work on a per task basis, the workday itself, and the actual presentation and receipt of payment) but concentrate on a variety of other rituals that provide the social meanings, associations, and contexts that make wine payments both desirable and problematic for those who pay and for those who work. In other words, I have attempted to locate the rituals that help to create and resolve the local tensions of economy by focusing on a particular kind of transaction that generates considerable discussion and debate among villagers.

From this perspective, several types of ritual contribute to the constitution of economy. Wine itself is an element widely used in Orthodox church rituals; the sharing of wine is also a ritual that punctuates much everyday activity and is incorporated into the structure of life-cycle rituals and most other commonly recognized categories of ritual (see Cash 2011). The arrangements of contemporary day labor partially replicate older work rituals, and the meaning of wine, when it is served to workers, borrows from rituals of hospitality. Across these rituals, the production, possession, and serving of wine symbolizes a man's individual respectability and a household's self-sufficiency; while the sharing of wine (temporarily) erases social difference and forges mutuality, commonality, and community.

The Problems of Paying in Wine

In the early 2000s, many rural households responded to the economic hardships that accompanied Moldova's privatization of agricultural land by reinvigorating traditional forms of labor exchange. Such a revitalization of presocialist work rituals was restricted in scope, and at the time of my research in 2009–2010, it had become preferable to pay workers rather than to be indebted for future requests for help from others. I found that households paid day laborers in varying combinations of cash and wine; most workers were only paid cash, but a category of people who were known to "work for wine" continually negotiated varying kinds of payment from the households that hired them.

In the years immediately preceding my fieldwork, paying day laborers in wine became a particularly valued but problematic option for many households. Although cash income has gradually risen since 2004 (mostly from remittances) (Laur 2005), Russian bans on the importation of Moldovan wine in 2005 and 2006 crippled the industry and many rural households now have an annual surplus of wine that they cannot sell to local wineries, as in the early post-Soviet years. In such conditions, substituting wine for cash is a rational solution for paying day laborers, but one that generates ongoing discussion as those who do the hiring remain distinctly uncomfortable with the arrangement, sometimes paying in cash and at other times offering to pay in food (i.e., meat, milk, wheat, or cheese) that can be eaten or resold in the local market. Such offers to pay in food are always refused by those who "work for wine," generating considerable discussion and a sense of moral dilemma as detailed below.

The moral dilemma faced by households that pay workers in wine rather than cash might be expected to revolve around the responsibility they bear for exploiting and furthering their workers' alcoholism. Such concerns do arise, particularly among women, and the alcohol dependency of female workers is generally of greater moral concern than that of male workers. Social concern for alcohol dependency, however, is generally limited; "alcoholism" is associated with the regular consumption of hard, falsified, or industrial alcohols; urban settings; ethnic Russians; and other people and places. "Real" alcoholics do not work. Regularly drinking wine in the village, even in substantial quantities, is considered normal and acceptable. Social disapproval, though not necessarily the label of "alcoholic," appears when drinking interferes with a person's ability to ensure his or her household's well-being, or when it leads to violence against family members. In the local understanding, therefore, the problems associated with paying workers in wine are more precisely related to how the working relationship between two households—one that pays in wine, and one that works for wine—reflects on the social status of each within the ideological framework of self-sufficiency that I describe in greater detail elsewhere (Cash forthcoming). While payment in cash symbolizes and creates autonomy between households, payment in wine symbolizes an interdependence of households that is rooted in mutual respect. The moral dilemma produced by paying workers in wine is thus both broad and deep as it requires households to confront and resolve the presence of mutuality, inequality, and social exclusion in a local model of economy that normally promotes independence, equality, and social respect between households.

The problems of paying workers in wine that have arisen in the postsocialist period become more evident when placed in a broader context of ritual life and meanings related to both work and hospitality. The practice of paying in wine itself can be linked to the continuation of pre-Soviet work rituals through the Soviet period. In the pre-Soviet period, various forms of work undertaken collectively by multiple households were quite literally, "work parties." Then, as now, well-fed workers were considered more likely to complete a given task. But, households that offered their workers wine as well as food also borrowed the meanings associated with offering wine and food from rituals of hospitality. In the context of work parties, the exchange of wine for labor allows for semantic slippage and transformation: work becomes celebration; relations of dependency or interdependency give way to social equality and mutual respect. During the Soviet period, households organized fewer work parties overall and some forms of work party ceased to be practiced at all, but the slippage of meaning between work and hospitality continued. In the language of closely related rituals of work and hospitality in the postsocialist period, workers who refuse to be paid in food but demand wine instead are also demanding social respect from their employers as well as the means to directly perform the sufficiency, autonomy, and respectability of their own household at the end of a workday by hosting guests of their own.

Economic Change in a Moldovan Village

I conducted fieldwork in the village of Răscăieți in 2009–2010.[1] Răscăieți is located in a climatic microzone capable of producing the well-regarded Purcari wines, and might well have been expected to prosper under new market conditions following socialism. Instead, like most of Moldova's villages, which have fewer claims to a distinctive product, Răscăieți has suffered general economic decline over the past two decades. The effects of changing border regimes on local economy is particularly visible in the village, as it is located on the banks of the Nistru River, only a few kilometers from Tiraspol, the capital of the secessionist region of Transnistria. A bridge and official crossing point to Transnistria are located at the northern edge of the village. During the Soviet period, regular boat services also connected the village to Odessa, Ukraine. The village's proximity to borders, towns, and river traffic may seem exceptional for a rural region, but it is actually quite typical for Moldova, due to its small size as a country, and the Soviet system of regional administration that supported the development of thirty-two regional towns and four cities in addition to the capital of Chișinău. In recent years, villagers have travelled more frequently to Chișinău—a 113 km or 2- to 2.5-hour drive—for shopping, healthcare, education, and administrative needs that cannot be met in the village or nearby towns.

Răscăieți is of medium size for a Moldovan village, with an official population of about 2,500 people, living in some 1,200 households. The small size of the average household reflects the village's aging population structure and declining birth rates over the past several decades.[2] Since the late 1980s, the official population has decreased by about 460 people, mostly through mortality. Villagers perceive a much more drastic decline in the population, however, because the official statistics do not reflect the high number of people who have left the village for work. Labor migrants rarely change their official registration in the village, even if they remain abroad for several years. In 2008, the village school conducted its own census, which revealed that 54 percent of school-aged children had at least one parent working abroad, and 30 percent had both parents working abroad (cf. Keough 2006). The small size of the average household makes it exceedingly difficult for a household to self-provision from its newly acquired lands without securing help from other households.

Răscăieți is an old village that developed significantly in the Soviet era. The newer settlements generally have poorer land than the old sections of the village—a factor that has become important in the self-provisioning strategies of families in the postsocialist period. Fruits and vegetables were plentiful under socialism: that which people could not, or did not, grow in their own private gardens could be purchased in the local store or taken from the two collective farms. One farm specialized in growing vegetables for seed stock, while the other specialized in grapes and produced bulk wine at its on-site factory. The factory had no bottling facilities, and wine could be easily purchased in bulk by villagers who found that their own supplies ran low. These farms were decollectivized in 1999 through the National Land Program (see Gorton and White 2003: 308, 314). In Moldova, decollectivization occurred relatively late, and the division of land was unusually equitable. Unlike in other cases throughout the postsocialist region, nearly all people who were entitled to land initially took it, and the method of distribution avoided much of the social contention that occurred elsewhere (cf. Verdery 1996; Kaneff and Yalçın-Heckmann 2003).[3]

Today, two successor cooperatives farm 55 percent of the village's total agricultural land.[4] Each cooperative has a "leader," an accountant and accounting assistants, a few tractor drivers and security guards, and a small number of seasonally paid workers; the total staff of the larger farm is fifty-three people, including the leader. Landowners receive a quantity of wheat and sunflower seeds calculated by a government-set formula based on the size of their land. The two farms specialize in grain production, so most of the best former vegetable-producing lands, vineyards, and orchards have not been rented from the individual households that now own them, and are used for household production needs. Some owners have uprooted vineyards to be turned to grain or vegetable plots.

Compared to the Soviet period when the two farms provided nearly universal employment, there are few employment options in the village today. Most salaried individuals work in the public sector, which includes the mayor's office, the school, two kindergartens, the Culture House, the post office, and a small medical center. There are very few businesses: ten stores, three bars, one internet and copy center, one small commercial vegetable producer that has greenhouses, one small flour mill, and the barely functioning wine factory. A small number of villagers work out of their houses as craftspeople and mechanics, and a few have regular employment in the regional center of Ştefan Vodă. A majority of villagers seek cash income through other sources—labor migration is the most common solution, with men most often working in construction in the "near abroad" of Russia and Ukraine, and women working most often as domestic help in southern Europe (Italy, Spain, Portugal). Networks for human trafficking, sex work, organized begging, the drug trade, and other smuggling activities have also cut through the village (Heintz 2006).

Changes in the postsocialist period have resulted in economic decline from several directions. The decollectivization of the village's two farms resulted in declining public services. Running water on demand in the central portion of the village was stopped; the public bath was closed; the central furnace that heated the school, kindergartens, and administrative buildings fell into disrepair; activities at the Culture House (including the showing of films) were severely curtailed; and streetlights were stolen, burned out, and not replaced. Roads also fell into disrepair; access to transportation declined; and river ferry traffic stopped. Changes in trade and production networks, the regulation of industry and markets, and the establishment of new state borders have also limited the economic opportunities of local households. It is perhaps not surprising that more than a decade after decollectivization, many villagers continue to feel that living standards and working conditions under socialism were better than their current conditions (cf. Hann 2003: 10–11).

Bread and Wine at the Base of the House Economy

Even in the postsocialist context, which is marked by multiple engagements of households with regional, national, and global markets, the dominant model of economy in rural Moldova remains one based on the principle of "householding" ("production for one's own use") (Polanyi 1944: 53). Villagers expect the state to regulate markets in the interest of households by controlling prices, enhancing the quality of available goods in local markets, and promoting export opportunities for agricultural products; trade is expected to exist, but "market principles" are morally questionable in village communities and households. As discussed elsewhere (Cash forthcoming), self-representations of the work undertaken by nuclear families to provision for themselves reveal an idealized vision of a rural household that still closely approximates Karl Bücher's classic definition of a "closed" or "independent" domestic economy (Spittler 2008: 93). Such self-sufficiency cannot be achieved at the household level (Sahlins 1972: 83), but actual instances of borrowing, debt, and dependence on others tend to be overlooked when individuals report on the well-being of their own household or that of others. Importantly, each of these principles and models of local economy should be understood from a symbolic perspective and as signaling the inseparability of economy from ritual. Decollectivization provided most village households with the resources to undertake actual self-provisioning, but few have pursued it with any seriousness.

As in many areas of the world, the dominant economic model is not merely based on householding, but is actually realized through a metaphor of the "house." Moldova's rural economy is a "house economy" because the house, as a physical structure and the social household that lives in it, is assumed, imagined, and expected to be the central economic institution responsible for both production and consumption (Gudeman 1986: 2; Gudeman and Rivera 1990: 48–53). Metaphors based on the physical and social attributes of houses are used to explain the goals and parameters of economic activity. Such metaphors are, accordingly, ripe for play and can be looked to for indications of the ritualization of economy.

In rural Moldova, bread and wine can be said to form what Gudeman has called the "base" of house economy (Gudeman 2008: 28–29). Although many foods are consumed, these two are the building blocks of a house's well-being and are vested with meanings that render them "sacra" (Gudeman 2001). Bread and wine are both omnipresent in daily and ritual life. The substances draw many of their symbolic resonances from Christianity. With more than 98 percent of Moldova's population declaring themselves Orthodox Christians, and a wide-reaching religious revival in the postsocialist period, villagers are well aware of the religious connotations of bread and wine. In interviews with me, religious specialists claimed that the widespread use of bread in life-cycle and commemorative rituals dramatically expands on biblical references and symbolism. But, since rituals such as weddings, baptisms, and commemorations of the dead are commonly assumed to be religious, the regular home consumption of bread used in such rituals also intensifies the sacredness of all bread. The same is probably true of wine, though local folklorists and ethnographers have compiled far less information about the ritual uses of wine than those of bread.

Bread is the basic staple of rural households.[5] When baked at home, bread "has no price;" it can only be given, not sold or exchanged, to non–household members.[6] A house cannot exist without adequate supplies of bread, and a new house is never established without it (Cash 2013a). As in much of Eastern Europe, bread is used in welcoming guests (Mesnil 1992: 7), but it also appears in wedding, baptismal, funerary, and commemorative rites. Bread is offered as part of the verbal invitation to a wedding, torn by a new couple to determine who will be the more powerful partner in the marriage, given to wedding sponsors, and exchanged between families; it is given to a baby's godparents at baptismal celebrations. It is placed on graves along with items such as clothing, and regularly given as *pomană* to relatives, friends, the church, and strangers to commemorate the deceased and help them reach heaven (Buzilă 1999). In short, bread is present at every life-cycle ritual, and would seem by association, if not explicit symbolism, to signify life itself. The archetypal bread is a round wheat loaf said to be "like the sun"—a metaphor that completes a circle of associations among solar energy, the land, and food (Gudeman 2012).

Wine is also essential to the social existence of a house. Visitors to a rural house are offered homemade wine from the cellar—a more important offering than food. One of the most visible markers of a house's social standing is in its display of barrels of wine, alongside preserved foods, in its cellar. As elsewhere in postsocialist Eurasia, household canning in Moldova serves the practical purposes of provisioning "healthy" food for winter, for times of market scarcity, and even for days when the household has little time for meal preparation or guests arrive unexpectedly (see Phillips 2002; Caldwell 2007; Jung 2009; cf. Alber and Kohler 2008; Jehlicka and Smith 2011; Smith 2002). But in rural Moldova, the canned vegetables, fruits, jams, and meats and barrels of wine stored in a house's cellar are also visible markers of everything important for a household to demonstrate about its members—self-sufficiency, hard work, and hospitality. The barrels of wine that line the walls of house cellars are the most important; they reflect more clearly on the household's commitment to providing hospitality to others and first-time visitors to a house are almost always taken into the cellar and offered a drink of wine drawn directly from a barrel. Wine reserves are so important for social reputation that even urban men often strive to construct "cellars" in the unused eaves, corners, and garages of their apartment buildings where they store bulk wine given by or purchased from relatives and acquaintances in rural areas.

Wine is also an integral component of many of the rituals listed above. It is offered alongside bread when inviting guests to a wedding, and appears on festive tables at weddings, baptismal parties, and all family celebrations. Wine is also offered as *pomană* in a series of commemorative services required by the church, and is poured on graves during funerals and commemorations. Wine sacralizes speech acts: it is indispensable for offering toasts on auspicious occasions, such as weddings, and for consoling and memorializing on more solemn occasions. Ethnic Moldovans insist that one does not "drink" (*a bea*) wine, but that through the consumption of wine one "partakes in honoring" (*a cinsti*) someone or something (see also Buzilă 2006: 489). Wine is most often consumed among close acquaintances because of its associations with respect, and for its capacity to bring those who drink together into relaxed and communal states (Buzilă 2006: 492).

Bread and wine are gendered and bear further associations that correspond with the economic domains of women and men. As a symbol of life baked by women, homemade bread only participates in economies based on mutuality. It cannot be denied to anyone who asks for it, and is exchanged between households without calculation. A house that lacks bread is not subject to moral critique, but it is considered desperately poor; even the poorest villagers (who may ask their neighbors for bread) do not publicly claim the offerings of *pomană* to which they are ritually entitled (Cash 2013b). On the other hand, wine is associated with men; "good wine" is said to be that which has been made by a "good man," and it is socially impossible to critique homemade wine without deeply offending its maker.[7] Like the men who make it, wine's contribution to a house's well-being rests in its capacity to broker extensive relations beyond the house and into the realms of the market. Wine can be given as a gift or a loan; and debts in wine are calculated. Unlike bread, wine also has a price, so it can be used in market relations as both a commodity and currency.

When used as a currency, wine's social meanings, uses, and associations increase, lending ambiguity to instances in which wine is exchanged between houses. Giving and taking wine is then manipulated creatively, and to different purposes, in social relations. From this brief discussion of the symbolism of bread and wine as the "base" of house economy, and their related uses in a broad range of rituals, it should be clear that offers to pay workers in wheat (i.e., "bread") or other foodstuffs also convey a social judgment of the workers as "poor," which cannot be contested if workers accept the offer. In contrast, payment in wine is ambiguous and can be manipulated to symbolize either the interdependence or autonomy of houses. Wine shared between individuals and houses in rituals of hospitality symbolizes respect and equality, as well as self-sufficiency. When served in work-related circumstances, such as work parties, wine also works to transform the situation into one that approximates hospitality. In most work relations, the worker who has helped another house should interpret an offering of wine to mean that his labor has been accepted as a "gift," that he is the respected social equal of the householder he helped, and that he can expect the other's help in the future.

When workers are not only served wine, but also paid in wine, the range of possible interpretations increases. Wine payments are problematic and closely managed because houses that have no wine (i.e., no base) of their own are hardly equal social partners with those that have a surplus. When a house has no wine of its own, its members are considered to not possess the moral strength, organizational capacity, or work ethic to provide for themselves. Such qualities are clearly not those with which houses that have a "base" want to associate. Yet neither do those who "work for wine" wish to be seen as inferior, and their demand for wine (and refusal of other food) entitles them to understanding their "payment" as a "gift" that conveys respect and recognition as well as the means to host guests of his own at the end of a workday. For such a worker, payment in wine can further his sense of equality in village life despite his obvious lack of material well-being.

Hospitality or Work? The Care and Feeding of Workers

When rural households engage external labor to help in the tasks of self-provisioning, the workers are offered food and wine. The various meanings and associations described above are thus transposed into the realm of production. An employer who offers a worker wine demonstrates his respect for the worker. Through the idiom of hospitality, the worker is temporarily incorporated into the household, with the expectation that, upon leaving it, he will testify to the house's merits. A household's economic decision to engage laborers is therefore fraught with ritual symbolism. Labor relations involve the negotiation of this meaning, as much as the negotiation of tasks and their just remuneration. In the postsocialist period, households with land holdings have regularly needed to secure additional labor at key points in the agricultural cycle in order to self-provision. Households that need labor choose between traditional forms of labor exchange and forms of paid labor. Of these forms, paying laborers "with wine" is the most popular solution, even though it leads to relationships that the hiring households find uncomfortable.

Most families use a mix of labor exchange and paid labor to meet their needs. In a survey of twenty-five households, seventeen responded that they make some use of hired labor. Of these seventeen, eleven use wine to pay workers for at least some tasks. Only seven households reported paying laborers in cash, although most of these specified that they prefer to pay with wine if possible. Some noted that cash payments are often reserved for specialized work, especially construction-related projects (for example, the construction of wells and heating stoves), whereas agricultural tasks such as weeding, grape picking, vine pruning, and corn husking are often paid with wine.

I was surprised to find a marked disinterest in labor exchange, especially considering the high rates of unemployment and widespread complaints about lack of income. Labor exchange could be a practical solution to the limited availability of cash, and it seems to have been one in the years immediately following decollectivization. But villagers tended to assign labor exchange, as various forms of work party (e.g., *clacă, şezătoare*),[8] to the realms of ritual and sociability, noting cyclical trajectories of decline that correspond with individual and household life cycles as well as longer-term declines that correspond with modernization. Indeed only a very few types of work party seem to have disappeared as a direct result of socialism. For example, work parties devoted to major agricultural tasks, such as corn husking, disappeared with the collectivization of agriculture; but women's sewing circles only began to disappear in the late 1960s as villages got electricity and women remained in their own homes at night. House-raising parties continued into the 1980s and 1990s, eventually disappearing with new trends in house design, building materials, and possibilities to renovate existing houses rather than building anew. While villagers say that younger families with many children have traditionally participated more extensively in labor exchange than older families (cf. Chayanov 1966: 56–69), survey results and my own observations indicate that younger families in fact prefer to use paid labor (in cash or wine) than to engage in work exchange (i.e., *pe ajutor*). Nor did younger families seem to participate more widely in the kinds of work party that continue to be practiced (e.g., preparations for wedding feasts).

In traditional forms of mutual aid across the presocialist, socialist, and postsocialist periods, a worker could expect to receive equivalent help in the near or more distant future. As noted, workers are also offered food and wine, often during, and certainly at the end, of work. As the etymology of the word *clacă* suggests,[9] the shared meal and wine transforms the workday into an enjoyable party. Eating and drinking together during work transform a potential employment relationship (back) into one of friendship, kinship, or neighborliness. By offering workers this hospitality, work is recognized as a "gift" that is given freely by the workers. Yet, though hospitality functions as an immediate form of reciprocity, it is not a full counter-gift for work; the gift of work still has to be returned. In paid labor arrangements, by contrast, both employer and worker are nominally free of obligations to the other once the work has been completed and paid. Yet paid laborers, whether remunerated in cash or in kind, are almost always fed in the same way as those who work *pe ajutor.*

The additional cost of feeding laborers is recognized, especially by the women who do the cooking, in financial, temporal, and social terms. Women are often reluctant to feed workers with preprepared foods because they cost additional money. But they also believe that it is important to cook because workers might choose to work for other families that feed them better, and that their reputations will suffer because workers will tell other villagers if they are poorly fed. As a result, households may put off hiring workers if they cannot prepare food in time, and women worry that food (and the time and effort of preparing it) may be wasted if the weather changes overnight and work cannot be done as scheduled.

One woman described the stresses and effects of the extra cooking before hiring workers as follows:

> They have a lower level of living, we do not consider ourselves to be very well off.… But then again, maybe they have it better. When we hire them to work for us, I have to get up at three or four in the morning to cook. They wake up at seven, maybe they wash their ears, maybe they don't, and then come here. I feed them; they eat. Then I clean up after them. Then we all go to work together, and we work in line with them. We do not go behind them and beat them, we work together. But we have to be there anyway to supervise. If you don't go, a worker who is less *gospodar*[10] might take a nap under a tree. If he drinks, he might get drunk. Then when it is time to eat, again I put out the food, and again, I clean it up. While I am cleaning, he smokes another cigarette or rests a bit more. Then, when we are done working for the day, I have to hurry home because they are already beating at the gate, and again, put out food for them, and again clean it up. They go home, full, without a care in the world. The next day they go to work for someone else and it is the same. I wouldn't say that their life is easy, but, for me, every extra moment (of work) exhausts me.

Hiring households expressed a sense of social duty and worker pressure to provide food. I was told repeatedly—with various mixtures of sympathy and moral critique—that most of the people available to work for others "hardly have anything at home." Anecdotes of workers who expressed the preference to be fed rather than receive a higher wage also circulated, and were retold to me, as proof that it was generally pointless to attempt to negotiate with one's workers to not feed them. Potential workers expected to be fed, I was told, and it was possible to lose a worker's help if one insisted that he bring his own food, even if he was paid a higher rate. The obligation to cater to the needs of one's workforce might be considered a gesture of respect toward a laborer one is paying in cash. However, the same gesture performed toward laborers who were paid in wine generated moral ambiguity and some resentment that one was paying "twice over." In the following section, I examine the roots of the resentment often expressed about the need to feed and offer wine to such workers.

Those Who Work for Wine

Each neighborhood in the village has at least one household known to "work for wine," and the individuals in these houses are engaged successively by their neighbors for one or a few days of labor at each point during the agricultural cycle. The neighborhood in which I lived hired from two families—one consisted of an elderly woman, her adult son, and his Russian wife; the other family consisted of four Gypsy sisters in their mid twenties and (more rarely) their parents.[11] Such individuals and their households are socially and economically marginal by any standard, but not fully excluded from village life. Rather, they create and maintain enduring social relations with the houses for whom they work.

Labor rates in the village are calculated in cash, and then converted into wine. During 2009—2010, a full day of labor cost between 70 and 100 lei.[12] The cost can vary slightly, and is generally higher in the summer when working hours are longer and lower in the fall and winter when workdays are shorter. The cost has increased slightly since 2008, by an average of 10 to 20 lei/day, an increase that is sometimes taken to reflect the country's "financial crisis." Some people calculated further, reaching an hourly rate of some 10 lei/hour, but workers do not always accept this conclusion. For example, when my host family paid three of the Gypsy sisters a total of 100 lei for three hours of cutting corn in the fall of 2009, the women's father appeared the next day to demand higher payment and to refuse further working relations. The cash equivalent of wine is 10 lei/liter, and wine is usually dispensed in two-liter bottles, making an average rate of pay 3 to 5 bottles of wine per day of work. In many cases, laborers are actually working off a wine debt accrued in the days or weeks immediately prior to being hired, or over the winter when there is less work for them. Most heads of household remember the size of the debt without making written notations.

The presence of people who "work for wine" is reminiscent of the payments for household labor made in vodka throughout Russia, but qualitatively different. For example, Myriam Hivon (1998) describes the payment system in rural northern Russia in the early 1990s as a continuation from the Soviet period when bottles of vodka were ideal forms of payment because they disguised the labor relations contracted between "private" individuals as gift relations; and because bottled vodka could be stored and recirculated. In his research in the Urals during the early 2000s, Douglas Rogers (2005) found that home-produced moonshine was serving as a new alternate currency, particularly in mediating the transfer of labor between households. In both cases, alcohol appeared as a substitute for cash, valued for its scarcity and pleasurable effects but with few other social or cultural meanings. In contrast, wine in rural Moldova is not scarce, and its production, storage, and consumption are deeply symbolic. Even when cash was in very short supply in the early 2000s, most village households in Moldova produced enough wine each fall for their annual consumption.[13] Few households ever find themselves without enough wine, and those that do usually pursue strategies other than "working for wine" to invisibly replenish their supply.

Working for wine is thus anomalous in Moldova and raises moral issues that appear not to be present in other ethnographically close regions. For households that hire workers, wine payments are both strategically useful and morally problematic. Working for wine conflicts with the values held by hiring households, both at the level of how work should be remunerated (either through exchange or in cash), and in the goals of work (i.e., to create a self-provisioning and self-subsistent household). People who pay workers in wine dimly perceive the exploitative nature of the relationship, but what they express more articulately is the way that "working for wine" departs from their own aspirations.

People who work for wine are not "alcoholics" by the strictest of local definitions because—after all, they work. Thus, one individual who is known to "work for wine" is distinguished from his wife who is an alcoholic; the wife barely tends her own house and is considered a poor worker who people prefer not to hire, while the husband is a good worker with "hands of gold." Although I had regular contacts with several people who work for wine, they regularly dissuaded me from ever visiting them at home, and for good reason: their houses really are in disrepair, the gardens are unkept, and the cellars are empty. They could not offer me the kind of hospitality that they, like those for whom they worked, considered normal and necessary. In the conversations we did have, they avoided discussions of both wine and work, focusing attention on their respect for those who paid them or other points of their lives that merited social respectability— such as their professed love of reading, anticipated visits from relatives, or long-awaited invitations to serve as godparents. Although marginal, such workers share many, and even most, of the basic values of those who hire them, and must therefore creatively manipulate the symbolic meanings of wine, work, and hospitality in ways that enable them to consider themselves socially respectable.

The marginality of these individuals and their houses has different root causes. Most do not have land of their own, but more importantly they have not pursued other forms of wage labor such as migration abroad; some have experienced debilitating personal traumas. The alcoholism of a spouse, parent, or close neighbors and acquaintances may correlate with an individual's willingness to work for wine, but villagers hesitate to say that it is so, and workers themselves deny it. Regularly working for others, however, certainly perpetuates marginality. Throughout the spring of 2010, one worker repeatedly tried to refuse work offers with the explanation that he needed to prepare his own garden; when pressured, he accepted all of the work offers and never completed his own planting.

The tensions surrounding the practice of paying workers in wine were brought out particularly well by a couple that has little access to cash, and feels a social and moral responsibility for their workers. Iurii and Pasha are in their mid fifties. During the Soviet period, Iurii worked as a driver on the village's main collective farm and Pasha worked in one of the two village kindergartens. Both lost their jobs during decollectivization, and the couple was among the first in the village to take their land out of the collective farm in 1999. The couple has not rented their land to either of the successor farms, but has made the decision to live off of the land as best they can, and with as little help as possible. Of the twenty-five households surveyed, their approach to self-provisioning is the most thorough and self-consciously pursued. They have a very small amount of cash income from the milk and cheese that Pasha sells among friends and neighbors, which they use to cover costs they cannot avoid paying in cash—petrol for periodic tractor hiring, pesticide (especially for their grapes), medicines, occasional store purchases, and unavoidable social costs. Although Iurii and Pasha strive to work their land themselves, they also rely on paid labor for help during critical points of the agricultural cycle. They make some use of labor exchange, but not very much, citing their own age and lack of physical stamina as reasons not to help others. They get some help from one son who has remained in the village, but they consider his primary responsibility to be to "his own family" and they are ashamed to be seen as needy vis-à-vis their son's parents-in-law.

Under these circumstances, Iurii and Pasha feel that they have little choice except to pay workers in kind rather than in cash. Conversations with them, more than with other families who have the ability to pay cash, reveal the moral and social ambiguities of paying workers in wine. In the extended quote below, Iurii attempts to explain to me why people work for wine, and why he pays workers with wine:

> [People who work for wine] do not have anything to eat at home. This is why they come to work. They know here you will feed them in the morning, at noon, and again in the evening. In the evening he goes home, goes to bed, and the next morning—hop—let's go to Ion's house. Oh, were we already at Ion's? Then, Vasia's, Gheorghe's … If I had money … I would give them money … if I had money.… But others have money, and do not want to give him money. They give him wine. But what can he possibly do with this wine? He drank it, he went to bed, and that's it. Bread he cannot buy; he cannot afford anything. He comes to a neighbor, and he begs, "Give me a bottle of wine," and the neighbor gives it to him, but on the condition that he will work it off later. If I had money, if I had money, I would not give him even one gram of wine. What does an hour of work cost? 10 lei? How many hours did you work—seven, eight, ten? Here, take 100 lei, go and buy something, do what you like with it. But others only want to give him wine, or something, as long as it is not money. Yet this wine ruins him. He drinks, continuously, continuously. Does he work? He works (and hard), and then drinks. Because he has no wine at home, he thinks, "Oh, today I will drink here, let him bring me a bottle of wine." I bring out a Pepsi-Cola bottle (two liters) of wine, he drinks it, and then I bring another one, and he drinks it. Let him drink. We also drink, but one glass, or two. He cannot drink like this, though. He has no wine at home. (whispering) They have none, and they want it, and they want a lot.

Like most people, Iurii lays a certain amount of personal responsibility on the workers for their "choice" to accept payment in wine. Certainly, many "blame the victim" for their own behavior, but Iurii and Pasha also recount numerous occasions when they tried to offer workers other food products instead of wine, and even attempts to give a calf as a gift (not payment) to one of the families that they regularly hire. Their workers refused them on all occasions, insisting instead that they be paid in wine. Although they "have no food at home," the workers did not want to accept food (e.g., cheese, flour, or lard) that could either be eaten or resold in the local market for cash. Despite these refusals, Iurii remains more explicitly sympathetic to his workers than most other villagers do, and would not dismiss them as drunkards. In his view, those who work for wine have a deep desire to drink because they do not have wine of their own, it is "normal" to drink wine as a means of punctuating and concluding work. "We also drink," he notes, but adds that he and his wife are able to drink in measured amounts because they have plenty of wine in reserve. They can drink as and when they like, and are not dependent on others to supply the wine.

Conclusion

On the surface, the relation between those who work for wine and those who hire them may be considered one of exploitation in which people encourage alcoholism to benefit from nearly free labor. Such an analysis, however, ignores local concepts of alcoholism, which defines as alcoholics only those people who do not work or who harm others. The consumption of alcohol, and specifically of wine, is generally understood as an integral part of (manual) work; the consumption of alcohol marks the progression and completion of work, and helps to transform labor into leisure; suffering into celebration; and the relations of presumed social hierarchy between boss and worker into the relations of equality between respectable individuals and houses that are expressed in hospitality. Moreover, an analysis that focuses on exploitation would be an overly cynical interpretation of labor relations in a village context where workers and those who hire them know each other well and must live together as neighbors over the long term.

Placed in the broader context of ritual life in rural Moldova, payment in wine is not merely an economic transaction fraught with moral ambiguity. Instead, payments in wine are themselves ritual acts that convey and create the tension of a house economy. Payment for day labor belongs to the realm of the ordinary, but payments made in wine are anomalous and ambiguous. Payments made in wine introduce the extraordinary meanings associated with wine and its use in other ritual settings into the domain of economy. Such payments are made possible by rational equations of the equivalences among labor, cash, and wine. But they also interrupt these equivalences with the reminder, drawn from across the ritual spectrum, that labor is ultimately incommensurable, a gift that cannot be repaid, and that offers of wine honor the worker by meeting his sacrifice of physical power and self-interest with the Christian symbol for the sacrifice of life.

Across the ritual spectrum, wine serves as a triple and contradictory symbol of an individual's social status, a house's self-sufficiency, and a house's connections to others. In some rituals, such as those related to hospitality and work, the paradox posed by wine about the compatibility of autarky and autonomy with mutuality and interdependence is resolved pragmatically by sharing wine only with houses of equal social standing. But payments in wine also challenge such an ordinary approach to resolving economy's tension through ritual. Are workers who accept, and even demand, payment in wine really the equals of those who hire them? Or, are such workers qualitatively different, motivated by other values and principles, never actually "working," but living life as a continual celebration, going from feast to feast? The answer to these questions turns on the ongoing negotiation of payment between houses and their workers and the evolving consensus among households that hire workers.

Notes

1. Răscăieți is the real name of the village. Its position within the wine industry would make it difficult to anonymize, and conversations with the mayor and villagers indicate there is no need to do so. Personal names, however, have been changed.

2. Households in Moldova generally consist of only a nuclear family; the small size of an average household, at just over two members, reflects a declining family size. I was frequently told that families with up to five children had been quite common through the 1960s, but historically, families have not been particularly large; Chayanov, for example, used published census data from 1891 that indicated an average family size of 4.5 individuals (i.e., 2 to 3 children) in Bessarabia (1966: 55). Since the 1980s, many young adults have also migrated out of the village and established their families in nearby towns and cities; this has also contributed to the aging of the village's population and an average decrease in household size for the village.

3. All villagers who were registered as farm workers or had been pensioned from the farms as of 1992 received land shares. This included people who had worked in the social service sectors of the farms (e.g., kindergarten teachers), but not those who were in state service (e.g., elementary school teachers). State workers received partial shares, but if both parties of a married couple were state workers only one could receive land. Although legislation allowed for the return of property to the descendants of its presocialist owners, no attempts were made to restore previous ownership in this village (or most others), and at the time of fieldwork no informants expressed any lingering emotional attachments to unrestored plots of land. Overall, Moldova's land restitution closely resembles that described for Ukraine (Kaneff and Yalçın-Heckmann 2003: 224–228).

4. In almost every village, at least one agricultural association exists to which people can rent their land. These associations are referred to as "cooperatives," even though "members" do not provide labor, participate in decision making, or receive a share of profits.

5. There is also a substitute for bread that can be eaten in times of extreme economizing—*mamaligă* (corn mush). *Mamaligă* is not supposed to be served to guests, but it is much loved by most people, and they often wonder why they do not eat it more often. Most of a house's corn is used to feed animals.

6. In rural Moldova, most households now bake the majority of their own bread—a change since the end of socialism. Bread produced by large commercial bakeries is sold in the local stores, but there is no demand or interest in establishing small local bakeries, even though women often complain about the work involved in baking bread. As I puzzled over this with ethnographers Virgiliu Bîrlădeanu and Ludmila Cojocariu, they drew my attention to the fact that a small bakery would

replicate home baking conditions, and that homemade bread cannot be sold, unlike other home-produced foods such as cheese, butter, meat, and milk.

7. During fieldwork, several men revealed that their wives actually made the wine, or at least supervised the wine-making process, because they had better "noses." In houses where women had been employed as laboratory workers in the wine factory, this was especially common. Nevertheless, the wine was publicly identified as belonging to the man.

8. Karl Bücher included both *clacă* and *şezatoare* in his study of work and rhythm, stressing how the food, song, and dance that accompanied both examples attracted voluntary laborers (1924: 309–311). His descriptions of the events, collected from informants in Romania and Bukovina, evoke the same festive mood as did the descriptions I heard. Thanks to Simon Schlegel for translating the relevant passage.

9. DEX (the authoritative Romanian dictionary) notes that the work done by a *clacă* is often followed by a party. This distinguishes it from more general labor exchange, which is referred to as working *pe ajutor*. Interestingly, the term originated in feudal labor relations when landless peasants were gathered to perform a task collectively, and without pay, for the landowner. The obligatory labor services of *clacă* were formally abolished throughout Romania in 1864; as a component of the Russian Empire, Bessarabia underwent similar agricultural reforms at about the same time (Hitchins 1994: 8, 85).

10. Here my informant is referring to an expanded set of associated meanings with household management. A worker who is *gospodar* should be industrious, hard-working, and orderly.

11. I use the term Gypsy as a reflection of local usage. Official statistics are beginning to record Gypsies in Moldova as Roma, but this particular family publicly claims to identify itself as Moldovan for official purposes and does not know Romani.

12. During fieldwork, 1 Euro was equal to approximately 16 Moldovan lei (s. *leu*); 1 USD was equal to approximately 12 Moldovan lei.

13. Villagers remember a variety of noncash strategies for exchange during the early 2000s, including a high prevalence of barter with people from Transnistria (villagers exchanged agricultural products including wine for clothing, soaps, and other industrially produced goods). Specialty alcohols, such as cognac and champagne, were also traded and bartered by those who had access to them. Within the village, labor exchange is said to have been practiced more intensely, but home-produced food products, including wine, seem not to have been needed to mediate these exchanges.

References

Alber, Jens, and Ulrich Kohler. 2008. "Informal Food Production in the Enlarged European Union." *Social Indicators Research* 89, no. 1: 113–127.

Alonso, Ana Maria. 1990. "Men in 'Rags' and the Devil on the Throne: A Study of Protest and Inversion in the Carnival of Post-Emancipation Trinidad." *Plantation Society in the Americas*, special issue "Carnival in Perspective," 73–120.

Bell, Catherine. 1992. *Ritual Theory, Ritual Practice.* Oxford: Oxford University Press.

Bücher, Karl. 1924. *Arbeit und Rhythmus.* Leipzig: Verlag Emmanuel Reinicke.

Buzilă, Varvara. 1999. *Pâinea, Aliment şi Simbol: Experienţa Sacrului (Bread, Food and Symbol: The Experience of the Sacred).* Ştiinţa: Chişinău, Moldova.

———. 2006. "Obiceiul cinstirii vinului la Moldoveni (The Custom of Partaking Wine among Moldovans)." *Tyragetia,* 488–498.

Caldwell, Melissa. 2007. "Feeding the Body and Nourishing the Soul: Natural Foods in Postsocialist Russia." *Food, Culture & Society* 10, no. 1: 43–71.

———, ed. 2009. *Food and Everyday Life in the Postsocialist World.* Bloomington: Indiana University Press.

Cash, Jennifer. 2011. "Capitalism, Nationalism, and Religious Revival: Transformations of the Ritual Cycle in Postsocialist Moldova." *Anthropology of East Europe Review* 29 no. 2: 181–203.

———. 2013a. "Performing Hospitality in Moldova: Ambiguous, Alternative and Undeveloped Models of National Identity." *History and Anthropology* 24, no. 1: 56–77.

———. 2013b. "Charity or Remembrance? Practices of Pomană in Rural Moldova." Working Paper No. 144, Max Planck Institute for Social Anthropology. Halle.

———. Forthcoming. "How Much Is Enough?: Household Provisioning, Self-Sufficiency, and Social Status." In *Oikos and the Market: Six Postsocialist Studies,* ed. Stephen Gudeman and Chris Hann. New York: Berghahn Books.

Chayanov, Alexander V. 1966. "Peasant Farm Organization." In *On the Theory of Peasant Economy,* ed. D. Thorner, B. Kerblay, and R.E.F. Smith. Homewood, IL: Richard D. Irwin Inc.

Gorton, Matthew, and John White. 2003. "The Politics of Agrarian Collapse: Decollectivisation in Moldova." *East European Politics and Societies* 17, no. 2: 305–331.

Gudeman, Stephen. 1986. *Economics as Culture: Models and Metaphors of Livelihood.* London and Boston: Routledge & Kegan Paul.

———. 2001. *The Anthropology of Economy: Community, Market, and Culture.* Malden, MA: Blackwell.

———. 2008. *Economy's Tension: The Dialectics of Community and Market.* New York and Oxford: Berghahn Books.

———. 2012. "Vital Energy: The Current of Relations." *Social Analysis* 66, no. 1: 57–73.

Gudeman, Stephen, and Alberto Rivera 1990. *Conversations in Colombia: The Domestic Economy in Life and Text.* Cambridge: Cambridge University Press.

Hivon, Myriam. 1998. "'Payer en liquide': L'Utilisation de la vodka dans les échanges en Russie rurale." *Ethnologie française* 28, no. 4: 515–524.

Hann, Chris. 2003. "Introduction: Decollectivisation and the Moral Economy." In *The Postsocialist Agrarian Question: Property Relations and the Rural Condition,* Chris Hann and the "Property Relations Group," 1–46. Münster: Lit Verlag.

Heintz, Monica. 2006. "Tolerance, Conformity, and Moral Relativism: Cases from Moldova." In *The Postsocialist Religious Question: Faith and Power in Central Asia and East-Central Europe,* ed. Chris Hann, 193–212. Berlin: Lit Verlag.

Hitchins, Keith. 1994. *Rumania 1866–1947.* Oxford: Clarendon Press.

Jehlicka, Petr, and Joe Smith. 2011. An Unsustainable State: Contrasting Food Practices and State Policies in the Czech Republic. *Geoforum* 42: 362–372.

Jung, Yuson. 2009. "From Canned Food to Canny Consumers." In *Food and Everyday Life in the Postsocialist World*, ed. Melissa Caldwell, 29–56. Bloomington: Indiana University Press.

Kaneff, Deema, and Lale Yalçın-Heckmann. 2003. "Retreat to the Cooperative or the Household?" In *The Postsocialist Agrarian Question: Property Relations and the Rural Condition*, ed. Chris Hann and the "Property Relations Group," 219–255. Münster: Lit Verlag.

Keough, Leyla. 2006. "Globalizing 'Postsocialism': Mobile Mothers and Neoliberalism on the Margins of Europe." *Anthropological Quarterly* 79, no. 3: 431–461.

Laur, Elena. 2005. "The Brief Characteristic of Creating and Developing the Poverty Monitoring and Analysis System in the Republic of Moldova." Paper prepared for the International Seminar on Poverty Measurement, National Institute of Statistics and Economic Studies, Paris, 30 November–2 December. Last accessed online at http://www.insee.fr/en/insee-statistique-publique/default.asp?page=colloques/pauvrete/pauvrete.htm, 11 October 2012.

Lukes, Steven. 1975. "Political Ritual and Social Integration." *Sociology* 9: 289–308.

Mesnil, Marianne. 1992. "Patience et longueur de temps: Les Leçons du pain." In *Du Grain au Pain: Symboles, Savoirs, Pratiques*, ed. M. Mesnil. Bruxelles: l'Institut de Sociologie de l'Université Libre de Bruxelles.

Phillips, Sarah. 2002. "Half-Lives and Healthy Bodies: Discourses on 'Contaminated' Foods and Healing in Post-Chernobyl Ukraine." *Food and Foodways* 10, no. 1–2: 27–53.

Polanyi, Karl. 1957 [1944]. *The Great Transformation*. Boston: Beacon Hill.

Rappaport, Roy. 2009. "Ritual." In *Folklore, Cultural Performances, and Popular Entertainments: A Communications-Centered Handbook*, ed. Richard Bauman, 249–260. New York: Oxford University Press.

Rogers, Douglas. 2005. "Moonshine, Money, and the Politics of Liquidity in Rural Russia." *American Ethnologist* 32, no. 1: 63–81.

Sahlins, Marshall. 1972. "The Domestic Mode of Production: The Structure of Underproduction." In *Stone Age Economics*, 41–100. New York: Aldine De Gruyter.

Smith, Adrian. 2002. "Economic Practices and Household Economies in Slovakia: Rethinking 'Survival' in Austerity." In *Work, Employment and Transition: Restructuring Livelihoods in Eastern Europe*, ed. Al Rainnie, Adrian Smith, and Adam Swain, 227–245. New York: Routledge.

Spittler, Gerd. 2008. *Founders of the Anthropology of Work: German Social Scientists of the 19th and Early 20th Centuries and the First Ethnogaphers*. Berlin: Lit Verlag.

Turner, Victor. 1969. *The Ritual Process: Structure and Anti-Structure*. Chicago: Aldine.

Verdery, Katherine. 1996. "The Elasticity of Land: Problems of Property Restitution in Transylvania." In *What was Socialism and What Comes Next?*, 133–167. Princeton, NJ: Princeton University Press.

2

Animals in the Kyrgyz Ritual Economy

Symbolic and Moral Dimensions of Economic Embedding

NATHAN LIGHT

This chapter is an attempt to understand the economic and social uses of animals and meat in a Kyrgyz village.[1] I present data about food and animal production, circulation, and consumption in one community, drawing comparisons to feasting and gift exchange in nearby regions of Central Asia. After describing profound changes in Kyrgyz economic and social life and the enduring importance of animal exchange as a cultural focus, I limit my anthropological analysis to discussing symbolic and moral dimensions of material exchange within ritual feasting. I argue that these are the key to the embedding of the animal economy within community life in ways that strengthen ties and produce sociality. In a virtuous circle, Kyrgyz use material exchanges to develop social ties, which in turn become the context for valuing material resources and personal success. Wider comparative questions about processes of meat distribution and feasting and their relationship to social and economic organization cannot be pursued in this chapter.[2]

Here I describe the complex gift economy and expressive practices through which animals and meat circulate among Kyrgyz village households, and show how local rituals realize symbolic potentials of animals beyond their value as nourishment or commodity. Rituals among villagers, friends, and kin give animals and meat a value that cannot be realized in other contexts. Most important social rituals involve feasting and gift exchange. Pastoral animals are the most valued gifts for close associates and at least one animal should be slaughtered for any household feast to mark "good or bad" events (celebrations or death commemorations). Animals represent the capacity of the household to produce resources that make possible participation in ritual exchange, both as meat for feasts and as the currency for important exchanges. Since animals can be bought and sold, their values are shaped by market prices on the one hand and ritual uses on the other. Animals and meat are key components of the complex performances that make feasts valued social experiences. The considerable work of keeping animals reflects the value people place on participating in rituals. Although most households raise goats, sheep, and cows for rituals, gifts, and hospitality, only some households can afford to keep horses for ritual consumption or transport. Raising animals generally requires placing them with professional herders in the summer and participating in household networks (*kezüü*) that share pasturing work during spring and fall.

Kyrgyz villagers raise crops and secure other income for use in the market economy, but animals have special value because they expand and maintain social ties. Kyrgyz generally subordinate market activities to social needs and exchange animals within the "moral economy" of social relations. Relations, respect, and recognition produced through hospitality and gifts are more desirable than what can be obtained through the market and few people pursue market opportunities at the expense of their social ties. Animals are not completely separated from the market in a different "sphere of exchange" (Bohannon 1955), but are more valuable when embedded and circulating in social activities. If sold in an impersonal market transaction, this potential social value goes unrealized. Thus people tend to hold onto animals, and only if they are able to produce more than needed for expected ritual needs do they sell the surplus animals on the market or consume them.

The Ritual Economy

In Kyrgyz villages, gift circulation and feasting are frequent and copious and require considerable effort and resources. Established householders, usually a couple with a separate house and children, are guests and hosts at numerous events and spend a lot of time planning travel, gifts, and contributions. Younger people without households of their own are not able to celebrate in the same way. They are more marginal participants in feasting, generally providing labor for events in the house of their parents or of close kin.

During the two autumn periods that I spent in the village of Beshbulak between 2007 and 2010, home-based *toy* (celebration feasts) were held approximately every other night in the village of 700 households, mostly for weddings. Other, café-based celebrations or commemorations took place every three or four days. Almost every weekend, middle-aged and older people attended *toy* or *ash* (death commemorations), or visited friends and kin for less formal events. For planned events with formal invitations, householders prepare a meat meal, usually of mutton, while more im-promptu visits call for tea, fruit, bread, milk products, and sometimes fowl to be served. Ritual feasts at home involve the slaughter of at least a goat or sheep.

Each event requires a repertoire of ritual gifts and ways of giving them. Any visitor to a home should bring a small gift such as a bag of sweets, but ritual visits require particular gifts appropriate to the event being marked, such as head scarves for new brides or bereaved daughters. Guests at most feasts and death commemorations bring gifts for other participants as well, such as items of clothing for elders and monetary contributions that serve as prizes for games and to remunerate those working at the event, and close relatives even contribute entire animals to the feast. These gifts are part of the complex system of expectations about how to express commit-ment and appreciation in particular relationships, and how to contribute to events. Many contributions and gifts are accompanied by formal public toasts describing the commitment and appreciation of the givers and con-veying their good wishes to the recipients. Food, entertainment, and gifts are similarly given to guests along with expressions of appreciation for their participation and contributions, and they are usually given food and treats to take away as well. Guests thus contribute to events and receive leftovers and gifts from them as well: elders in particular receive clothing and food in appreciation of their attendance and the blessings they give through their presence and their good words.

It is important to note that because of the emphasis on producing pos-itive and harmonious relations, gifts are not given competitively. Compe-tition or reference to the indebtedness of others would spoil the sense of reciprocal generosity and shared participation in producing a good event that is both socially and spiritually efficacious.[3] Relationships are guided by an ideal of sustainability: people should hold events that they can af-ford and give affordable gifts. No one should be expected to hold an event and not receive gifts, nor should they go bankrupt in order to reciprocate. Bridewealth is not given until the giver can accumulate enough surplus, and the dowry (*sep*) might not be given to the couple by the bride's parents for several years after the bridewealth.[4] The dowry should be roughly com-parable in value to the bridewealth—although it consists mostly of house-hold furnishings rather than animals or money—but it also expresses the parents' affection and appreciation for the couple.

Generosity is strongly valued but bragging about it only earns nega-tive responses.[5] Each ritual event or even ordinary visit creates a moral economic context in which people communicate about their relationship through expectations and performance of hospitality and gift giving. People rely upon their broad knowledge of how to perform these transactions in order to achieve valued social results. They create conditions and carry out exchanges that maximize material and symbolic benefits, while avoiding the many pitfalls through which people might feel insulted or neglected.[6]

I argue that this symbolic moral economy should be seen in terms of James Scott's idea that close communities of peasants support a "right to subsistence" for all members. Social arrangements should "minimize the danger of going under" and the well-off should be openhanded with those worse off (1976: 176). I extend this moral approach to the ritual economy: in Kyrgyz villagers' moral ideals, harmony (*ïntïmak*) is created when people give and receive respect and are not offended by inadequate symbolic or material treatment. Social activities are thus guided by the ideal of "minimizing the danger of going under" within the symbolic system of mutual respect, appreciation, and participation. Respect for community members extends to both material aid for ensuring subsistence and help in carrying out important rituals. This moral economy produces what Joel Robbins (2009) describes as "recognition": shared expectations about morality guide Kyrgyz villagers in giving and receiving recognition through rituals consisting of words, actions, and material transactions.

This moral economy is important for understanding ritual because it explains how products, particularly animals, become especially valuable within the context of feasts: the moral economy of feasting maximizes their value. Animals as gifts, especially when served as meat, communicate recognition of personal value to the recipient. Pieces of meat, other foods, and drinks given in appropriate feast contexts produce shared positive feelings and maintain ties among people. The frequent *ooz tiyuu* ritual provides a vivid example of the symbolic value of hospitality: a visitor who is invited but has no time to stay as a guest is brought bread by a household member. The bread is set on a cloth, which represents the *dastorkon* tablecloth on which food is served and the symbolic guests take and eat small pinches of bread and then pass the palms of their hands down across their face while saying "*omïn*" in the conventional prayer that closes a meal. These acts connote the ritual of giving and receiving hospitality but need only minimal food and time to produce. In keeping with Marcel Mauss's (1925) observations about the obligation to both give and receive gifts, the *ooz tiyuu* ritual carries strong moral compulsion: those invited to partake of *ooz tiyuu* must do so or risk insulting their host.

The Village and Its Material Economy

The village of Beshbulak is a typical pastoral and agricultural community in northern Kyrgyzstan and consists of roughly 4,000 inhabitants in 700 homesteads lying along the northern flank of the Alatau Mountains in the western part of Talas oblast. It was initially a Kyrgyz winter quarters (*kïshtak*) that was made into a permanent settlement and incorporated into a collective farm during the collectivization of pastoral nomads in the early 1930s. By the 1960s Beshbulak had grown to more than 300 families and was converted to a state farm (*sovkhoz*) focused on producing fine wool and some horses for Soviet and international markets, along with milk and meat for regional markets. As a state farm, Beshbulak received additional technical and financial assistance, and was streamlined to increase production of sheep and wool (cf. Humphrey 1998: 14; Trevisani 2010: 67–70; Jacquesson 2010). By the 1980s Beshbulak was one of the eighty-six state farms in Kyrgyzstan that specialized in breeding sheep (Tsentral'noe 1984: 124). Its herds reached a peak of 40,000 to 50,000 sheep or roughly one-half percent of the total sheep population of Kyrgyzstan at the time.

As in many state and collective farms, the managerial and technological systems that made Beshbulak a successful farm enterprise declined very quickly after the dissolution of the Soviet Union. Without the large-scale, centralized animal production of the *sovkhoz*, the equipment used for breeding, shearing, feeding, and dairy production fell into disuse and was no longer maintained, along with barns, supply buildings, storehouses, and silage pits. The village infrastructure also decayed (as in the case described by Cash in this volume). Before a new water system was installed in 2007–2009, children and teenagers hauled water by hand from the river and canals with carts and old milk canisters. The long abandoned public baths have only recently been replaced through grant funding. The only Soviet-era institutions maintained by the post-Soviet local government were the public school, a health clinic with dental and childbirth services, and a pharmacy.

Unlike some other post-Soviet states, privatization of land in Kyrgyzstan resulted in most land being given directly to families, rather than being held in larger plots and managed according to contracts with the state as in Uzbekistan (Trevisani 2010), or maintained as large cooperative farms as in the Ukraine (Allina-Pisano 2008). Village families in Kyrgyzstan received titles to plots of irrigated land, although in many villages people opted to continue some cooperative farming as well (Beyer 2011; Yoshida 2005). The average household of six people received 1.5 hectares of irrigated state farm lands. Irrigated land from the large *sovkhoz* fields was distributed as strips from 200 to 500 meters long, so a small parcel could be quite narrow (a one-hectare field could measure 20 by 500 meters, and some small families received even less). Additional land can be rented from the local village government or in nearby communities where households received more land per capita. The animals and other equipment and facilities of the *sovkhoz* were sold to local people in a variety of transactions: those few who risked buying items on credit were fortunate to be able to repay with devalued currency after the financial crises of the mid 1990s.

Kyrgyz engaged in a variety of market activities even before the socialist period but production of commodities expanded considerably under the Soviet economic system, and changed again after 1991. Following radical reorganization of production and trade, postsocialist Beshbulak is connected to commodity markets through the sale of cash crops and animals, and to consumer markets through small shops selling fuel, staple foods, and household needs. The initial financial crises and decline of markets, trade networks, and financial stability meant that people focused on subsistence activities after the Soviet period. They stopped growing tobacco because market networks failed and the government stopped supporting tobacco production. With the loss of heated barns and other technology people turned to raising hardier traditional breeds of goats and sheep and local breeds of cows that give less milk. People continued to raise mixed flocks of chickens, ducks, turkeys, and guinea fowl. Few families specialize in raising horses for milk and meat, and less than 30 percent of families keep horses for transport. Meat production in Kyrgyzstan in general decreased dramatically, while crop production increased somewhat in an effort to reduce dependence on imported food crops (Fitzherbert 2000; Dekker 2003; Jacquesson 2010).

Reduced economic activity and poor transport meant the 1990s were a period of limited market participation in Beshbulak. People attempted to start businesses but customers had little money, obtaining goods was difficult, and credit was largely unavailable. Only over time and through trial and error did people expand their ability to produce and sell through wholesale and retail market outlets. Some took over *sovkhoz* orchards or planted their own fruit trees and now grow fruit and vegetables to sell in the large city of Jambul (Taraz), Kazakhstan, but most avoid the expense and three hours of travel by selling to itinerant buyers who come to the village. Selling milk by the pail to daily collection trucks is also common, and buyers frequently pass through villages seeking animal hides, beans, vegetables, and fruit.

Since 2000, bean exports from northwest Kyrgyzstan have risen significantly, putting it among the top twenty dry bean exporting countries worldwide in 2008 (Akibode and Maredia 2011: 73). This extensive trade has led to a variety of local commodity trading activities: some households buy beans, process them, and find wholesale buyers, while others buy them during the harvest with money from savings or from out-of-town investors and store them in hopes of higher prices. Hand-lettered signs outside many homes announce how much the homeowner is paying for different varieties of beans. The ease of local sales means that many growers store beans as a reserve they can sell when they need money. Although people also harvest potatoes and apples they generally sell these quickly because they do not store well. The greater value per unit weight and ease of storage explain why most families prefer to raise beans as their primary cash crop.

Since 2000, new crops and market opportunities have increased prosperity in much of Talas oblast. The village economy has become a popular alternative to high prices and poorly paid work opportunities in cities such as Bishkek, or living precarious lives as migrant workers in Kazakhstan and Russia.[7] Despite opportunities, few farmers in Beshbulak invest in intensifying farm production. Most families only seek two to three tons of beans or ten tons of potatoes from one hectare; either crop is worth roughly 1,200 Euros. However, some farmers are expanding their cultivated land and hiring villagers to cultivate, harvest, and process their crops. The workers are either day laborers recruited the same morning or more organized labor brigades that contract with landowners in advance and offer more disciplined workers.

Despite the relatively good pay (6–7 Euros per day in 2009) most villagers avoid wage labor because of the hierarchical relations it introduces. People prefer to work in *ashar* mutual aid groups because of the sense of cooperative sociality. *Ashar* are social events in which people help kin and close associates with farming, cooking, construction and other tasks, and these cooperative work parties are also key to preparing ritual events. The most important categories of people to draw on for *ashar* are agnatic kin, friends, and, particularly for younger men, middle school classmates. People join these events out of a sense of reciprocal responsibility and often travel considerable distance to do so. People come from Bishkek, an eight-hour trip, in order to help with the harvest in Beshbulak. They are fed well, younger kin are usually paid a small amount, and town-dwellers often receive gifts of rural produce, but the pleasure of working together and the duty of ongoing reciprocity are the primary motivations.[8] Those who must work for wages forgo this atmosphere and resent nascent class divisions in the village; a middle-aged single mother and brigade-leader who I interviewed commented: "now you understand the life of the working class in Beshbulak."

There are numerous small businesses in the village. Food and automotive fuel shops can be found on almost every other block (fifteen in total in the village). Such shops have very limited stock in trade, usually basic household necessities and occasionally cellular phone credits as well (cf. von der Dunk and Schmidt 2010). Some people provide transport services taking people and produce to nearby towns and cities. Women usually take produce for sale in Kazakhstan because it is considered risky for Kyrgyz men. As one man put it, "Right now, men cannot go to Kazakhstan because they get beat up and no one can help them out of jail. Women can go because they cannot be shut up. They will yell enough."

Purchases at village shops are small: most people have little cash and spend little. They often purchase on credit and end up with debts that must be paid off with income from their crops. Household cash budgets are limited: between 5 and 15 Euros per month per person is spent on food and basic needs. Families purchase flour and cooking oil, and cook and do some heating with electricity. They rarely buy coal or natural gas fuel but burn sheep dung instead. Few households own working vehicles in the village, so they must pay others for transport or use horses and donkeys. Above the basic subsistence budget and the costs of farm inputs such as irrigation fees, taxes, and rented machinery, any extra income is divided roughly half and half between the costs of social events and special purchases such as televisions, cars, or university tuition.

Households and Social Events

Social life in the village revolves around the house. Almost all social events and hospitality take place at home (the only alternatives are the mosque for religious events and two cafés that have opened since 2005 that are used for large feasts with over 100 guests). Women manage the household space and do most of the preparation and serving of food. Houses generally have large rooms to accommodate twenty or more people gathered around a large *dastorkon* cloth, which is spread upon felt carpets. Guests sit on mats along the sides of the room. The room can also accommodate overnight guests by simply rearranging the mats. At less formal male social events, such as drinking or playing cards, men sit outside in a courtyard or in public spaces, usually on mats on the ground. Cafés with their chairs and tables are used only for formal gatherings because people prefer to spend money on increasing the quality and quantity of domestic hospitality.

The household is also the center of the social and economic activity of a married couple who accumulate economic and social resources through their activities. People expand and reinforce their social ties by ritual events based in the household, and couples enter community life by creating a household and producing a family. The birth of a child begins the sequence of feasts held in family and community venues celebrating birth, first steps, completion of the first year of school, circumcision for a boy, graduation from school, and finally marriage (cf. Werner 1999: 64). The marriages of one's children generally lead to strong ties and large gift transactions with the affines known as *kuda* (parents-in-law of one's son or daughter). *Kuda* are the most important in the broader category of nonagnatic kin known collectively as *jekjaat*. One woman described the importance of relations with *jekjaat* as follows: "My *törkün* [a married woman's natal family] are *jekjaat*, my younger brother's in-laws are *jekjaat*. My son's in-laws are *jekjaat*. My daughter's husband's parents are *jekjaat*. Thank god, we interact with all them. If I have a *toy* I invite them, if they have a *toy* they invite me." A couple with growing children needs to produce resources for feasts and hospitality, and contribute to the events of others in order to establish and ramify ties with allies. By inviting respected guests, particularly elders, mullahs (*moldo*), and affinal kin, as well as colleagues, classmates, and neighbors to a feast the household receives blessings and properly marks weddings, births, circumcisions, and deaths. The household relies on close patrilineal kin to help prepare events and to loan animals for larger events. If the household has adequate resources it can draw more workers from its patrilineal kin group (*uruu*) and hold a larger feast to mark multiple ritual occasions—such as an important birthday (fiftieth, sixtieth), a son's marriage or circumcision, and a new home—in a single celebration, now usually held in a café.

The exchange relations around life-cycle events are essential not for material survival, but because holding rituals is a crucial part of household social life. In the face of real dearth people help community members with basic needs but it is through feasts that a household becomes a full member of the community. As some villagers pointed out, the mutual aid given by close associates and affines for major rituals serves as a kind of rotating savings association: one must contribute to others when they need to hold a ritual feast, and can in turn expect to receive assistance from them for one's own event. Rotating saving associations are generally called *chërnaya kassa* (see Abramzon et al. 1958: 259–260; Yoshida 2005: 244 n.16). Despite the overtly stated motivation of access to resources from kin, neighbors and friends, people also value participation and sociality for their own sake. Rather than using sociality to maximize access to resources, people seem to maximize the sociality attainable with limited material resources.

Some of the largest and most costly feasts are those for death commemorations. However, contributions by guests, kin, neighbors, and lineage members mean that households commemorating deaths do not usually lose money on these occasions. After a death in Beshbulak, the body remains at the home for two or three days of mourning visits by relatives, colleagues, and community members. On the final day hundreds of fellow villagers and kin attend the ritual of removing and burying the deceased, and share in a large but simple meal made up of horse and sometimes other meat. During this initial period, mourners donate money to the family when they visit, and patrilineal kin usually take up a collection of money to give to the spouse or children of the deceased to support funeral costs.

In addition, affinal kin bring carpets and money to the funeral (cf. Beyer 2009). The family slaughters a sheep each week in a sequence of smaller feasts that culminate in a larger one on the fortieth day after the death. The more elaborate commemorative ritual feast known as *ash* should happen the following year, but it may be delayed if resources have to be gathered. It should include the slaughter of at least one horse, although a cow may be substituted if one has limited resources or if the deceased is a woman (Jacquesson 2008: 299). The ritual generally extends over a whole day with many groups of guests attending in sequence. *Kuda* are expected to contribute animals or money to these events, and other *jekjaat* are also expected to bring significant gifts and money.

Ritual participation requires that households carefully manage production to be able to fulfill future ritual needs as well as participate in reciprocal support relations around more costly or sudden events such as funerals. Ritual events create social ties with allies who serve as donors for later events. The most important ties should be permanent, although there is always the possibility that relations will fade and people will stop contributing to each other's events. If a couple divorces, *kuda* usually stop supporting each other, but they may remain friends and stay in close contact regardless of the relations between their children. Relations may break down through simple neglect but can be restarted. In one case, Bekbosun and Cholpon had not made reciprocal visits or gift exchanges with Cholpon's brother for many years, but when the brother and his wife hosted an *ash* commemoration feast after the death of Cholpon's mother, they invited Bekbosun and Cholpon and were able to restart relations. As *jekjaat* Bekbosun made a donation worth 40 Euros to the event to demonstrate his commitment to renewing the relationship.

The "developmental cycle" (Goody 1958) of Kyrgyz households leads young married couples to gradually expand household production and reproduction and build social ties through rituals. Households vary in organization with a major difference between extended families that include parents and a number of younger married sons working together to sustain production and reproduction, and households managed separately by mature brothers who only sometimes work together. Rituals also vary widely, with weddings and funerals varying from 50 to 300 people and 300 to 2,000 Euros in costs. Flexible ritual forms give people options, but the frequently quoted local "standard" for a bridewealth of 100,000 som or roughly 2,000 Euros serves as a symbolic benchmark for people to express commitment to a relationship.[9] In fact, most bridewealths are less than this, at least in the village, because most people cannot afford so much. For all but the most prosperous households, anything in the range of 50 to 100,000 *som* is considered acceptable. The wide range of acceptable ritual forms allows most families to afford ritual meals regardless of household capacity or number of dependents. Marriage processes are flexible enough to overcome resource shortages.

Public opinion tends to prioritize the interests of families that need brides over those of the brides and bride-giving families, and kin and friends will contribute to the weddings of those with limited resources. Young women are encouraged to marry within a few years of graduating from secondary school, and even members of their natal family may discourage them from leaving a new household after they have been kidnapped for marriage. Such marriage by kidnapping (*ala kachuu*) is widely tolerated despite its violence, partly because the village moral economy avoids excluding young men and their households from the ritual cycle and delaying the household developmental cycle.[10]

Valuing Animals

Animals have a wide variety of uses and values. Bridewealth gifts may include up to nine equine, bovine, and ovine animals of differing age and sex (Jacquesson 2010: 57–64). Goats are believed better for *kuday tamak* sacred meals while sheep are more appropriate for honoring important guests. Keeping animals for ritual needs and contributions is central to social participation. People save money or sell crops for such purposes but having animals in reserve is felt to be more reliable. Most villagers treat them as illiquid because buying and selling them is time-consuming and uncertain. They prefer to earmark animals for rituals, while crops can be more readily sold to cover other expenses. Even when people have debts at high rates of interest they may prefer not to sell large animals to pay them off (cf. Douglas 1967: 140). The costs associated with animals, such as winter fodder, taxes, and fees for inoculations and pasturing are considered low relative to the animal's increasing value, and caring for animals is felt to be less onerous and demeaning than tending crops.[11] Raising crops is generally household-based work with occasional cooperative work days, while raising animals involves domestic work, rotating cooperative pasturing and some paid herders.

Animals extract value from land that would otherwise have to be worked through human labor. They provide milk, skins, wool, and fuel in the form of dung, as well as meat, although the wool currently produced has little use or market value. Sheep dung is preferred for fuel because of its low cost and the steady heat it provides—although people do comment on its nonmodernity and mention the convenience and low cost of Soviet-era coal—and they value animal foods more than those from plants. Keeping animals represents prosperity and self-sufficiency in ways that crops cannot because they stop growing and are difficult to keep after harvesting. Animals are kept until needed, continue to gain weight, and may provide useful products. Life is felt to be poor if one lacks animals: they improve life through richer foods and enable participation in rituals.

Having animals shows social commitment, readiness to fulfill obligations, and ability to participate in events and offer hospitality. For settled village Kyrgyz with relatively egalitarian distribution of agricultural land, the few animals that most people can raise are reserved for hospitality and social rituals as well as subsistence needs. Cows are now one of the more popular animals for long-term holding, because they provide milk and are large enough to be a suitable contribution to major ritual feasts (cf. Behnke 2003). Sheep are valuable as gifts and for their meat, but their milk and wool are of little value, so dung and lambs are the primary products they create while alive. Many people store beans as a reserve for urgent expenses: they are exclusively a cash crop because people do not eat them or serve them to guests.[12] Unlike animals, beans have no symbolic value in social circulation.

Animal gifts ease accounting and reciprocation because each age and sex of animal is appropriate for a particular category of gift, just as different cuts of meat are suited for different categories of guests at feasts. Animals thus provide a stable symbolic currency: although money is often substituted for animals, gifts are usually remembered in terms of animal equivalents because this prevents distortions due to inflation and changing currencies. When gifts are matched to social categories, accounting is easier: one remembers getting a conventional gift rather than recording each gift individually. Textiles and items of clothing also provide a system of gift categories suited to many different social relations and events, but people are often less satisfied by these because one can easily end up with too many carpets and suits of clothes.

Poverty and other economic problems affect access to animals as well as money. In Beshbulak during the relative poverty of the 1920s through the early 1950s few animals were given for ritual events or bridewealth. But even in the 1950s, some dowries in Kyrgyzstan were reportedly large enough to receive counter-gifts of a cow and 1,000 roubles (Abramzon et al. 1958: 246), representing at least a year's salary for a collective farm worker at that time.

Animals and Feasts

Managing animals for hospitality and feasts is a central concern of Kyrgyz villagers. The social consumption of animals has increased although animal production declined after the end of the Soviet Union, indicating that with private ownership, a larger proportion of animals circulate through social transactions, rather than at markets. Although the decline in the sheep population in Kyrgyzstan stabilized and began to rise again around 2000, the use of animals in feasts has increased more than the number of animals themselves. During the Soviet period villagers often bought meat in local markets for domestic consumption, but now most meat is consumed during feasts with leftovers taken home for family consumption.[13]

Even when sociality and business are combined sociality remains a dominant goal, and overt pursuit of personal gain at another's expense is generally avoided.[14] The traditional social events known as *sherne*, in which people pooled resources to hold a feast, are now considered to be the same as rotating savings associations. (The *sherne* is the most calculating and equitable way to enjoy the pleasures of a social event while sharing costs equally: the occasion is limited to the social pleasures of friendly reciprocity among peers. People leaving are given *shïbaga* (shares) from the leftovers rather than the *keshik* leftovers one takes home from most feasts.)

This calculated sharing contrasts with the sharing of the *kuday tamak* (sacred meal), in which the host household provides all of the resources for a feast and invites both people recognized as Islamic ritual specialists (mullahs and elders who can recite prayers) and neighbors without regard for social ties.[15] Guests are not expected to bring gifts or make other contributions to *kuday tamak* and everyone leaving is expected to take home *keshik* (ritual leftovers that carry blessings). By sharing with others without expecting return, the household benefits spiritually and the food it produces is sacralized: the guests contribute their presence and benefit both spiritually and materially by consuming the food. Funerals should also have many guests because they contribute spiritual benefits and social recognition by sharing the food offered by the family of the deceased. Ritual feasts have multiplied because each one maximizes the people and food brought together while minimizing the trouble for any individual household: whether for a monthly feast held by a different household in rotation or a wedding, material and work contributions reduce costs. Celebrations usually result in net costs to the household (except for death commemorations), but the general pattern of sharing expenses reduces the burden on hosts and increases their capacity to hold events.

Rituals are part display, part entertainment, and part shared recognition of a celebration or commemoration. In addition to inviting community members to join in commemorating deaths or offer blessings against bad fortune in the *kuday tamak*, Beshbulak villagers offer food and drink in commensal rituals to share their good fortune when they have a new baby, a new bride, a birthday, or a major acquisition such as a new home or car. The events interweave material, spiritual, and symbolic offerings and benefits. People exchange good words, blessings (*bata*), and collective concern along with material gifts. Attention to others' fortunes and misfortunes helps suppress differentiation and offense that might lead to conflicts. Food, particularly meat, carries important spiritual and social meanings, but other material exchanges are important as well. Cloth, clothing, and even items of jewelry can become sacralized gifts when given to participants at a funeral. Often the most significant gifts are given to the guests from the greatest geographic or genealogical distance (cf. Jacquesson 2008: 291; Hardenberg 2010).

Animal Economics and Social Ties

At least 80 percent of households in Beshbulak raise at least a few sheep and goats that they reserve for ritual events, with an average holding of 15 animals. Buying animals from the market is inconvenient and expensive. It violates the expectation that one raise animals or have access to them through local associates. Most households can afford to slaughter an animal at home only when they are holding a significant ritual. A few households with larger flocks may slaughter a sheep for domestic consumption as often as once a week, but the meat is still usually shared among related households. Only 10 percent of households regularly sell animals in the nearest market town or the oblast capital. Although the nearest market serves a region of 58,000 people in an area of 4,200 square kilometers with at least 100,000 sheep, 10,000 cows, and 5,000 horses,[16] the usual presence of less than 100 animals for sale at any one time indicates how illiquid the livestock market is.

Because of the labor and expense, less than 30 percent of households keep one or two horses, although both alive and as ritual meat they are an important source of status. Less than 10 percent can keep a herd of around ten horses because of the work involved (see Jacquesson 2007, 2010: 60, 223). A two-year-old horse is worth as much as 30,000 *som* (600 Euros), or almost twice as much as a cow of the same age. As a result, many households slaughter cows rather than horses, even for death commemorations.

The Kyrgyz case demonstrates that animal production can be a central part of economic exchange but remain distinct from market activities. Both animal and crop production are adjusted to market conditions. When buyers had little cash and commodity chains no longer connected to more distant markets, as in the 1990s, Kyrgyz produced animals and crops for greater self-sufficiency but continued to participate in local exchange and sharing, particularly through rituals. Peter Finke's (2003) analysis of commoditization among Kazakhs in western Mongolia shows that the value of products for ritual and subsistence activities shape decisions about market exchange. For Kazakhs, horse milk and melons have high prestige value as gifts and people avoid selling them. Their cultural values influence decisions more than economic considerations such as transaction costs, market risks, and transport costs.[17] Similarly sheep heads are ritually valuable among Kyrgyz at feasts because they are given to show respect to the eldest male guest. However, they have little value when bought from market butchers. The market price is based on nutritional value and convenience of preparation, but in commensal rituals the head stands as the eldest male stands in relation to the gathered guests. Presenting the elder with a sheep's head confirms the group's respect for him.[18]

In ritual contexts, food and drink are given to guests in orderly and meaningful displays of respect. Guests similarly offer toasts, prayers, blessings, stories and even jokes in an effort to entertain and show respect for those present and convey sincere sympathy or congratulations, good wishes for the future, and so on. Elders in particular usually deliver *bata* or words of blessing for selected younger people among the host household, who stand to receive these words at the close of a feast.

Animal exchanges in local kin networks are a common element of mutual aid. One farmer, Amanbek, usually raises a bit more than one hectare of beans, and depends upon a well-off *kuda* to provide a tractor-cultivator for cultivating his fields. This increases his yield by 30 percent over what most people get with little additional work for himself. However, in 2009 he was raising a cow that he planned to give to this *kuda* for a major birthday that would take place in two years. In addition, members of this *kuda* family are the most honored guests when they visit Amanbek's home. Another of Amanbek's daughters married the son of his tenants in an isolated homestead that he bought from the Beshbulak *sovkhoz* when it was broken up. These tenants take care of his small herd of 30 sheep and goats as well as tending their own sheep and horses and raising potatoes. They do not have a systematic agreement about rent or other payments.

Both these cases reflect the ways that kinship and economic relations overlap in flexible mutual support outside of contractual relations. People enter relationships to extend the household and its resources. Linked households work to their mutual benefit in what Stephen Gudeman describes as extending and sharing the base (2001: 80–93). *Kuda* do not always rely upon each other for material help in raising crops and animals, but they generally share care for grandchildren (although paternal grandparents generally invest more in their care). Some firstborn children are even adopted by paternal grandparents and refer to their biological parents with the kin terms for elder siblings.

The close sharing among *kuda* does not eliminate formality. Sharing is tempered by displays of politeness and mutual respect. Agnatic kin ties tend to be more hierarchical and plagued with tensions that do not arise in the more respectful, cooperative ties among affines. Some wealthier families in Beshbulak have expanded their herds and land holdings, with each son taking responsibility for some animals and land, but sustained cooperation of this sort is often difficult. Brothers tend to get into conflicts with each other and require strong parental authority to impose cooperation. By the time their parents retire or pass on, the sons may not continue to work together. Khalid, an eighty-year-old retired herder and hero of Soviet labor was able to build each of his five sons a home in the same neighborhood, but they do not cooperate economically. They maintain separate houses and work independently. Even Khalid and his wife live relatively independently in a separate small house in the compound of the youngest son.

Animal and Meat Transactions

As symbols in many social transactions, animals and meat are parts of communicative routines. At large celebrations (*toy*), male guests are expected to donate money to be given as prizes in a game of *kök börü* (buzkashi) that will be played the following day. The games allow local men who are not invited to the feast to share in the celebration by competing for monetary prizes. When arriving at the entrance to the feast, each male guest is confronted with the carcass of a goat placed in front of him as a signal that he should give 1 or 2 Euros for the *kök börü* game that will be played using this carcass. Sometimes money collectors will continue to block the guest's path and joke with them to extract more money. Food can also be used to extract donations: when *jekjaat* guests attend a feast, they are first seated in a separate room and served meat and hot tea to extract donations of 2 to 10 Euros in a process called *terdetüü* ("making sweat"). If they do not give money quickly or it appears to be too little, they are ostentatiously served more food and tea amid joking. In addition to being used to extract contributions, meat is exchanged socially when elders give bones with meat on them (*jilik*) to younger people during feasts. The proper acknowledgement is simply the word "*kulduk*" said by the younger to the elder, meaning roughly "[I am your grateful] servant."

Preparation for rituals revolves around slaughtering animals and dividing the meat, which is served on top of platters of noodles or rice pilaf. During the event the meat should be carefully arranged on the platters according to the guests' status. This distribution of meat takes place in a room set off from the rest of the group, where middle-aged male agnatic kin of the hosts known as *chïktanchï* are in charge, while women and younger men bring them platters and describe who will be eating from each one. Although most boys by age twelve or so are relatively proficient in slaughtering sheep, the processing of larger animals and proper serving of meat to show appropriate respect for the guests are valued skills. Like the servers and other working agnatic kin, *chïktanchï* are not guests at the feast, nor are they paid. However they can serve meat and tea to get *terdetüü* money from men who enter their work room.

The production and serving of food in general, and the preparing and arranging of meat as part of it, are central to creating ritual value. Seating patterns, the meat and other food served, games and prizes, gifts, toasts, and blessings all contribute to a successful event. The material substance of animals becomes more valuable when it circulates and is used as part of symbolic ritual transactions.

The Dialectic of Bridewealth

Giving bridewealth is a central event in shaping the relationship between the two sets of parents of the newly married couple. This alliance is one of the most important in a person's social life. Until the giving of bridewealth (*kalïng*), the groom's parents are morally and socially in debt to the bride's parents. Bridewealth is often given within the first year after marriage, but it may not be transferred until two or more years later. This is traditionally the first time that the two kin groups meet formally. The bride's parents organize a large party and the groom's parents usually bring both cash and a variety of large animals and several sheep. Some animals are specifically designated for the bride's paternal uncles and her mother. The formal term for this event is "to come and bow" (*jïgïlïp kelüü*), which implies that the wife-takers acknowledge their debt and show gratitude for the bride, and are willing to be the slightly subordinate partners in a long-term affinal relationship involving reciprocal respect and material support. One telling aspect of giving bridewealth is that it involves no negotiation: the groom's parents give what they decide is right and set the time when they feel able to give it.[19]

The voluntary timing and quantity of bridewealth makes it a way to communicate about the relationship one seeks with the new *kuda*. A *kuda* should not negotiate or make demands about the amount given because this limits the opportunity for displaying cooperative goodwill and generosity. Partners build social relations through demonstrations of mutual recognition as autonomous, honorable, self-sufficient, and generous. People are expected to treat *kuda* well but when accepting hospitality or bridewealth it should be acknowledged as voluntary. A household should voluntarily place its responsibilities to *kuda* ahead of other obligations.

If a bride's parents ask for a specific amount of bridewealth, then the animal givers (wife-takers) will feel that their autonomy is not respected. This transaction is an opportunity to publicly display one's generosity in relationships and thus promote one's reputation. Each side avoids offending the other but also tries to display a friendly and unconcerned demeanor. People generally give as much bridewealth as they can in order to show respect to their *kuda* and promote their own reputation. The dowry (*sep*), usually given from two to five years after the bridewealth, is similarly a point of pride: it is the mother's opportunity to show her appreciation for her daughter and her desire to maintain good relations with her and with the *kuda*. A woman who was not well-off but still had given a dowry of greater value than the bridewealth they had received explained, "What else could I do, she is my daughter?"

Bridewealth may include both cash and animals, but the cash has to be conceived of as its animal equivalent. It would be insulting for this money to be known to come from raising crops. A middle-aged Kyrgyz man with a fondness for jokes mentioned to me that a neighbor received a bridewealth that people knew was raised through selling potatoes but public mention of this would offend all involved. A joke about "the bride who came for potatoes" could only be told among close friends. Indeed, the main term for wealth, *mal*, literally means animals—and giving animals, or money that is explicitly specified as their equivalent, is the best way to demonstrate one's respect for close associates.

Animals as Models of Loan Transactions

Given their central role in production, ritual exchange, and accumulation, it is not surprising that animal transactions shape ways of thinking about the economy in Beshbulak in the most fundamental ways. For example, in local systems of credit, high interest rates (10 to 15 percent per month) are justified in part because animals grow rapidly. Because pasture access traditionally was free and one did not pay for herding services but treated them as a loan of animals, even now most Kyrgyz in Beshbulak do not consider land and labor as costs of production in raising animals. Rather, they conceive of the rate of return on an animal as equal to its growth rate. Animal weights increase by 60 to 100 percent per year, often almost doubling, and their market value increases similarly. Relying on this concept of increasing animal value, villagers feel it is reasonable to pay 10 or even 15 percent per month on loans of money between unrelated parties, and in fact prefer to pay this than to sell an animal and pay off the debt. The underlying concept is that when one loans an animal, one should repay with an equivalent animal, as if it had continued growing during the time of the debt. A loan of a one-year-old animal should be repaid the following year with a two-year-old animal. The loan is considered a favor and the borrower benefits from the wool, dung, milk and even offspring, and so should return the equivalent animal regardless of the fact that the lender did not have to raise the animal. The return to the lender should be commensurate with having kept the animal personally.

Animal loans share features with traditional loans of animals from those with large herds to poorer kin: the person tending the animal would keep offspring, wool, and milk from it (Shahrani 2002: 179; Jacquesson 2010: 67). After keeping the animal for a year, the lender receives the older, larger animal, while the borrower benefits from its production during this period. Despite this conventional return on such loans, in practice people are trying to shift away from the dominant model. A farmer with a small family, Kasïm, told me about loaning a one-year-old sheep to the widow of a deceased colleague when she had to hold a ritual event. The following year she returned a sheep of the same age she had borrowed, rather than a two-year-old sheep. Kasïm accepted this but only because he felt sorry for her and because he had been friends with her dead husband. In another case a man complained about loaning a one-year-old horse for someone's memorial feast and not being offered an adequate return. The horse loaned was worth around 15,000 to 18,000 *som*, and a year later he should have received 27,000 *som* or a two-year-old horse, but the borrower was asking to repay only 22,000 *som*.

The high rates of interest on animal loans can also be linked to the return expected from advance payments in spring for the fall harvest. This involves risks to both seller and buyer because prices may change significantly, but the price paid in spring is usually only 50 to 60 percent of what a crop should sell for in the autumn. The interest rate on this loan during the six-month growing season is thus around 10 percent per month but this is the only way some people can afford to plant in the spring. Money loans, thus, are viewed as variants of animal loans or advance purchases and a high rate of return is considered normal. Although people pay less or no interest when borrowing from friends and relatives, moneylenders in the village charge 10 to 15 percent per month. People's low esteem for money lenders and the risk they run of not being repaid means that only a few people try to make money in this way in the village.[20]

Conclusion

Kyrgyz animals and animal transactions are clearly not entirely separated from the market. Animals are valued in monetary terms and their growth rate validates the terms of monetary loans. Nonetheless, animals are also deeply embedded in community social life and they convey messages that money or other gifts cannot when given or consumed within ritual contexts. They are central to the public display of good relations through respectful (and yet entertaining and enjoyable) performances of hospitality and gift giving.

As Joel Robbins suggests, gift exchange is part of emotional regulation of community relations. Urapmin explicitly say that bridewealth serves to reduce the anger of the bride's parents upon her marriage (Robbins 2009). Similarly, Kyrgyz lineage elders travel immediately to the home of a girl when she is kidnapped for marriage in order to apologize for the insult and start building good relations. They give a sheep and 200 Euros in a conventional gift known as *achuu basar* ("suppressing bitterness") that is intended to placate these future *kuda*. Its importance is suggested by its invariability: to give less would compound rather than mitigate the insult. Kyrgyz gifts and hospitality in other rituals are also carefully managed to prevent offense and improve harmony.

A slaughtered animal served without expectation of material reciprocity is the "pure" gift that generates blessings in *kuday tamak* meals as well as the food eaten at sacred sites (*mazar*). But even the feasts held by rotating savings associations serve to realize the social value of a sheep rather than reducing it only to its market value. Commensal sharing of resources, particularly animals, helps reduce material inequalities among people of the same age or status while promoting hierarchies based on age and authority rather than wealth as ideals for orderly community life.

Ritual feasts in Beshbulak, in contrast to more politicized events reported elsewhere in Kyrgyzstan (Ismailbekova 2012), are venues organized around the ascribed status of age and do not produce authority or power.[21] Those with local political authority in Beshbulak usually do not sponsor feasts because they receive little benefit from them. Feasts have limited capacity to create either political power or the "security of mutual indebtedness" (Werner 1998) because there is no guarantee that others will help later, and respect does not translate into authority. Rather, as expressions of mutual respect, gifts provide a symbolic idiom that promotes social ties and enhances opportunities for further gift exchange. Rather than being driven by the obligation to give and to receive, Kyrgyz in Beshbulak seem to give with pleasure when they can and as long as they feel their gifts are appreciated. Gifts and contributions to a feast increase the host's capacity to offer hospitality, and recognition from the host for the gifts and contributions encourages further giving. The circulation of support and recognition makes celebrations into socially rewarding events in which every participant is both donor and recipient. Participatory give and take eases the burdens of sharing and allows Kyrgyz to hold more feasts and give more gifts.

Sources of prestige in Beshbulak include age, good public speaking in toasts, prayers and blessings, authoritative speech about political and world affairs, and demonstrated healing abilities. Being a good householder, producing food, taking care of one's family, being hospitable, participating in community events, and supporting community causes also lead to respect. The moral economy of mutual recognition requires an audience of guests to whom one extends hospitality and appreciation. People should display their pleasure in cooperative sociality rather than appearing competitive or looking forward to future reciprocation.

Beshbulak is a community in transition toward greater social and economic hierarchy and opportunities to accumulate wealth, but most people also strive to preserve and respect egalitarian community values. Villagers often mentioned that wealth, which had been politically suspect during the Soviet period, was now something to which they aspired, in both traditional and new forms. Some try to expand their wealth through larger herds and rented fields, some buy imported cars, and some construct more attractive homes with a second story or install indoor plumbing. A few dream of creating tourist attractions to bring well-off visitors to Beshbulak, and there is a growing divide between those who work for a living and those who hire them. Nonetheless, unless people move away from the village or withdraw from its social life, nicer homes and cars and higher incomes are locally shared. Aspirations to differentiate are held in check through strong moral principles that prescribe egalitarian treatment of community members and recognition of everyone's right to respect and inclusion. As long as the local moral community remains the context in which personal material success is most satisfyingly recognized, most villagers will continue to participate in village social events and relations. For the time being, few people live much better than others: they may eat more meat, but it is the same meat, and in the end, commensal feasting with fellow villagers remains more enjoyable than eating alone with one's household.

Notes

1. For many helpful discussions and suggestions I thank my colleagues in the Economy and Ritual group at the Max Planck Institute for Social Anthropology. In addition, Svetlana Jacquesson's close reading and detailed comments helped me refine my argument, as have numerous discussions with Judith Beyer. This articles

draws on ten months of fieldwork (and farm work) in Beshbulak and the surrounding region between 2007 and 2010. I have changed the names of people and the local communities to preserve their anonymity. I try to provide local terms when possible in order to facilitate comparisons among different areas of Kyrgyzstan, as well as abroad.

2. Research on the sharing of hunted animals from an evolutionary perspective is quite well known (e.g., Hawkes et al. 2001; Gurven and Hill 2009). However, economic anthropology has surprisingly little comparative analysis of public exchanges of animals and meat. Some important starting points for a comparative study of this kind of ritual feasting and exchange include Stevenson 1943, Leach 1954, Volkman 1985, Junker 1999, Hoskins 1993, Thompson 2000, Whitehead 2000, Stammler 2005, and Russell 2007.

3. An unusual example of the effort to display cooperation and connection is a case in which, after many years of good relations, the parents of the bride offered to hold the celebration for receiving bridewealth while not expecting the impoverished parents of the groom actually to give anything. They wished to celebrate their good relations rather than receive the prestation. In a contrasting and also unusual case, the father of a bride complained publicly in the presence of the givers that the small bridewealth he received meant that his big celebration would bankrupt him.

4. I use the term bridewealth in the sense of John Comaroff (1980: 4) to indicate wealth transferred from the kin of the husband to those of the wife. It might be better described as a "bride gift" because neither the value nor the time of giving are set through negotiations; several of the contributors to the Comaroff volume also describe societies where bridewealth is more a voluntary gift than a negotiated payment. In a valuable comparative discussion of nomadic ideas about collective property rights to bridewealth and dowry animals, Abramzon (1978) translates the Russian-Turkic term *kalym* as "bride money," although it refers mostly to animals. The *enchi* animal part of dowry that Abramzon discusses is now usually small compared to *sep* household goods.

5. One should not be seen as trying benefit from one's own generosity nor as taking advantage of that of another. Generosity should generate reciprocity and positive recognition; calling attention to one's own generosity can produce conflict. However, during a competitive game such as *kök börü*, a long and noisy debate about fairness of the teams is an appropriate show of self-interest. Slightly less acceptable is showing off or bragging about one's skill in *kök börü*. Lack of humility can damage a good reputation.

6. This harmonious ideal is not universal, and there are tolerated zones of banter and insults even at rituals. However, the ease of insult and conflict and the risk of violence and permanent rifts that might result do lead most people to consistent displays of mutual respect, or at least concealment of animosity.

7. After declines in the 1990s, rural populations in northern Kyrgyzstan have begun to increase in the 2000s (National Statistical Committee 2009: 39). Approximately 2 percent of the northern population works abroad, compared with 10 percent of the population from the south.

8. Compare the work parties motivated by millet beer in Darfur, in which sociality and reciprocity are highly valued appreciated by the workers (Barth 1967). Barth

shows that their enjoyment of the beer allows the "employer" to profit more than if he paid wages and that the workers would earn much more in wages than the beer they consume is worth.

9. Bridewealth in Beshbulak from the 1950s through 1980s was usually around three to seven large animals (*kara mal*, cows and horses of various ages). It was accumulated from multiple kin because no one could own these privately. In the more impoverished 1930s and 1940s many people did not give bridewealth at all and wedding feasts were very small: some people reported only being able to afford a chicken. During the Soviet period those wishing to follow more "socialist" practices were encouraged to marry through dating, engagement, and a *Komsomol'skaia svadba* ("Komsomol" civil wedding) without religious ceremonies or bridewealth.

10. A long history of Soviet tolerance for private rural customs allowed the practice of bride kidnapping (*kïz ala kachuu*) to expand. It remains common despite legal and moral sanctions and extensive public criticism. The practice has many varieties but the most dramatic and common are those against the will of the young woman. For evidence of its historical increase during and possibly after the Soviet period, see Kleinbach, Ablesova, and Aitieva 2005 and Werner 2004.

11. These opinions closely parallel those of herding families in Colombia according to Gudeman and Rivera (1990: 86–87), and also among African herders such as the Gogo (Gudeman 1986: 116–117).

12. People in Talas like to discuss why they do not eat beans. The obvious answer is that beans are not part of local cuisine and people know little about cooking them, but the discussion remains popular because it gives vent to ironic commentary about cash crops that are not consumed. The value of relative independence from the market is violated by producing beans, especially since people have largely given up producing wheat and instead buy flour with some of the cash they obtain through selling beans.

13. It bears noting that because visiting and ritual participation are activities of middle-aged and older people, younger people often have less access to meat and other rich foods. Werner (1997) argues that gifts required for feasting deplete the resources of poorer households and reduce the food available to children.

14. People often described the profits made by others in business (usually other ethnic groups) but stressed that they had not thought about doing such business themselves. Stories of trying to run a shop or other business while extending credit and not being able to collect one's debts were also common. Successful local entrepreneurs running the two "cafés" and numerous shops are generally appreciated as part of the community, but money lenders are more suspect. Some villagers do successfully invest in and operate transport and farm equipment, or buy beans wholesale and hire workers to clean them.

15. *Kuday tamak* are clearly related to the *qatïm quran* in Kazakhstan described by Bruce Privratsky (2001: 145–146), since both rituals are intended to provide the host family with spiritual benefits and both involve prayers. Privratsky describes events that involve more extensive "reading from the Quran" (i.e., prayer), while the Kyrgyz events usually include briefer prayers by invited mullahs.

16. These numbers are estimates calculated by taking one-fourth of the whole of Talas oblast's livestock population in 2007: see Животноводство Кыргызстана, last accessed online at http://www.agro.kg/ru/cattle_breeding/515/, 13 February 2012.
17. This analysis can be extended to other products and services in rural Kyrgyzstan. Handmade woolen articles, wool, or brightly colored market textiles are commonly given as gifts or as part of a dowry. Handcrafted wool hats and cloaks and leather whips or bottles are also ritual gifts. All of these products have some market value, but are more valuable when given in the correct ritual context with accompanying performances to display respect and appreciation. The characteristic felt hats worn by Kyrgyz men are important for formal wear and sold in large quantities because they make convenient inexpensive gifts, while still conveying significant respect for the recipient.
18. In some other regions of Kyrgyzstan the head is given to a young man.
19. This differs from the practice in other regions of Kyrgyzstan, particularly the south, when the bridewealth is often given at the time of marriage and negotiated in advance. Within Kyrgyzstan, the Talas region is felt to have a high bridewealth with a conventional level of 2,000 Euros.
20. In parts of southern Kyrgyzstan, people do not charge interest on loans because of Islamic prohibitions, but shopkeepers can circumvent this by accepting walnuts at a submarket price as repayment for credit accounts (von der Dunk and Schmidt 2010: 240).
21. See Beyer 2010 concerning the political ineffectiveness of Kyrgyz village political rituals.

References

Abramzon, Saul M. 1978. "Family-group, Family, and Individual Property Categories among Nomads." In *The Nomadic Alternative: Modes and Models of Interaction in the African-Asian Deserts and Steppes,* ed. Wolfgang Weissleder, 179–188. The Hague: Mouton de Gruyter.

Abramazon, Saul M., K. Antipina, G. Vasil'eva, E. Makhova, and D. Sulaimanov. 1958. *Byt kolkhoznikov kirgizskikh selenii Darkhan i Chichkan.* Moscow: Akademiia Nauk SSSR.

Akibode, Sitou, and Mywish Maredia. 2011. "Global and Regional Trends in Production, Trade and Consumption of Food Legume Crops." Department of Agricultural, Food and Resource Economics, Michigan State University. Last accessed online at http://impact.cgiar.org/sites/default/files/images/Legumetrendsv2.pdf, 21 September 2011.

Allina-Pisano, Jessica. 2008. *The Post-Soviet Potemkin Village: Politics and Property Rights in the Black Earth.* Cambridge: Cambridge University Press.

Barth, Fredrik. 1967. "Economic Spheres in Darfur." In *Themes in Economic Anthropology,* ed. Raymond Firth, 149–174. London: Tavistock.

Behnke, Roy H. 2003. "Reconfiguring Property Rights and Land Use." In *Prospects for Pastoralism in Kazakstan and Turkmenistan,* ed. Carol Kerven, 75–107. London: Routledge Curzon.

Beyer, Judith. 2009. *According to Salt: An Ethnography of Customary Law in Talas, Kyrgyzstan.* (Dissertation, Martin Luther University, Halle-Saale, Germany.)

———. 2010. "Authority as Accomplishment: Intergenerational Dynamics in Talas, Northern Kyrgyzstan." In *Eurasian Perspectives: In Search of Alternatives,* ed. Anita Sengupta and Suchandana Chatterjee, 78–92. Kalkutta: Maulana Abul Kalam Azad Institute of Asian Studies.

———. 2011. "Settling Descent: Place Making and Genealogy in Talas, Kyrgyzstan." *Central Asian Survey* 30, no. 3–4: 455–468.

Bohannan, Paul. 1955. "Some Principles of Exchange and Investment Among the Tiv." *American Anthropologist* 57: 60–70.

Comaroff, John, ed. 1980. *The Meaning of Marriage Payments.* London: Academic Press.

Dekker, Henri. 2003. *Property Regimes in Transition: Land Reform, Food Security and Economic Development: A Case Study in the Kyrgyz Republic.* Aldershot: Ashgate.

Douglas, Mary. 1967. "Primitive Rationing: A Study in Controlled Exchange." In *Themes in Economic Anthropology,* ed. Raymond Firth, 119–148. London: Tavistock.

Finke, Peter. 2003. "Does Privatisation Mean Commoditisation?: Market Exchange, Barter, and Gift Giving in Post-Socialist Mongolia." In *Research in Economic Anthropology,* Vol. 22 *Anthropological Perspectives on Economic Development and Integration,* ed. N. Dannhaeuser and C. Werner, 199–223. Amsterdam: Elsevier JAI.

Fitzherbert, Anthony. R. 2000. *Pastoral Resource Profile for Kyrgyzstan.* Last accessed online at http://www.fao.org/ag/AGP/AGPC/doc/Counprof/kyrgi.htm, 18 January 2012.

Goody, Jack. 1958. *The Developmental Cycle in Domestic Groups.* Cambridge: Cambridge University Press.

Gudeman, Stephen. 1986. *Economics as Culture: Models and Metaphors of Livelihood.* London: Routledge & Kegan Paul.

———. 2001. *The Anthropology of Economy: Community, Market, and Culture.* Malden, MA: Blackwell.

Gudeman, Stephen, and Alberto Rivera. 1990. *Conversations in Colombia: The Domestic Economy in Life and Text.* Cambridge: Cambridge University Press.

Gurven, Michael, and Kim Hill. 2009. "Why Do Men Hunt? A Reevaluation of 'Man the Hunter' and the Sexual Division of Labor." *Current Anthropology* 50, no. 1: 51–74.

Hardenberg, Roland. 2010. "How to Overcome Death? The Efficacy of Funeral Rituals in Kyrgyzstan." *Journal of Ritual Studies* 24, no. 1: 29–43.

Hawkes, K., J. F. O'Connell, and N. G. Blurton Jones. 2001. "Hadza Meat Sharing." *Evolution and Human Behavior* 22, no. 2: 113–142.

Hoskins, Janet. 1993. *The Play of Time: Kodi Perspectives on Calendars, History, and Exchange.* Berkeley: University of California Press.

Humphrey, Caroline. 1998. *Marx Went Away—But Karl Stayed Behind.* Ann Arbor: University of Michigan Press.

Ismailbekova, Aksana. 2012. *"The Native Son and Blood Ties": Kinship and Poetics of Patronage in Rural Kyrgyzstan.* (Dissertation, Martin Luther University, Halle-Saale, Germany.)

Jacquesson, Svetlana. 2007. "Integration Among Northern Kirghiz: Kinship and Descent in Practice." Paper presented at the *10th Conference of the European Society*

for Central Asian Studies, Ankara, Turkey. Last accessed online at http://halle
.academia.edu/svetlanajacquesson/Papers, 12 February 2012.

———. 2008. "The Sore Zones of Identity: Past and Present Debates on Funerals in Kyrgyzstan." *Inner Asia* 10, no. 2: 281–303.

———. 2010. *Pastoréalismes: Anthropologie Historique des Processus d'Intégration Chez Les Kirghiz du Tian Shan Intérieur.* Wiesbaden: Reichert.

Junker, Laura Lee. 1999. *Raiding, Trading, and Feasting: The Political Economy of Philippine Chiefdoms.* Honolulu: University of Hawai'i Press.

Kleinbach, Russell, Mehrigiul Ablezova, and Medina Aitieva. 2005. "Kidnapping for Marriage (ala kachuu) in a Kyrgyz Village." *Central Asian Survey* 24, no. 2: 191–202.

Leach, Edmund. 1954. *Political Systems of Highland Burma: A Study of Kachin Social Structure.* London School of Economics Monographs on Social Anthropology, no. 44. London: G. Bell & Co.

National Statistical Committee of the Kyrgyz Republic. 2009. *Population and Housing Census of the Kyrgyz Republic of 2009. Book I: Main Social and Demographic Characteristics of Population and Number of Housing Units.* Bishkek.

Privratsky, Bruce. 2001. *Muslim Turkistan: Kazak Religion and Collective Memory.* London: Routledge.

Robbins, Joel. 2009. "Rethinking Gifts and Commodities: Reciprocity, Recognition, and the Morality of Exchange." In *Economics and Morality: Anthropological Approaches,* ed. Katherine E. Browne and B. Lynne Milgram, 43–58. Lanham, MD: AltaMira Press.

Russell, Susan. 2007. "Feasts of Merit: The Politics of Ethnography and Ethnic Icons in the Luzon Highlands." *Cordillera in June: Essays Celebrating June Prill-Brett, Anthropologist,* 30–61. Quezon: The University of the Philippines Press.

Scott, James C. 1976. *The Moral Economy of the Peasant: Rebellion and Subsistence in Southeast Asia.* New Haven: Yale University Press.

Shahrani, M. Nazif. 2002. *The Kirghiz and Wakhi of Afghanistan: Adaptation to Closed Frontiers and War.* Seattle: University of Washington Press.

Stammler, Florian. 2005. *Reindeer Nomads Meet the Market: Culture, Property and Globalisation at the End of the Land.* Münster: LIT Verlag.

Stevenson, Henry Noel Cochrane. 1943. *The Economics of the Central Chin Tribes.* Bombay: Times of India Press.

Thompson, Robyn. 2000. "Playing the Stockmarket in Tana Toraja." *The Australian Journal of Anthropology* 11, no. 1: 42–58.

Trevisani, Tommaso. 2010. *Land and Power in Khorezm: Farmers, Communities, and the State in Uzbekistan's Decollectivisation.* Münster: LIT-Verlag.

Tsentral'noe statisticheskoe upravlenie Kirgizskoi SSR. 1984. *Kirgizstan k 60 letiiu obrazovaniia.* Frunze: Izdatel'stvo Kyrgyzstan.

Volkman, Toby Alice. 1985. *Feasts of Honor: Ritual and Change in the Toraja Highlands.* Urbana: University of Illinois Press.

von der Dunk, Andreas, and Matthias Schmidt. 2010. "Flourishing Retail in the Post-Soviet Sphere? Potentials and Constraints of Small-Scale Retail Activities in Rural Kyrgyzstan." *Communist and Post-Communist Studies* 43, no. 2: 233–243.

Werner, Cynthia. 1997. "Women and the Art of Household Networking in Rural Kazakstan." *Islamic Quarterly* 41: 52–68.

———. 1998. "Household Networks and the Security of Mutual Indebtedness in Rural Kazakstan." *Central Asian Survey* 17, no. 4: 597–612.

———. 1999. "The Dynamics of Feasting and Gift Exchange in Rural Kazakstan." In *Contemporary Kazaks: Cultural and Social Perspectives,* ed. Ingvar Svanberg, 47–72. New York: St. Martin's Press.

———. 2004. "Women, Marriage and the Nation-State: The Rise of Nonconsensual Bride Kidnapping in Post-Soviet Kazakhstan." In *The Transformation of Central Asia. States and Societies from Soviet Rule to Independence,* ed. Pauline J. Luong, 59–89. Ithaca, NY: Cornell University Press.

Whitehead, Harriet. 2000. *Food Rules: Hunting, Sharing, and Tabooing Game in Papua New Guinea.* University of Michigan Press.

Yoshida, Setsuko. 2005. "Ethnographic Study of Privatisation in a Kyrgyz Village: Patrilineal Kin and Independent Farmers." *Inner Asia.* 7, no. 2: 215–247.

3

From Pig-Sticking to Festival

Changes in Pig-Sticking Practices in the Hungarian Countryside

BEA VIDACS

In this chapter I examine the practice of pig-sticking (the winter slaughtering of a pig for home use, *disznóölés*) in the eastern Hungarian village of Szentpéterszeg, which I have known for more than three decades.[1] More specifically, I analyze its impending disappearance or transformation from a private (house-based) event to a community-based public celebration. The practice had great significance in traditional peasant life for provisioning households with meat, bacon, and sausages, and above all lard, which used to be the sole form of fat used in cooking. Edit Fél and Tamás Hofer described the economic role of the practice in everyday subsistence in the village of Átány as follows:

> On the average, a family of four has sufficient meat, fat, and bacon from a pig weighing 160 to 180 kg to last for a year, provided that poultry is raised also so that the lack of fat in the autumn months before pigsticking can be supplied by ducks and geese. However, in a year of a good harvest the same family may consume two pigs of that weight, and in other years they may have to make do with a pig of only 100 kg. (Fél and Hofer 1969: 119)

Now, the practice of pig-sticking is slowly disappearing, or at the very least, is significantly changing. At the same time, another process is taking place in the village, one that we could call the festivalization of pig-sticking, its reinvention as a festival, as a public ritual: the "*Hurka* and Sausage-Making Festival."[2] This event follows a very different logic from both that of the traditional practice of pig-sticking and that of the newer practices of house-based pig-sticking I will discuss below. Before launching into the pig-sticking story, some background information is needed on the general parameters of the village and on the economic and political changes that have affected it with the demise of socialism.

Background: The Village

Szentpéterszeg is a small village in eastern Hungary, near the Romanian border. The nearest town is 8 km away (population 15,000) and the village is about 30 km from the county capital and 220 km from the national capital, Budapest. In 2009 there were 1,173 inhabitants, whereas 30 years earlier there were 1,485. The current figure would be even lower, but for in-migration.[3] Today, practically all young people go to secondary school and quite a few of them continue on to university or other tertiary education. They do not come back. There is very little to come back for, and parents measure the success of their children by their ability to go away. This demographic decline is characteristic of many rural settlements in Hungary (Váradi 2008). I will argue that the creation of public rituals in the village is at least in part motivated by a conscious effort on the part of its leaders to make it a "livable" community, attractive to both its current inhabitants and potential in-migrants.

The many civic organizations of the village organize several such public rituals.[4] These include village-wide events such as Welcoming Spring, Mayday, Goodbye to Summer (or Village Day), Harvest Festival (which in 2009 was replaced by a "Fake" Wedding), and a New Year's Eve Party. Most end in a lively party with a live band. There are also smaller events catering to particular constituencies within the village, for example, the school organizes a Mardi Gras party and a Christmas party, both of which serve as fundraisers for the graduation ceremony in June. In addition, at the Day of the Elderly, schoolchildren entertain the elderly with a performance. I have chosen to analyze pig-sticking rather than any of the other events for several reasons. First, the slaughtering of pigs in the winter was formerly one of the most characteristic practices of peasant life in Hungary and also in Eastern Europe in general (see Minnich 1979). Second, the changes taking place in the home-based practice as well as the creation of the "festival" are closely intertwined with the economic changes that have taken place in the wake of socialism. And finally, most of the abovementioned events are newly invented or revivals of earlier communal practices (e.g., the harvest festival). *Disznóölés* is the only case of a house-based economic practice being "elevated" to community ritual.

Although in many Hungarian villages during the 1950s there was an aggressive drive for collectivization, this was not the case in Szentpéterszeg; in fact, there was no attempt to collectivize at that time. The Producer Cooperative or collective farm (*termelőszövetkezet*) was formed in 1960 and until its disappearance in 2000 it was the most decisive factor in the life of the village. This was due partly to the fact that it provided jobs to a large proportion of the population, and partly to the economic symbiosis that developed between the collective farm and the household-based production of the villagers. By comparison, the local council was insignificant. Many of its activities were intertwined with those of the *termelőszövetkezet*. Following the end of socialism in 1989, the Cooperative gradually became less and less successful until eventually it folded. The majority of villagers think that this was the worst thing that could have happened, but agree that at this point there is no use crying over spilt milk. They also remember forced collectivization with various degrees of resentment, as well as the hardships they had to endure in the early days of the collective farm when it could barely pay its members. But by the 1980s the Cooperative provided employment to about 300 people and acted very much like a benevolent tyrant. On the repressive side, in the early 1980s about half of the population did not baptize their children because the Cooperative ran a competition between its various brigades and deducted points from the entire group if a member had his or her child baptized, rather than resorting to the civil ceremony, rather unimaginatively called "name giving ceremony" (*névadó ünnepség*).[5]

On the enabling side, the *termelőszövetkezet* provided its members with animal feed in the form of maize, which in many villages in Hungary served in lieu of the "household plot." The latter was the cornerstone of the post-1956 reorganization of Hungarian agricultural policy. Instead of merely forcing people to join the collective, as they did before 1956, in Hungary the government introduced measures to institutionalize collective membership in such a way as to increase productivity and prosperity in rural communities. Some of these measures led to decentralized decision making and increased autonomy for collective farms and material incentives for household producers. The household plots, where cooperative members could grow crops, and which could serve as the base to raise animals, were the cornerstone of household-based productive activities of cooperative members and their significance increased as several administrative measures were taken to strengthen them during the late sixties and throughout the 1970s (Swain 1985; Harcsa, Kovách, and Szelényi 1998a). The extent to which cooperatives supported household production is shown by the fact that after 1977 all over Hungary the household plots ceased to be distributed as individual plots of land. Rather, the Cooperative worked the land with the superior technology (tractors, mechanical hoeing, pesticides) at its disposal. In this village, members only had to harvest the maize, which they did by hand, along with neighbors, relatives, *komas* (ritualized best friends, some of whom were also *compadres*), and friends in systems of mutual labor exchange. Delivering the maize to each household was again accomplished with the help of the *termelőszövetkezet,* which provided the transport. Maize was essential to the household economy as it was used in feeding pigs and poultry, which were among the most important elements of the diet, and—especially in the case of pigs—were a significant source of cash incomes. All villagers agree (and analysts would concur) that the steady rise in their living standards during the 1970s and early 1980s was due to the sale of livestock raised in households with the active aid of the Cooperative, and that this was what made Hungarian agriculture the most flourishing part of the Hungarian economy in socialist times. Given the essential role of the *termelőszövetkezet* in this system, as elsewhere in Hungary (cf. Hann 1980; Swain 1985) there was a symbiosis between cooperatives and villagers in which the collective farm (and the economy at large) both enabled and relied on the labor of the villagers outside the confines of the socialist institution itself.

The Cooperative was intertwined with the power structure of the village in other ways too. Some of these can be seen as positive, and certainly are seen as such by many in retrospect. The building of the water treatment plant as well as the paving of roads were carried out with the workforce of the *termelőszövetkezet,* which had a 26-member "construction brigade" that not only built and repaired buildings for the Cooperative but also for the village, such as the nursery school, the club for the elderly, and the House of Culture. The Cooperative would also repair roads: when potholes developed it sent a truck with gravel to fill them up. It was also involved in activities of a more social nature. For example, it regularly lent one of its trucks for the purpose of school excursions and did the same for the football club, transporting players to away games.

In postsocialist times councils were replaced by the Municipality (*Önkormányzat*). Its seat is the Mayor's Office (*Polgármesteri Hivatal*), which gives rise to the name by which the villagers refer to local officialdom, that is to say, the *Hivatal* or Office.[6] While the Municipality is primarily the inheritor of the functions of the local council, in many ways it also follows in the footsteps of the Cooperative. Similarly to the collective farm, the Office also provides a bus to take schoolchildren to events, such as competitions in town or on excursions, as needed, and the football club uses it to take the players to away matches.

A significant difference between the Office and the Cooperative is that the latter was able to bankroll much of this from its own activities and provide work as well. The Office does not have the resources of the Cooperative. It has a state-allocated budget, but there is always a shortfall, even though, as a small village belonging to a disadvantaged region of the country, it is entitled to some extra funds allocated to "small communities in a disadvantaged condition beyond their control" (abbreviated as *ÖNHIKI*, literally: "through no fault of their own"). Nevertheless, the mayor has to struggle to find ways and means of running the village. This state of affairs is not unique to this community; most small rural settlements in Hungary face similar problems (Váradi 2008).

Funding for most public activities in Szentpéterszeg comes from external sources. That is to say, funds for the improvement of the infrastructure of the village, such as road repair, the reconstruction of public buildings such as the old people's day-care center, and the installation of security cameras come from grant moneys rather than from the regular budget. Whenever possible the Office or one of the civic associations also applies for funds to support the frequent cultural events they organize. They do not employ a full-time grant writer but hire one as needed.

The Office is the largest employer with forty-one employees.[7] In addition to running such institutions as the Mayor's Office itself, the Village House (cultural center), and the school and nursery school, it takes care of the physical upkeep of the community: public roads, the school and the nursery school, street lighting, plowing snow, and landscaping. Most of this work is done by people on workfare (*közhasznú munkások*, or *közmunkások*). Unemployment is very high in the village, due in part to the final dissolution of the Cooperative in 2000 and in part to the drying up of job opportunities in the neighboring town.[8] Once unemployment benefits run out, after six months, the unemployed can be invited to perform various tasks for the community. For this they receive payment, but it falls into the category of social aid, which is why I refer to it as workfare, rather than employment. It often has limited duration, most commonly ranging from three to six months.[9] The village has to pay only 5 percent of the workfare workers' wages; the rest is provided by the state. Workfare recipients typically get the minimum wage (in 2009 amounting to 75,000 Ft per month, which is about 300 Euros). They do a variety of jobs, and it is not always obvious which positions are workfare positions. I was sometimes taken completely aback to find out that somebody was actually working in that capacity.

The economic consequences of the demise of socialist agriculture were accentuated by deindustrialization in the nearby town. Several factories that used to provide jobs for the villagers closed or drastically reduced their activities (the most significant were a dairy, a textile factory, and a light manufacturing factory). The only large employer that continues to provide work to several villagers is the hospital. The loss of employment can be gleaned from the figures of the official census: the number of persons employed in 1980 was 626, which by 2001 had shrunk to 308.[10]

After the regime change many people saw the writing on the wall and got themselves on disability pensions. These provided less than what they could get if they were to retire when they are supposed to, but it was more certain than finding a job under the changed economic circumstances that arose after 1989. As one woman put it, regarding why she did not get a certificate to show that she was computer literate: "it won't change the fact that I am fifty-four years old!" Even during socialism people whose health had deteriorated could, when certified by a medical practitioner, go on disability pension. Though in most cases the medical condition was real enough, some recipients promptly devoted themselves to full-time activity in the "second economy."[11] After 1989 there was a rise in the number of people requesting disability pensions, as many hastened to ensure they had a fixed income (Szalai 1991, 2006).

In 2009, nearly 38 percent of villagers over the age of eighteen had "pension-like" provisions. While 19.35 percent (227) of the 1,173 inhabitants were over sixty, according to the official census figures, in the same year 356 persons (30.35 percent) received "pension-like" provisions, which most likely means that about 11 percent (129 people) were on disability pensions. By comparison, the number of inhabitants under eighteen was 235 (20.03 percent), and those between eighteen and fifty-nine (711) made up 60.61 percent of the population. Those who have a regular pension usually do not have much more than 70,000 to 80,000 forints per month (250–300 Euros), and there are some who get even less. Most people rely on a combination of sources for income. For most, security is attained through a salary or a pension. Only for a handful of entrepreneurs is this not the case.

Upon the folding of the Cooperative, members who had contributed land to it in 1960 were supposed to get back what they took in. In addition, those who had worked for the Cooperative for at least two years received a fixed value in land (30 gold crowns).[12] There is a lot of confusion as to what people got and why. Many do not cultivate these lands themselves. Rather, they rent them out to one of two large entities: a cooperative in a neighboring community or a large private enterprise based in the neighboring town. Others rent their land to one of the few local farmers who engage in agriculture in a serious way. The payment can be in kind (maize, wheat, or barley) or in cash or a mix of the two.

Most people grow vegetables in their gardens surrounding their house, except if they are quite old, in which case they just stop altogether or let someone use it for growing fodder, so that the land does not get overgrown by weeds. Most of those who engage in this kind of garden production claim that they grow enough vegetables and fruit to cover most of their families' needs during the summer months. Some of the produce is even left over for the winter in the form of jam and preserves that women make in large quantities, especially if they have small children. The many teenagers in boarding schools outside the village also carry large packs of food prepared for them by their mothers every week. Even grown-up children living elsewhere receive these products. Some families do not bother to produce anything and their relatives in the village help them out. But the villagers are not completely self-sufficient in fruits and vegetables as indicated by the fact that there is a greengrocer in the village. She mostly sells produce she obtains from commercial channels outside the village and only sells local produce very rarely.

Pig-Keeping and the Tradition of Pig-Sticking

Beyond producing pigs for home use, during socialism Hungarian rural households raised a large number of pigs for sale: most had contracts to deliver a certain number of pigs every year to a state company or the cooperative at fixed prices. Under current conditions, the number of pigs being raised has drastically decreased, as did that of all other livestock. According to the Hungarian Central Statistical Office, nationwide, the number of pigs in individual economic units (*egyéni gazdaság*) decreased from 2,375,000 to 846,000 between 1995 and 2010.[13] This trend is certainly felt in Szentpéterszeg too; people complain bitterly that they used to be able to count on an income from raising animals, and explain that they built houses for their sons with the help of the money thus raised. They also complain in the abstract, nostalgically bemoaning how the number of cows or pigs decreased in the village. In addition to the decline in raising pigs for commercial purposes, these days even pig-sticking is on the wane or at least its characteristics are changing drastically. There is much more variation in pig-keeping and pig-sticking practices than during my earlier fieldwork.

In 1980–1981 practically every household held a pig-sticking. The work required the cooperation of at least four people or even as many as six or seven, and thus, it usually involved two or three families, who tended to be relatives. In 1980, my host regularly did the pig-sticking with one of his brothers and the sister of his wife and their spouses. However, he did not invite his sister, who lived at some distance, because, as he put it, "they have developed another set [of people] over there." She carried out the pig-sticking with her husband and his siblings, even though the two groups did mix in other forms of labor exchange. The slaughtering was done by a butcher or by one of the (male) members of the work party.

The butchering began around 5 A.M. and the processing lasted into the evening. The slaughtering of the pig was followed by singeing (*perzselés*).[14] Subsequently the animal was carved up and the intestines were removed, washed several times, and scraped to serve as sausage skin. The fat of the pig was rendered into lard, a by-product being the much loved cracklings. Other fatty parts were kept as bacon. Most of the organ meats went into the *hurkas*, and quite a bit of the meat was turned into sausage or salami.

The *hurka* had to be consumed immediately or within a few days; some of the sausage was also consumed fresh, but most of it was either dried or smoked. Part of the meat was served immediately in a meal at the end of the day of the slaughtering; however, the primary purpose of pig-sticking was to preserve and store meat and its products for the future.

An important feature of pig-sticking was the sending of a sample (*kóstoló*) to neighbors, relatives (on both sides), ritualized best friends (*komas*), and others, going well beyond the circle of people who participated in the event. Thus, even though, as mentioned above, my host did not cooperate with his sister's family in pig-sticking, they did send each other the *kóstoló*. People felt obliged to reciprocate when they did their own pig-sticking. Because pig-stickings were spread over the entire winter, most people had access to fresh meat products throughout the winter season. Another way the *kóstoló* was distributed during the 1980s was through the over-fourteen children and young adults of the community, many of whom were going to school outside the village. Some of the products of pig-sticking traveled with them to their halls of residence, or digs, weekly and were shared among friends.

The advent of deep freezers in the Hungarian countryside (along with some other factors) changed this picture.[15] A few years before the regime change (1989), the entire country was gripped by *gorenje*-fever, that is to say, a very large number of people traveled to Austria with the purpose of buying a freezer made by a Yugoslav company named Gorenje. There were so many travelers that tourism experts spoke of "*gorenje* tourism" (Michalkó and Rátz, 2006). The freezer changed the possibilities for preserving meat and influenced pig-sticking practices as well as the keeping of chickens. It is now much easier to kill the chicken at the age considered to be optimal for preparing breaded chicken, a very popular dish in Hungarian cuisine (see Dienes 2005; Guillou 1991).

During the early 1980s there were no butcher shops in Szentpéterszeg.[16] Meat was obtained almost exclusively from their own poultry, and from pig-sticking and all its ancillary products. Whenever there was a forced butchering (*kényszervágás*) of a cow or bull the word would get around and the villagers would immediately buy up the meat in portions of a few kilos. The nearby town could have served as a source of meat, but villagers only purchased meat in town on very exceptional occasions.

The day before a wedding was held, a group of women came to the house of the bride to help pluck the chickens for one of the main attractions of the wedding meal the next day: the chicken soup with special pasta. In preparation for feeding the work party, the previous day (two days before the wedding) the bride's family slaughtered a pig to feed the participants of the group. The chickens were brought along by the mother or wife of each man who planned to attend the wedding. The part of the slaughtered pig that was not fed to the work group was made into sausage rather than into other meat products and became part of the event. It was served roasted to the guests late at night during the dancing that followed the wedding dinner. Another extraordinary occasion for slaughtering a pig was house-building, which, under socialism, was almost always done with help from relatives, *compadres* (*komas*, i.e., ritualized best friends), neighbors, and other friends. The large number of people who came to help were "rewarded" by being fed.

Changing Tastes, Changing Traditions— Pig-Sticking Transformed

In the early 1980s many people were engaged in home-based pig-raising for delivery to state-owned companies, aided significantly by the collective farm. In 1980–1981, the fifty-one households for which I have information about animal husbandry practices had 259 pigs (not counting piglets).[17] Eight families did not have pigs at all. Two of these were young couples living with parents, in which case the parents did have pigs, and one informant explained that they had just delivered their pigs, i.e., they just happened to be at the end of the pig-raising cycle.[18] There was, however, significant variation between how many pigs people raised: eighteen households raised between 1 and 3, another eighteen families had between 4 and 9, and seven families had 10 to 24 pigs. Currently many people simply do not keep pigs. The combined number of pigs in forty-seven households interviewed in 2009–2010 was 116. Of these households, twenty-five did not keep pigs at all.[19] Members of four of these were over the age of seventy at the time of the interview; however, members of the remaining twenty-two households were quite young or middle-aged and physically capable of animal husbandry. In fact, age was no barrier to pig-keeping in 1980, as evidenced by my material: out of seven families in which the principals were seventy years old or older, five kept pigs and in 2009–2010 there were still five households in the same age group who continued to raise pigs. Among the twenty-two households that did raise pigs eleven had between 1 and 3, four raised 4 to 9 pigs, and another four had 10 to 30 pigs. If we consider that one of these households alone had 30 pigs, the decline in the number of pigs raised in households becomes much more striking.

Thus, during the early 1980s, at least half of the households questioned raised pigs for sale and only held back 1 or 2 for household consumption.[20] Today, by contrast, the majority of those who keep pigs at all do so for the purpose of self-provisioning. Among the forty-seven families interviewed in 2009–2010, only five raise pigs to sell on the market. This does not exclude the possibility of some pigs changing hands locally, but instead of the overall pattern of producing pigs for the market under socialism, now we see evidence of withdrawal from the market accompanied by continuity in self-provisioning.

These days, those who carry out pig-stickings slaughter 1 to 3 pigs in the course of the year and keep the meat in the freezer (less meat needs to be worked into sausage or *hurka* because the meat can be kept as is). Those who do not keep pigs may still hold a pig-sticking by buying the required pig, as some say, "ready-made," only to be slaughtered, or just a few weeks before the pig-sticking is to take place, thus avoiding having to take care of them or feed them for a long time. When people buy they may do so from covillagers who raise pigs, or from outsiders. Others may buy half a pig, sometimes sharing with family or friends, and process it; yet others may just make a simple trip to town and purchase a few kilos of meat for the sausage or other ingredients for liver sausage (they can only make the latter type of *hurka*, as buying blood for blood sausage is not possible.) They also purchase the intestines for the casing, and although they will wash it again and scrape it a bit, basically the "dirtiest" part and the bulk of the work of preparing the casing into which the sausages or *hurka* will be filled no longer needs to be carried out.

The people who resort to these practices are varied. For example, an old couple, both of them in their eighties, declared that just a few weeks earlier they had had a fancy for sausages, so they bought a few kilos of meat to process into sausage. Unfortunately, the meat had gone bad, so it was a waste. They do not keep pigs anymore, on account of their age. But they have two grown sons in the village, who will send them a *kóstoló* when they slaughter a pig; however, even one of those does not raise his own pigs, but rather buys the animal to be slaughtered. Another couple (the husband has been retired since 1997 and the wife worked for the Municipality) share their house with one of their grown-up sons. During the winter, one Saturday they had bought a few kilograms of meat as well as internal organs and sausage casing in the neighboring town, and, together with their other son, a university student visiting for the weekend, made it into sausage and *hurka*. The quantity was larger than what they could immediately consume, but the work was done in a few hours. Some of the products were eaten immediately, some traveled with the university student to town, and the rest was frozen. I also received a plate of *kóstoló*, having helped in the process.

The commentary people offer to explain why they do not do pig-sticking anymore reveals the changing values in the village. Earlier, doing "peasant work" was a matter of course, but now more and more people seem to think of it as a hardship, smelly, demanding, and in one way or another unpleasant. Older people are likely to explain that they are too old to take care of a pig or to carry out a pig-sticking. However, as mentioned above, age did not used to be such an important determining factor in the keeping of pigs or the holding of pig-stickings.[21] In my view, the waning of the practice also indicates a changed attitude to the human life course. Some people explicitly do not wish to work until they drop, but rather would like to "enjoy" their retirement and they think that as one gets older one should cut back on activities. This is not always completely voluntary. An elderly lady, who lives in the same household with her daughter and well-to-do son-in-law as well as her grandchild, in a well-appointed modern house, declared that "they forbade me to keep animals because it was too smelly, although I would still be willing to bother with a few chickens."[22]

Retiring from "peasant work" may not be always possible, but most of the elderly are entitled to a pension. Many of them also derive some income from renting out the land that they received back after the cooperative was dismantled. It is less clear what will become of the younger generation of people who do not have the same secure future for their retirement.

Another, quite common, explanation for not holding a pig-sticking anymore is that personal preferences in the family make slaughtering a pig impractical, unnecessary, or wasteful. Changes in taste, not liking meat, and not liking the fatty parts are often cited reasons. For example, a middle-aged woman explained that neither she nor her husband could eat the fatty parts, so a lot would be wasted; therefore they prefer to buy the parts that they do like. Another woman, a widow who lives together with her son and daughter-in-law, explained that they no longer held pig-stickings because "they [her other son living in a small town] did not eat it, or ask for it, because we used to fatten one for them as well, then we slaughtered it and they took it away. But even with us, the truth is that many parts of the pig are not needed. And then, it is already a waste when they don't eat the fatty part, when they are choosy ..."

Since the early 1980s, most activities that required cooperation and were important events from the point of view of the reproduction of the village have been shortened and commercialized (especially weddings and funerals). In the case of pig-sticking, this is manifested in the hiring of a butcher to do the entire work process. Earlier, people might have hired a butcher to slaughter the animal, but the processing was done by the owner of the pig and his helpers, consisting mostly of family members. According to the Hungarian Ethnographic Lexicon, hiring a butcher used to be a sign of being better off. These days, it seems that this is partly a question of efficiency, as one woman said with satisfaction: "we are done by noon" (whereas the traditional work party took an entire day). It costs 5,000–6,000 forints (20–24 Euros) to have the work done. This may be considered a reasonable cost for the service provided or exorbitant. An elderly man and his wife (both pensioners) explained with great relish how efficient it was to have a butcher do the job:

> He does everything, fills everything (*megtölt*), the *hurka*, the sausage, he cuts up the meat ready to use.… [in answer to my question whether any help was needed, his wife added,] Well, they bring it out of the pigsty, then the butcher shoots [stuns] and stabs it, and then it's not a problem even if nobody is with him!
>
> [Her husband continued:]
>
> He says, "Uncle Gyula, sit over there on the chair!" Well, 6,000 forints are 6,000 forints. [again, his wife took over:] That's how much it costs. He is here by 7 in the morning, and at 11:30 we shut the door after him.

Until three years before this interview, when their daughter got divorced, they did the pig-sticking with their son-in-law. They only resorted to hiring a butcher when, due to the divorce, he was no longer there to help.

A young woman (thirty-two), who raises her three children alone, relies on her half-brothers from a nearby village to help her with slaughtering the pig. In answer to my question whether she hired a butcher to do the pig-sticking, she replied: "we don't waste money on such things! The relatives come from K., stab it [the pig], take it apart; we put it in the freezer. Well, let's say, we make the *hurka* with Janó [her twelve-year-old son]." In this case, poverty made it impossible for the woman to think of hiring a butcher, and although she did not have relatives in the village she could call upon relatives from a nearby village. In general, those who hire butchers to do the bulk of the work marvel at the ease hiring a butcher affords them, whereas those who do the work themselves stress the value of self-reliance. Thus, it is easy to find a justification for either practice.

Another consequence of the decrease in and transformation of traditional pig-sticking is the breakdown in sharing and reciprocity occasioned by the diminishing number of people participating in the custom. When I asked whether they send or receive *kóstoló* several people answered that they do not receive it, because they do not send it. For example, people who do a "limited" pig-sticking, just buying the ingredients for sausage or perhaps liver *hurka*, will not offer a sample to neighbors or friends, though they might still give some to relatives. Instead, they will freeze the leftovers.

There is a consensus about the norm that there should be balanced reciprocity in the sending and receiving of samples. With unrelated parties this is adhered to fairly strictly. When it comes to relatives, however, this "rule" is not always kept. An elderly informant, a widow in her late sixties, explained that ever since her husband had died she no longer did pig-sticking. She then mentioned that she still received a *kóstoló* every year from her brothers, even though she told them not to give her any since she was not going to be able to reciprocate. Children who do pig-sticking typically reserve *kóstoló* for their parents, despite the fact that they are not going to receive anything in return.

I have outlined the process of transformation that has been taking place in Szentpéterszeg with regard to raising and slaughtering pigs. Whereas during the early 1980s pig-sticking was a regular annual and seasonal event that satisfied an economic necessity, which could not otherwise be met very easily, thirty years later it has become an increasingly flexible practice with many elements of choice built into it. Today, there is equal scope for intensifying pig-sticking by the expedient of the freezer or for abandoning the custom. The latter is partly due to the availability of other channels through which one can acquire the products of pig-sticking and partly to a change in values and needs. All items that used to be obtainable only through pig-sticking are readily available at the four local food stores of the village, and of course the town, with its supermarkets (*Penny, Lidl, Tesco*) and smaller stores, is only 8 km away, and many people claim that it is ultimately cheaper to buy these items in the stores.

In addition to the decline of pig-raising as an entrepreneurial activity, there is also a decrease in the number of households that carry out pig-sticking and an even greater decrease in the number of people who slaughter pigs that they had raised. So, as the market as a mechanism through which people can dispose of the animals they raised is retreating, another segment of the market is more present and enables people to make lifestyle choices about what aspects of the meat processing procedure to keep or whether to forgo it completely and only purchase the processed products in a store. Some of these changes have to do with economic realities, that is to say, with such factors as lack of a secure demand for pigs combined with the rising costs of raising pigs, which some people claim make it economically unviable to engage in animal husbandry. But there is also an important element of lifestyle choices, including loss of skill and dislike of or distaste for the more onerous parts of life in the countryside. As it becomes increasingly possible to skip these, more and more people are opting for these shortcuts.

The Festivalization (Ritualization) of Pig-Sticking

The greatest change with regard to pig-sticking in the village has been the appearance of the *Hurka* and Sausage-Making Festival. Such gastronomic festivals have become widespread all over Hungary and thus can be said to belong to a larger set of phenomena encompassing practically the whole country (Bali 2007; Bódi and Járosi 2008; Pusztai and Martin 2007). The creation of such events is not unique to Hungary. Laurent Sébastien Fournier (2007) analyzes "thematic festivals" in rural France as they emerged in the context of increasing affluence in the 1970s. They signal the opening of these communities to the outside world. In Hungary, too, it is hoped that the festival, if successful, will give a name to the community and have beneficial effects on its economy. Rural tourism has been a buzzword ever since the regime change. Such festivals do often attract a large number of people, even from outside the community.

Since there is a proliferation of such events, most do not really make that much of a wave. Nonetheless, organizers devise them in order to emphasize the uniqueness of a locality, sometimes inventing a story to accompany the celebrations, sometimes tapping into a pre-existing local event or characteristic.[23] This phenomenon is often described in the anthropological literature as "branding" (Pusztai 2007; Wengrow 2008). Success is more likely when the publicity surrounding the event manages to frame it in such a way as to create some kind of a historic or cultural continuity in the public imagination. Discussing the conditions under which such events can thrive is beyond the scope of this chapter. Suffice it to say that several factors have to come together for such an event to have more than local significance: advertising, location, accessibility, financial resources, organizational power, and the quality of the product are the most important factors (cf. Fournier 2007).

But sometimes festivals are simply invented without any seeming excuse, which is the case in the village under discussion. Other than the traditional custom of pig-sticking, which has been part of the winter season in all Hungarian villages, there is no "historical" precedent or cultural referent claimed for the event, although the larger region the village belongs to is quite famous for its sausages and meat products. The Sausage Festival of Békéscsaba, a nearby town, has been in existence since 1997 and it attracts 60,000 to 70,000 visitors. Among other prominent public personalities, Viktor Orbán, the current prime minister of Hungary, has participated in this event several times since its inception.

The festival under discussion is of more recent origin: in 2010 it was held for the fourth time.[24] In principle, it is organized by the civic association called "Friends of Szentpéterszeg."[25] People who originate from the village but live elsewhere receive the village newsletter that appears three to five times a year through their membership of the organization. The newsletter is distributed to all households free of charge. The association acts as an umbrella organization in the sense that the events it creates require the cooperation of many villagers, which is usually obtained through working closely together with other civic associations. The *Hurka* and Sausage-Making Festival, in which every civic association took part, was a prime example of this cooperation. Without their labor inputs it would not have been possible to hold it.

In 2010, the festival took place on February 13. Beginning in December, two months in advance, representatives of these groups began to meet and discuss the organization of the event, debating logistics, the sequence of events and actions, work groups and individuals responsible for certain processes. Each civic association delegated several of its members to contribute their labor power to the event on one of the three days that it lasted; in addition, the Folklore Circle for Women had been making 7 kg of special pasta (*csigatészta*) and also promised to help out both in the preparations for the festival and at the event itself. There was also a "cultural program," which in 2010 was provided by the visiting anthropologist, who exhibited the photographs she had taken of the villagers in the previous six months. Such cultural programs have been a regular part of the event ever since its inception. In previous years it had consisted of an exhibition representing some traditional aspect of village life. In 2009 it displayed traditional hand-icraft items with the implements used to make them; thus the purpose was representing the villagers to themselves.

Although the festival proper (the public part of the event) took place on a single day, a Saturday, the two preceding days were taken up with preparations. On Thursday, with the help of mostly workfare people, the premises of the Village House (formerly the House of Culture) were set up for the reception of the workers who would process the meat the next day. The Friday activities were already part of the event, albeit backstage. Three huge pigs, bought from villagers, were killed at the abattoir and transported back into the village, to the Village House. There, a group of men and women were already waiting to start the processing of the meat into sausages and *hurka* for sale to visitors on the morrow. Some of the meat was kept for the cooking of the "typical" pig-sticking dishes to be sold as sustenance to visitors during the festival. Some of these workers were representatives of the various civic associations; some of them were workfare recipients and some of them were employees of the old people's day-care center. The latter were drawn into the process by virtue of being employees of the center. The kitchen staff of the nursery school should also have been involved, but a conflict between the head cook and the organizers led to the nursery school's personnel withdrawing from the event, with the exception of two individuals.

The task was an enormous one: three pigs, weighing in total about 600 kg, had to be processed in the course of the day. The meat was made into sausages, cracklings, and liver sausage (*hurka*). In addition, they also made a very large quantity of *kocsonya*, a dish of meat in jelly, similar to the German *Sülze*. It was apportioned into individual plastic containers to be jellified individually and sold the next day. The workers also processed the meat to be made into a traditional soup (*orjaleves*) and a main course (*lucskos káposzta*), which were also to be sold to guests and participants the following day. One of the organizers went around quite early in the morning asking the participants in the day's work to place their orders for sausage, *hurka*, and cracklings, because the previous year they had run out of sausages and *hurka* early, and the workers who did not make a purchase in time, because they were busy working, went home empty-handed. The *kocsonya*, not quite as difficult to come by as "homemade" sausages, was only put on sale the next day. By late afternoon the sausages were ready and the people in charge of making them started filling the orders of the participants of the day's work. Afterward the cracklings had to be made and the cleaning up needed to be done. Despite the efficient coordination, it was late in the evening before people went home.

The next day, Saturday, was the actual festival, centering on a *hurka* and sausage-making contest. Before the competition, a fourth pig had to be killed. This was held back, so that at least one pig would be slaughtered "traditionally," i.e., not at the abattoir but rather "at the house"; in this case, the deed was done in the backyard of the Village House (the animal was clubbed first to stun it, and then stabbed in the heart). Barely any outsiders watched this or the subsequent singeing of the pig with a blowtorch. The only spectators consisted of a group from a Transylvanian village that is twinned with Szentpéterszeg, which had come to participate in the contest.[26]

In 2010, twenty-three teams, consisting of five persons each, participated in the contest. All the civic organizations of the village participated: the Association of Large Families, Civic Guard, Fishing Association, Friends of Szentpéterszeg, Volunteer Fire Brigade, Sport Association, Shooting Club, and the Folklore Circle for Women. In addition, the employees of the day-care center for the mentally handicapped that operates in the village also took part, and the Church had a team too. Other teams included the immediate neighbor of the village, with which it shares certain administrative functions, as well as other villages in the region and the neighboring town. Notable among them was the team of the county-level association of the Civic Guard and of the MP of the Hungarian Socialist Party (soon to be voted out of Parliament) with a team named "We shall never give up!" There was also a team from the town of Békéscsaba, famed for its sausages, and a team of locally based border guards.[27] The son of the retired Headmaster of the local school, a university student, came with his friends from Budapest to take part. Each team paid a participation fee of 5,000 forints (25 Euros).[28] In return they were each given 2 kilos of meat and internal organs from which to make sausage and *hurka*. They brought their own spices and flavoring agents. They had to submit to the jury only a portion of this amount; the rest of the raw materials were theirs to keep.

Thirteen of the twenty-three teams came from the outside, thus bearing out Fournier's argument that thematic festivals are connected to modernization and not inward looking, as traditional feasts had been.[29] All contestants from the village came from the ranks of civic associations or other official bodies. So, not only were the associations instrumental in organizing and providing labor in the preparatory phases of the event, they were also the ones who, by participating in the contest, represented the village to the outside world. At these gastronomic events, usually the organizers invite a team of professional cooks from outside the community. They are dressed in their cooks' uniforms, taste every entry, and after due deliberation, announce the winners, collecting a hefty fee for doing so. There was also a "star guest": in 2010 it was Péter Poór, one of the great pop stars of the 1970s, with two young women.

The event started with the slaughtering of the fourth pig at 6:30 A.M.; between 8 and 9 the teams registered themselves, occupied their allotted places, and set up for the competition. From around 9 A.M. on, traditional pig-sticking breakfast dishes were on offer and those who wished could purchase them with coupons sold in the vestibule of the Village House. The official opening of the event at 10 A.M. meant the beginning of the competition and also the opening of the photo exhibition that took place to great popular acclaim. While the competitors were busy seasoning sausages and *hurka* and then filling the casings, they, and all those who gathered for the occasion, were entertained by the pop singer. Lunch was served starting at noon. As at breakfast, there was an array of "traditional" pig-sticking fare that had been prepared at the day-care center for the elderly and could be purchased with the special coupons. The sausages and *hurka* prepared by the competitors had to be baked in the outdoor brick ovens before they could be presented to the jury. The task of the contestants was not over yet; the items still had to be arranged in an aesthetically pleasing way, which the competitors did with great energy and creativity. Many of them had brought material with which to decorate the plates. The judges retired to a separate room to make their decisions.

Around 3 P.M., the results of the competition were announced in a ceremonial manner: the chef-judges stood on stage in their starched white uniforms and declared the winners, one by one, and concluded with some overall remarks about what they had seen and tasted and advice for the organizers. Their remarks also stressed the importance of maintaining traditions. There were two categories of the competition (sausage and *hurka*) each with first, second, and third prizes, as well as three special prizes. The honor of winning was thus spread out over a large number of people. Following the announcement of the winners there was some dancing and people chatted to friends and acquaintances until around 5 P.M., when the eagerly awaited raffle draw began. The raffle is an important source of income at this event and a source of suspense and entertainment for the participants. The prizes included practical and less practical household items, toiletries, and sometimes even upscale food items purchased by the organizers. But the prizes also included contributions from some of the local businesses, thus serving as a form of advertising and garnering respect for the people who make these offerings. Some people, especially those who come in a group, end up buying quite a number of raffle tickets (ten to twenty not being unusual) and wait impatiently for the numbers to be called out. When they win they cheer loudly and joyfully. The raffle drawing lasts until the late afternoon, and is followed by some dancing, while others drink peaceably until about 8 P.M. at the cash bar.

Regina Bendix (1989) has argued that the significance of Swiss cultural festivals lies in their manifold meaning(s) for the locals rather than for the tourists.[30] In order to understand the significance of the festival for the villagers, we first have to see how it differs from the event that it is supposed to recall, the pig-stickings of yore. A household-based, family event with a fundamentally economic goal is elevated into a public ritual. In reframing it as a festival, despite the very real labor that goes into the event, the traditional, practical economic aspect of pig-sticking has been removed. The event was devised by village elites to make a profit for the community (or at least for some of its members). However, at least so far it has not fulfilled such hopes and thus remains primarily a form of entertainment, where the gains are more symbolic than economic. In the course of de- and recontextualizing pig-sticking, its meaning changes completely. The changed context is no longer economic, but rather ludic, with symbolic and political overtones.[31] It is ludic because it is done for entertainment, to have a good time. Many of the elements that structure the actual Saturday festival are entirely novel: the presence of the star guest, the playfulness of the competition, the cultural element (in the form of the exhibition of photographs), the raffle, and the opportunity to dance afterward all move the festival from the realm of work to that of play. The presence of the team of university students in the competition underlined the ludic element, as the seasoning of the sausages they produced was in open mockery of the traditional product. The activities of Friday correspond directly to the traditional pig-sticking with the obvious difference of scale and personnel, and, of course, location (the Village House instead of the family house).

The festival has little practical economic significance. It certainly does not provide the household with lard, sausages, or meat for the remainder of the year. It is redistributive in that everyone who wants to can buy a piece of sausage, but the items are paid for directly and taken home, not shared. One does not send a *kóstoló* sample of something for which one has paid cash. The festival is an economic event only in a limited way. The funds for it were mostly raised locally (through competition entry fees, entrance fees to the event, sale of sausages and *hurka,* raffle tickets, etc.). In other words, most of the costs of the event had to be advanced: from the Friends of Szentpéterszeg, or from a separate foundation that was set up to provide such loans, or from discretionary funds in the Mayor's Office.[32] Outside money only came in in the form of a relatively small grant (50,000 forints) from the Main Library and Cultural Center of the county capital. This sum was allocated at the last minute and was more of symbolic significance. The festival had a slight loss, offset in part by leftover food and drinks that were used at a subsequent community event.[33]

The changed context of the event is also evident in the presence of a large number of outsiders at the festival, including external entrants into the competition. Some of them are political allies of the mayor, some personal friends of one or several of the organizers, thus representing orientations to the outside world. But outsiders could also come as visitors because the event is widely publicized on the internet and in regional media. Many former inhabitants of the village have settled in the nearby town. They are likely to be members of the association Friends of Szentpéterszeg, but even if they are not, they would know about the event from relatives or friends or the local media. Some of them came to the festival to see relatives or old friends and to buy homemade sausage and *hurka.*[34] People came at least in part because it was a "traditional" event, because the sausage was "homemade, village sausage."

Discussion and Analysis

Clifford Geertz has famously described the Balinese cockfight as "a story they tell themselves about themselves" (1973: 448). No doubt, the *Hurka* and Sausage-Making Festival is also a story the villagers tell themselves about themselves. The festival tells not one story, but many. It is an invented tradition and nobody in the community would claim otherwise. The essence of the notion of invented tradition (Hobsbawm and Ranger 1983) is that it should parade itself as age-old and not invented, but this is very far from being the case here.

Many villagers still engage in pig-sticking (even if often in an attenuated form), which makes it difficult to present the event as the revival or survival of something otherwise long gone. This aspect of the festival cannot be completely dismissed, however, because to at least some of the outsiders, especially those coming from urban milieus, the festival is likely to appear as an example of "living tradition," of traditional peasant culture and the products that could be bought at it as more authentic than what could be bought in stores.[35] Even some of the villagers, especially those who no longer engage in pig-sticking at home, see these products in the same light. At the festival the popularity of these items was such that the organizers increased the number of pigs from the previous year's event because the demand proved to be much larger than they had anticipated. Some of this enthusiasm was likely to come from notions about the authenticity of "homemade" products. The valuation of the authentic implies nostalgia, which is indexing the disappearance of what one is being nostalgic for. As I have indicated, on the preparatory day of Friday, the workers (volunteers, workfare workers, as well as organizers) made sure they got their share before the general public could have access to it the next day.

The events taking place on the day of the festival are sufficiently different from the household type of pig-sticking that it is difficult to credit the idea that the villagers see it as a recreation or representation of the traditional event. What takes place on the previous day, however, is an oversized version of the traditional pig-sticking, where much larger amounts of meat, with the help of many unrelated people, are processed into pork products. The closest the event came to the kind of commensality that traditional pig-sticking meant was the lunch that all workers shared on the Friday. This differed from the kind of eating that took place on the Saturday, when everybody paid for food individually, with coupons that could either be purchased in the entrance hall or alternately were given to the workers free of charge. In fact, the Friday preparations were reminiscent of the communal preparations and cooking that regularly took place in connection with weddings during the early 1980s. On these occasions, women (relatives, neighbors, and *komas*) came together to help prepare for the wedding feast, which was held at the House of Culture (now the Village House, the site of the festival). Thus, despite some of the novel aspects of the event, the festival does draw on certain pre-existing modes of cooperation in the community.

In moving pig-sticking from the household to the community level, the story (or one of the stories) that is being told also takes on a wider significance. It represents, creates, and reinforces openness to the outside world. This story is meant for outside consumption as much as for insiders, but there is a difference between how the message works on these two "constituencies." The message for the outside world could be called the overt message of the festival. It is one that is consciously formulated by the organizers. The festival creates a story of solidarity, a story of a well-integrated community capable of impressing the outside world. In this respect the presence of outsiders of some political significance among the contestants is very important. Some of them are simply partners of the mayor, but some may also be in a position to benefit the village through their administrative decisions. Another, less political aspect of presenting this positive image is that, given the demographic decline in the village, attracting "suitable" outsiders to move in from elsewhere is very important for the community. This story told for the outside world is personally beneficial to the mayor, and makes his tasks as mayor easier because of the connections he is able to maintain through welcoming his associates at such events, but it is also beneficial to the village.

A version of the same story is also told to the villagers. For internal consumption the emphasis was put on the benefits the event brought to the village. But this story bifurcates in that for those who participated as volunteers and organizers the success of the event built and reinforced solidarity; through working together they restated and re-created their commitment to the village and to each other. For those who remained outside the event, however, the story told was one of exclusion and differentiation. Some complained that the festival was only an occasion for the mayor to shine in front of outsiders, and to "party."[36] Others remarked rather sharply (and in my opinion somewhat unjustly) that the roads were suddenly cleaned of snow when outsiders were likely to visit. Yet others complained that the prices at the festival were too high, "they are not for us."

The workfare workers had their own version of the story. When I asked one of them on Friday night whether he would be there the following day, he answered "I am *obliged* to be here," explaining that he would rather stay at home with his four children, whom he is raising alone. Another person complained that the people (most but not all of them workfare recipients) working in the backyard were not given the opportunity to buy raffle tickets and thereby lost the chance to win something.

The festival also tells a story of power. It shows the ability of the mayor, and more generally of the leadership of the village, to dispose over the labor of members of the community, their ability to make others do their bidding and thereby further the agenda of the leadership (which may or may not coincide with the interests of the village). Only one person questioned this power. The head cook at the nursery school was called into a planning meeting for the festival, together with the heads of the various civic associations and elected representatives of the village. After listening to the discussion for a while, she asked why she had been summoned to this meeting when she neither represented a civic association nor was an elected representative. She was in a somewhat veiled fashion pointing to the fact that she and her staff were called upon to "volunteer" their time and labor for the event without being properly consulted. By asking the question, she questioned the right of the leadership to dispose over her labor. The mayor called the next day to placate her, but he was unsuccessful and the staff of the nursery kitchen pulled out of the event.

More skeptical authors, dissatisfied with a Durkheimian explanation of ritual serving primarily to create social solidarity and integration, argue that one of the main things that ritual does is hide something. Steven Lukes (1975: 301), for example, argues that ritual "helps to define as authoritative certain ways of seeing society," but even more importantly he adds that "every way of seeing [is] also a way of not seeing." Catherine Bell (1992) offers a similar but more elaborate explanatory framework. She talks about ritualization rather than ritual and regards ritual as a practice. She defines the features of practice as being fourfold: "1) situational, 2) strategic, 3) embedded in a misrecognition of what it is in fact doing, and 4) able to reproduce or reconfigure a vision of the order of power in the world" through what she calls "redemptive hegemony." Bell takes the notion of misrecognition back to what she calls "the Marxist argument that a society could not exist 'unless it disguised to itself the real basis of that existence'" (Bell 1992: 82, quoting Sahlins's *Culture and Practical Reason*).

Bell's notion implies a more all-encompassing mystification than that of Lukes. In her view, none of the participants of ritual can have a clear sense of what ritual does. While his formulation suggests the possibility of someone knowingly being able to control the effects of ritual, hers implies an ultimate inability to do so on the part of anyone who is taking part in the ritual (including its organizers and most likely the analyst as well). With this in mind, I would suggest that at least some aspects of the festival (or the story it tells) are accessible to the participants as well as to the outsiders. What I labeled the official story above is the intention of the event, and most of those concerned in the event one way or another were aware of it, regardless of whether they "accepted" the story or not. On some level at least, the organizers were aware of the alternative readings of the event. Some of the other versions of the story (the points of view of those who did not come to the event and of the workfare workers) were not part of the official story, yet they were created (at least in part) by the event itself. The enactment of the festival also re-created the inequalities present in the village, whether this was intentional or not. But what the event ultimately concealed, and directed attention away from, was the community's rather dismal economic prospects. One could counter that the event was intended to change these prospects in a positive direction, but can such ritual trump economic realities even as it draws from them?

Notes

1. I first carried out fieldwork in Szentpéterszeg in the winter of 1980–1981 (see Vidacs 1985) on strategies of choosing godparents. I worked there again in 2009–2010 in the framework of the Economy and Ritual group. I wish to thank the inhab-

itants of Szentpéterszeg for the welcome and help they extended to me during both sojourns. Thanks are also due to numerous colleagues, but especially to Mihály Sárkány and my colleagues in the group.

2. *Hurka* is the generic term for blood and liver sausage.
3. Between 1970 and 1979 natural growth was 23, and the difference due to migration was −87; between 1980 and 1989 natural growth was 29 and migration led to a decrease of 160 persons; between 1990 and 2001 there was negative natural growth of −27, but there was still a positive balance of 26, which means that over the ten-year period there had to have been an in-migration of 53 people.
4. These are: Volunteer Fire Brigade, Football Club, Civic Guard, Fishing Association, Shooting Club, Friends of Szentpéterszeg, and the Association of Large Families. These associations have a nonprofit status and thus are legally considered to be civic associations. Two other groups without such a legal status are also very active in the creation of public events. These are the Folklore Circle for Women, comprising mostly retirement-age women, and the Folk Dance Group, organized for teenagers.
5. The Hungarian socialist regime created this ceremony in imitation of the Soviet system, which had devised a much wider array of such civil ceremonies that were meant to discourage religiosity, but nonetheless afforded an opportunity for people to celebrate the most important turning points of the life cycle (see Lane 1981).
6. Although the word "Office" sounds ominous, in fact in the usage of the village it does not seem to have negative connotations.
7. The "Office" itself, besides the mayor and the notary, employs seven people, but the personnel of the cultural center (Village House) as well as the school and the nursery school are also on the payroll of the Municipality. In 2009, the Village House had two regular employees and the school had fourteen teachers and four people working in various caretaking capacities. The nursery school employed twelve people: in addition to four teachers and two helpers, this number included five kitchen staff and one caretaker.
8. Officially registered unemployed numbered 116 in 2009, which is 10.5 percent of the population of 1,095; however, not all unemployed people are registered.
9. The regulations of social welfare provisions change frequently. For example, during my fieldwork there was a major shift in how social aid (*szociális segély*) could be allocated. During 2009 it was possible for both members of a married couple to receive it at the same time; starting in 2010 only one member was entitled to receive it. Other regulations also change often.
10. This may also reflect the "aging" of the village.
11. The term "second economy" entered popular and social scientific parlance in the later decades of socialism to refer to all economic activities outside those of the planned economy. It did not disappear with the demise of socialism and now corresponds approximately to the Western European usage of "informal economy." See Hann 1990.
12. The gold crown (*arany korona*) was the unit devised by the cadastral surveyors of the late Habsburg period to measure the quality of agricultural land (cf. Hann: 2006: 61–62).
13. http://portal.ksh.hu/pls/ksh/docs/hun/xstadat/xstadat_eves/i_oma.003.html, last accessed 21 May 2011.

14. The technology of singeing is a temporal marker of change for the elderly members of the village who recall when singeing was practiced with straw (*szalma*) rather than a blowtorch.

15. In 1979, I carried out fieldwork in Etyek, a village about 30 km from Budapest, where the population was mixed Swabian (German) and Hungarian from Transylvania. The arrival of Hungarians in the village was the result of the population movements that were initiated during the Second World War, and the Hungarians were settled in the village in the place of Swabians expelled from Hungary to Germany after the war (Vidacs 1984). Those Swabians who stayed were frequent recipients of the bounty of their relatives in (West) Germany and one of the main items that they supplied were large deep freezers. At the time deep freezers counted as signs of prestige and privilege, and they were only affordable (and even available) due to Western relatives.

16. There are no butcher shops today either; the one that was there during 2009 closed in 2010 because it could not survive even on the limited schedule of being open two mornings a week. However, people are able to go to the nearby town and buy meat at one of the many stores available there, and sausages and other meat products are readily available at the local stores.

17. I interviewed fifty-seven households in 1980–1981; however, in six of the questionnaires the information regarding number and kind of animals raised is missing, so data are only available for fifty-one households.

18. Additionally, many households also kept cows or raised bulls for sale: thirty of the fifty-one households had 63 heads of cattle, and twenty-one households had none.

19. One of these had butchered their pig just before the interview. Not having a pig did not necessarily mean not having access to home-made pig-sticking products. Several of the younger people not raising pigs reported that they did participate in pig-sticking with their parents or received the products from them. Conversely, some of the elderly interviewees benefitted from the pig-sticking carried out by their children.

20. In my 1980 research, which was about strategies of choosing godparents, I did not inquire after whether people were selling pigs or not, nor did I ask whether they held pig-stickings or to whom they offered *kóstoló*. I did ask whether they had any other source of income than wages or salaries, and thirty-nine out of fifty-one households claimed to get additional income from animal husbandry. However, there is some imprecision in the numbers as, for example, when there is no statement about additional income despite the household having 7 or 8 pigs, clearly a much larger number than what can be consumed.

21. I did not collect data about pig-sticking practices during my earlier fieldwork.

22. Compare this with the following statement about the 1970s from a different region of Hungary (Varsány, Nógrád County): "Many of the new two-storey houses had no outbuildings for pigs and no gardens. Younger people preferred to live in a 'clean' environment, with a lawn in front of their house, but they still kept pigs in the sties belonging to their parents, who continued to live in traditional housing but contributed to the construction of the new houses with both money and labour" (Hann-Sárkány 2003: 126).

23. Well-known examples include *miskolci kocsonya* (the meat jelly of Miskolc) and *bajai halászlé* (the fish soup of Baja). Both of these items were well established in popular gastronomy long before festivals arose around them.

24. The festival grew out of a demonstration event held by the elected representatives of the Municipality together with those of a neighboring village in 2002. The purpose of the event was to "revive" tradition. It was held in the yard of the *tájház*, a traditional peasant house that had been restored and furnished with items from the preindustrial era.

25. Friends of Szentpéterszeg is a nonprofit organization founded in 1995. Its declared goals include uniting all those who wish to do something for the village and exploring and reviving the past while at the same time bringing together older and younger generations. The organization runs several communal events, including a biennial meeting of people who have moved away from the village and a competition for the most beautifully arranged gardens in the village.

26. On the increased number of twinned communities since 1989, see Giczi and Sík 2003.

27. The village lies near the Romanian border and quite a few men work or have worked as border guards.

28. The Folklore Circle for Women constituted an exception to this rule, in acknowledgement of their contribution of the special pasta, the ingredients of which they provided from their own resources; the affiliation fee was waved for them. The two teams from Romania were also exceptions; the mayor personally paid their affiliations.

29. I am not suggesting here that traditional feasts had been completely inward looking, but the number of teams coming from the outside and the distances they came from do indicate that the relationships are more far-flung than they would have been in earlier times.

30. Admittedly, the events she talks about are of much greater historical depth. The oldest she discusses first took place at the beginning of the nineteenth century and has been held several times since, although its second occurrence was at the beginning of the twentieth century. However, even the newest was established in 1955 and has been held regularly ever since.

31. This is not to say that there were no ludic elements in traditional peasant culture, here or elsewhere, in Hungary. Among others, the grape harvest (*szüret*), which corresponded to pig-sticking in that it had an important economic function, was always interspersed with ludic elements. And there were of course various other occasions where young people, especially, were supposed to have fun apart from the immediate economic task they were to perform. In addition, in this village as well as elsewhere in Hungary, there have been "balls" (*bál*) and other party-like occasions held for a long time. Amateur theater productions began in the 1920s.

32. Expenses included the following: hiring the tent, paying for three pigs (the fourth one was a gift from one of the villagers), raffle prizes, ingredients of the foods to be served at the event, ingredients for the sausage/*hurka* making, such as sausage skins, and additional internal organs to go into the *hurka*. Furthermore, honoraria had to be paid to the chef-judges, the entertainers, and the two butchers.

33. The overall costs of the event were 953,000 forints (circa 3,800 Euros) and it brought in 816,000 forints (3,260 Euros), the difference being paid for by the foundation mentioned above.
34. In total, about 300 to 400 people participated, including contestants, workers, and visitors, many of whom did not stay for the entire day. Setting aside the contestants, the locals outnumbered the visitors from outside significantly.
35. For a more detailed discussion of the implications of creating "living tradition," see Kaneff and King (2004); Eriksen (2004).
36. Such charges, however, are not rare. Bódi and Járosi (2008) describe very similar charges in connection with a communal festival in another region of the country.

References

Bali, János. 1999. "Disznóölés—egy paraszti rítus továbbélése Magyarországon napjaink falusi társadalmában. (Pig-sticking—The Survival of a Peasant Rite in Contemporary Rural Society in Hungary.)" In *Menyeruwa*, ed. Géza Kézdi Nagy, 159–166. Budapest.

———. 2007. "A lokális tradíció és a helyi közösségszerveződés a falusi főzőfesztiválok tükrében. (Local Tradition and Community Organization in Light of Rural Cooking Festivals.)" In *A vidéki Magyarország az EU csatlakozás után. VII. Falukonferencia* [Rural Hungary after Accession to the European Union. 7th Village Conference], ed. Teréz Kovács, 376–384. Pécs: MTA Regionális Kutatások Központja.

Bell, Catherine. 1992. *Ritual Theory, Ritual Practice.* Oxford: Oxford University Press.

Bendix, Regina. 1989. "Tourism and Cultural Displays. Inventing Traditions for Whom?" *The Journal of American Folklore* 102 no. 404: 131–146.

Bod, Tamás. 2001. "Szép siker a Csabai Kolbászfesztiválon," Last accessed online at http://www.hdsz.tag.hu/keret.cgi?/00/6/00_06_09.html, 7 April 2012.

Bódi, Jenő, and Katalin Járosi. 2008. "'Itt nyolcvanháromféle külön világ van'—Nagyszakácsi mozaik. ('There Are Eighty-three Kinds of Separate Worlds Here'–Nagyszakácsi Mosaic)." In *Kistelepülések lépéskényszerben* (Small Communities That Must Act), ed. Monika Mária Váradi, 323–367. Budapest: Új Mandátum Kiadó.

Dienes, Beáta. 2005. "'Jó dolog ez a hűtő!' A disznóölés és sertésfeldolgozás mai formája Bárándon. ('Fridges Are Good Things!' Contemporary Pig-sticking and Pork Processing in Báránd)." In *Parasztélet, Kultúra, Adaptáció* (Peasant Lifestyle, Culture, Adaptation), ed. Anikó Báti et al., 165–174. Budapest: Akadémiai Kiadó.

Eriksen, Thomas Hylland. 2004. "Keeping the Recipe: Norwegian Folk Costumes and Cultural Capital." *Focaal: European Journal of Anthropology* 44: 20–34.

Fél, Edit, and Tamás Hofer. 1969. *Proper Peasants.* Chicago: Aldine.

Fournier, Laurent S. 2007. "La fête thématique, nouveau visage de la fête locale en Provence (France)." *Recherches sociologiques et anthropologiques* 38, no. 2: 165–174. Last accessed online at http://rsa.revues.org/474, 24 May 2011.

Geertz, Clifford. 1973. "Deep Play: Notes on the Balinese Cockfight." In *The Interpretation of Cultures: Selected Essays,* 412–453. New York: Basic Books.

Giczi, Johanna, and Endre Sík. 2003. "A települések kapcsolati tőkéjének egy típusa—a testvértelepülések. (A Type of Social Capital for Settlements—Twinning)." *Szociológiai Szemle* 13, no. 4: 34–54.

Guillou, Anne. 1991. "Food Habits, the Freezer and Gender Relations in the Countryside." *Journal of Rural Studies* 7, no. 1–2: 67–70.

Hann, Chris. 1980. *Tázlár: A Village in Hungary.* Cambridge: Cambridge University Press.

———. 1990 "Second Economy and Civil Society." In *Market Economy and Civil Society in Hungary,* ed. C. M. Hann. London: Frank Cass.

———. 2006. "'Not the Horse We Wanted!' Procedure and Legitimacy in Postsocialist Privatisation in Tázlár." In *"Not the Horse We Wanted!": Postsocialism, Neoliberalism, and Eurasia,* Chris Hann, 42–90. Münster: LIT Verlag.

Hann, Chris, and Mihály Sárkány. 2003. "The Great Transformation in Rural Hungary: Property, Life Strategies and Living Standards." In *The Postsocialist Agrarian Question: Property Relations and the Rural Condition,* Chris Hann and the "Property Relations Group," 117–141. Münster: LIT Verlag.

Harcsa, István, Imre Kovách, and Iván Szelényi. 1998a. "The Hungarian Agricultural 'Miracle' and the Limits of Socialist Reforms." In *Privatizing the Land. Rural Political Economy in Post-Communist Societies,* ed. Iván Szelényi, 21–42. London: Routledge.

Harcsa, István, Imre Kovách, and Iván Szelényi. 1998b. "The Price of Privatization: The Post-Communist Transformational Crisis of the Hungarian Agrarian System." In *Privatizing the Land: Rural Political Economy in Post-Communist Societies,* ed. Iván Szelényi, 214–244. London: Routledge.

Hobsbawm, Eric, and Terence Ranger. 1983. *The Invention of Tradition.* Cambridge: Cambridge University Press.

Hoppál, Mihály. 1980. "Elosztás és egyenlőség (Sharing and Equality)." *MTA Nyelv- és Irodalomtudományok Osztályának Közleményei* 32 no. 1–2: 139–154.

Kaneff, Deema, and Alexander D. King. 2004. "Introduction: Owning Culture." *Focaal: European Journal of Anthropology* 44: 3–19.

Kovach, Imre. 1999. "Hungary: Cooperative Farms and Household Plots." In *Many Shades of Red: State Policy and Collective Agriculture,* ed. Mieke Meurs, 125–149.

Lane, Christel. 1981. *The Rites of Rulers: Ritual in Industrial Society—The Soviet Case.* Cambridge: Cambridge University Press.

Lukes, Steven. 1975. "Political Ritual and Social Integration." *Sociology* 9: 289–308.

Michalkó, Gábor, and Tamara Rátz. 2006. "Typically Female Features in Hungarian Shopping Tourism." *Migracijske i etničke teme* 22 (1–2): 79–93. Last accessed online at http://hrcak.srce.hr/index.php?show=clanak&id_clanak_jezik=8131, 24 May 2011.

Minnich, Robert G. 1979. *The Homemade World of Zagaj.* "An Interpretation of the "Practical Life" Among Traditional Peasant-Farmers in West Haloze–Slovenia, Yugoslavia." Occasional Paper No. 18. Bergen.

Pusztai, Bertalan. 2007. "Identity, Canonisation and Branding at the Baja Festival." In *Tourism, Festivals and Local Identity: Fish Soup Cooking in Baja, Hungary,* ed. Bertalan Pusztai and Neill Martin. Edinburgh/Szeged: University of Edinburgh—Szegedi Tudományegyetem Néprajzi és Kulturális Antropológiai Tanszék, 83–100.

Pusztai, Bertalan, and Neill Martin. 2007. *Tourism, Festivals and Local Identity: Fish Soup Cooking in Baja, Hungary* (Turizmus, fesztiválok és helyi identitás: Halászléfőzés Baján). Edinburgh/Szeged: University of Edinburgh—Szegedi Tudományegyetem Néprajzi és Kulturális Antropológiai Tanszék.

Rockefeller, Stuart A. 1999. "'There is a Culture Here': Spectacle and the Inculcation of Folklore in Highland Bolivia." *Journal of Latin American Anthropology* 3, no. 2: 118–149.

Sárkány, Mihály. 1983. "A lakodalom funkciójának megváltozása falusi közösségekben (The Changing Functions of the Wedding Feast in Rural Communities)." *Ethnographia* 94: 279–285.

———. 2005. "Re-study of Varsány: Entrepreneurs and Property in Rural Hungary after 1989." In *Anthropology of Europe: Teaching and Research*, ed. Peter Skalník, 143–151. Prague: Set Out.

Stan, Sabina. 2000. "What's in a Pig? 'State,' 'Market' and Process in Private Pig Production and Consumption in Romania." *Dialectical Anthropology* 25: 151–160.

Swain, Nigel. 1985. *Collective Farms Which Work?* Cambridge: Cambridge University Press.

Szalai, Julia. 1991. "Hungary: Exit from the State Economy." In *Time for Retirement: Comparative Studies of Early Exit from the Labor Force*, ed. Martin Kohli et al., 324–362. Cambridge: Cambridge University Press.

———. 2006. "Poverty and the Traps of Postcommunist Welfare Reforms in Hungary: The New Challenges of EU-accession." *Revija za socijalnu politiku* 13, no. 3–4: 309–333.

Váradi, Monika Mária, ed. 2008 *Kistelepülések lépéskényszerben* (Small Communities That Must Act), Budapest: Új Mandátum Kiadó.

Varga, Zsuzsanna. 2009. *The Hungarian Agriculture and Rural Society: Changes, Problems and Possibilities.* Budapest: Szaktudás Kiadó Ház.

Vidacs, Bea. 1984. "Food as Ethnic Identity in Etyek, Hungary." *Journal of Folklore Research* 21, no. 2–3: 226–228.

———. 1985. "Komaság és kölcsönösség Szentpéterszegen (Godparenthood and Reciprocity in Szentpéterszeg)." *Ethnographia* 96, no. 4: 509–529.

Wengrow, David. 2008. "Prehistories of Commodity Branding." *Current Anthropology* 49, no. 1: 7–34.

4

Kurban

Shifting Economy and the Transformations of a Ritual

DETELINA TOCHEVA

The profound economic upheavals in the Bulgarian countryside after the fall of socialism were accompanied by significant transformations in ritual life. If in some respects ritual activity sharply declined as a result of the economic downturn (Creed 2002), in other respects rural areas became the cradle of ritual creativity (Creed 2011). Instead of following the economic depression, the ritual that I examine has been thriving in a period marked by social disjuncture and a crumbling economy. In the village of Belan in the southern Rhodope Mountains, a new type of spring *kurban* ritual, related to sheep breeding in the past and first established in its present form in 1992, grew in importance as making a living became harder.[1] The term *kurban* is of Muslim Turkish origin and means "sacrifice." In this region it designates both a Muslim and an Orthodox ritual comprising a blood sacrifice and a sacrificial meal shared among the participants. The word spread in the Balkans during the Ottoman period, but it is not known when and under what circumstances it came to be applied to communal feasts with slaughtered animals at Orthodox churches.

The postsocialist village *kurban* in Belan is relatively disconnected from religion, which may be viewed as a legacy of socialist secularizing policies. Its egalitarian spirit, however, is clearly a postsocialist invention. Individualism, competition, and economistic maximization of outputs and minimization of inputs have become prominent in many areas of village life. In contrast, this ritual transcends individual interests and deploys an egalitarian grammar. The stronger the economic fracturing since the early 1990s, the wider and more important the ritual of sharing, opposed to calculative reasoning and self-interest. I argue that the new *kurban* is the annual realization of a consensual model of egalitarian relationships; it promotes sharing and negates self-interest and differentiation according to wealth and power. The ritual encapsulates a model of an alternative economy and sociality that partakes in the making of social cohesion.

To concentrate on sheep in order to examine social, economic, and ritual life in a Balkan country in the twenty-first century may appear as an anachronistic reference back to the classical Mediterranean anthropology of an earlier era (Campbell 1964). I argue that this approach provides a privileged insight into both long-term transformation and the surprising creativity of the human economy in Bulgarian postsocialist capitalism. Looking back over the last century, I notice a reversal of the relationship between the prominence and role of *kurban,* and the economic role of sheep breeding in the local economy, a trend comparable to the trajectory of pig-sticking in Hungary analyzed by Vidacs (this volume). While in the past sheep breeding was of crucial importance for almost every house (Light, this volume), now the number of sheep holders has shrunk in relation to the village population and their economic role is much smaller. Before socialist collectivization started in the late 1940s, the spring ritual of *kurban* in Belan involved only sheep-owning families. At present, it has reached major prominence as a village-wide event. Thus, the current *kurban* unites a village community whose economic resources are more diverse and stretch far beyond sheep breeding. In comparison with the end of the nineteenth and the beginning of the twentieth century, the early postsocialist period saw a reversal of the relationship between the economy of sheep breeding and the ritual. Whereas the shrinking economic importance of sheep followed the general rural decline in the country, the new communal *kurban,* fruit of villagers' creativity, has become extremely popular. This ritual is an instance of a stunningly wide phenomenon. Various forms of *kurban* have risen across the country as the economy became more fragmented and social stratification sharper after 1989. How are we to make sense of this?

Anthropologists have argued for an approach to the economy that accounts for economic practices and ideas as rooted in broader ideological and social logics, for ways to understand economy as culture (Gudeman 1986). As Polanyi argued, while "the human economy … is embedded and enmeshed in institutions, economic and noneconomic" (Polanyi 1957: 250), global policies tend to create markets that are increasingly disembedded from society. Keeping this tension in mind, the lived, human economy (Hart, Laville, and Cattani 2010) needs to be approached in its social and cultural embeddedness. Ritual can also provide a model of economic thought and operation; it can effectively make social cohesion. The postsocialist spring *kurban* in Belan is an enactment in ritual of alternative, noninstrumental economy and egalitarian social organization.

This is not the only village-wide event where villagers and guests get together. The villagers look forward to their summer fair (*sabor*), initiated in 1991, probably as much as to their *kurban.* At the fair, local political leaders, folkloric ensembles, and singers occupy the stage. Large quantities of food and drink are sold. The village fair belongs to the category of events that legitimate the existing social and economic order, and dominant ideologies of consumption and leisure. To paraphrase Godelier, such rituals are the visible expressions of mental superstructures underlying the social order (1984). But rituals can also express a reversal of the actual social order, contest it, or undermine it. Rituals can also express potentialities present in shared thought, although not necessarily formulated as such. For example, Gerald Creed's *Masquerade and Postsocialism* (2011) examines mumming festivals in rural Bulgaria as the ritual enactment of social relationships, different from those imposed on Bulgarian society after 1989. For Creed, mummers and their covillagers practice festivals of various scales and elaboration, thus compensating for the cultural dispossession through which they have been deprived of any meaningful participation in the politically and economically reformed society. Different sorts of *kurban* have been equally widespread since 1989 and subject to variation and adaptation (Givre 2006). If mumming is, among other things, a reflection on the integration of conflict and tension within community (Creed 2011; see also Creed 2006), the type of *kurban* that I analyze is a reflection on a noninstrumental economy and egalitarian community. While in many respects competition, acquisitiveness, and stratification characterize village life, in Belan, this ritual, thriving since its creation in 1992, hints at the opposite of self-interest, competition, and differentiation. In contrast to Marxist approaches, it does not legitimate or disguise the extant social order. It rather enacts diametrically opposed economic and organizational principles once per year and thereby generates social cohesion by effacing individual interests and actual stratification at the ritual moment.

After a brief depiction of the social structure of the local economy, I describe the ritual and how its messages contradict both the officially promoted principles of the economy and social hierarchy and the effects of the postsocialist reforms. After examining long-term transformations of livelihood in the region, I pay close attention to a reversal of the relation between the economic prominence of sheep breeding, to which the predecessor of the current ritual was related, and the affirmation of the postsocialist *kurban.*

The Social Structure of the Local Economy

Generally, after 1989 the elite-organized dismantlement of entire sectors of the economy for selfish gain and the concomitant undermining of crucial state functions (Ganev 2007) have had painful effects throughout the Bulgarian countryside. In Belan, the state-run collective farm was the heart of economic life under socialism. It employed most locals. With its disbanding in 1992, the small industries closed down; the school, the kindergarten and local administration have continually downsized their personnel since that moment. The few local entrepreneurial ventures in the 1990s did not compensate for the loss of jobs and villagers did not become agricultural entrepreneurs. Agriculture has become only an occasional source of cash. Increasingly, out-migration affected Belan. The earlier principles that structured the local social hierarchy, such as proximity to the regional Party leadership, or membership in the managerial apparatus, were redefined according to the new economic principles, with political connections remaining important for entrepreneurs. In practice, some of the formerly powerful figures have retained some power. Success in rural tourism has propelled a small local economic elite.

In 2010 Belan had 151 inhabited houses containing 182 households.[2] Overall, the Rhodope villages have a mixed economy. In contrast with the presocialist past, now no one sees a high number of sheep as a sign of wealth. In Belan, the most significant income comes from salaries, wages, pensions, five small grocery stores, and house-based tourism for some families. The main employers are the mayor's office, the school, the kindergarten, a shirt-making factory and a small wood-processing plant. An overwhelming majority of households are unable to cope only with their monetary income from wages and salaries. They grow potatoes, beans, and vegetables and keep a few sheep; some have a cow and a calf. Home-grown food is seen as an insufficient fallback.[3] Hence, the majority of sheep-owning houses use them as one branch of their complex domestic economy and many do so through participation in common pasturing.

For a few houses sheep, among other assets, constitute a connection to the market of rural tourism. Since the late 1990s, the expansion of rural tourism has partially alleviated the bitter sense of political and economic abandonment. In Belan and in nearby Radino, house-based tourism has brought additional income and more life in the summer, permitting the villagers to retrieve a sense of self-esteem. This enterprise largely depends on domestic farming, nonwage labor, and local networks of cooperation. It is a form of engagement with the market through the assets held by the domestic economy. Home-grown potatoes, beans, vegetables, cow milk, veal, lamb, and dairy products from sheep milk are highly valued. Two families who take in tourists, one in Belan and one in Radino, have clearly outdistanced all the others; both keep sheep. Therefore, rural tourism has been the major source of social stratification over the last ten years, with the domestic economy as its key supplier and marketing argument.

In 2010, a wealthy house in the village is one that successfully combines various incomes from salaries, wages, old-age pensions, and small businesses with the sale of agricultural produce (potatoes, beans, milk, meat) and produces all these along with other foods to be eaten by the household members. As in socialist times, food produced in the countryside feeds relatives in the town. This food fulfills the important task of supplying urban residents who chronically experience money shortages and are faced with generalized employment instability. The situation has the twofold effect of putting stronger pressure on rural domestic food production while simultaneously encouraging migration to the largest cities that offer more attractive salaries. The pressure on the rural house relaxes when former small-town residents move on to cities, or migrate abroad. They tend then to come back less often to the village house, inhabited usually by the elderly. Relatively well-off houses comprise three or four generations, with steady income from salaries and pensions.

In a worse-off house, money income is irregular, coming most often from precarious wages and short-term unemployment benefits. Usually these households do not produce enough to sustain themselves. Thus, when the incomes are limited and irregular, pensioners become precious house members, as their income is guaranteed. Most often pensions are used to pay the monthly bills for the whole house. Elderly couples or solitaries, if they receive a relatively solid pension, can afford not to keep animals or to grow any foods. Intergenerational solidarity intermingles with rural-urban solidarities, as old-age pensions and domestic farming often support younger urbanites or commuting household members. These solidarities alleviate the pressure stemming from the low salaries, delayed payments, and job insecurity that those who move to the city accept as an alternative to complete unemployment in the village.

Togetherness, Sharing, and Equity

The annual village *kurban* in Belan enacts an economic model of gift and sharing, and an egalitarian social organization from which hierarchies and competition are completely absent. As noted above, the Balkan *kurban* is a ritual adopted during the Ottoman period that became characteristic of the Christian and Muslim traditions (Givre 2006; Hristov and Sikimić 2007). Different sorts of *kurban* provided an enduring frame for the continuation of religious practices under socialism, although they were not necessarily understood as religious by the participants (see Blagoev 2004; Hristov and Manova 2007; Iankov 2006; Kolev 2006; about the Rhodope region see Iordanova 2006; Stamenova 1995: 137–186). *Kurban* is practiced at Muslim religious celebrations, Orthodox saints' days, village days, and at life-cycle rituals, and to commemorate personal events (e.g., a sacrificial *kurban* meal may be offered annually on the date when a person miraculously survived a car accident). "To slaughter *kurban*" (*koli se kurban*) means that an animal is slaughtered, cooked, and shared as a free meal with kin, friends, acquaintances, and other people. The animal is not necessarily a sheep or a lamb. It can also be a calf, though in the Rhodopes it is most commonly a sheep. The blood sacrifice constitutes the symbolic religious matrix of this ritual for Muslims and Christians (Givre 2006).

In Belan, there is a large Bulgarian Muslim majority and a Bulgarian Christian minority. The two groups practice some forms of *kurban* separately, and participate together in others. First, the annual Muslim Kurban Bairam celebration is marked by the domestic slaughter of one sheep per married pair, so up to three or four animals per house in Belan. A small portion of the meat is given to neighbors and to the village poor, usually elderly living alone on a tiny pension; the rest is cooked, canned, or frozen. The distribution is not ritualized. Second, ritual gatherings in the Muslim houses are organized for life-cycle events, such as childbirth, wedding, or commemoration of deceased relatives. Then, a house opens up and invites fellow villagers, work colleagues, friends, and kin, irrespective of their religious identity. Third, the village spring *kurban* transcends the houses; the village acts as a community that hosts itself and its guests. The village *kurban* has much in common with the symbolism of sharing and equality of the Muslim house-based *kurban*: the foods are almost identical, the guests use only spoons (as in everyday life in the past), and three or four people eat from the same plate, all being received with no differentiation of status, wealth, gender, or age. Fourth, the two Orthodox churches in Belan also hold *kurban* on the day of their respective patron saints, but these attract less people than the village *kurban*. There is no equivalent ritual practiced at the local mosque. While Kurban Bairam and the *kurban* of the churches were officially forbidden under socialism as religious practice, villagers report that the solidarity between Muslims and Christians allowed keeping their respective ritual hidden from the authorities, and thus permitted them to continue, though on a limited scale. Whereas the celebrations in the Muslim houses are marked with long-term continuity, as they seem to have changed little under socialism and after, even though more guests were hosted with the rising living standard in the 1970s and 1980s, the village *kurban* is a postsocialist invention inspired by an earlier spring *kurban* related to sheep breeding.

All neighboring villages offer their own *kurban* in the spring; the villages coordinate with each other in order to avoid overlapping dates. *Kurban* in Belan is said to be the one in the area attended by the most numerous guests. The total number of participants was estimated as 1,000 in 2010. In fact, neighboring Radino claimed this number for their *kurban* in 2009. If very accurate figures are hard to establish, claiming higher numbers attests to the fact that *kurban* fosters competition over prestige between the villages.

The village *kurban* in Belan was initiated in 1992 by several villagers, most of them Muslim. Ethnographic records of the Rhodopes show that before World War II Muslims offered a spring *kurban* on the day of the first milk measuring; no data evidence such practice among the Christians. However, as pointed out above, Christians as much as Muslims in the Balkans consider *kurban* as their traditional ritual. In Belan, the Muslim religious elements are easier to identify, but both Christians and Muslims see the spring *kurban* as a request for protection and prosperity that bridges the two religions. Most villagers spoke of the event in remotely religious terms, or drew no religious association at all: "This is good for the sheep, for the people, for the village." Many of those who left the village or originate from neighboring villages emphasized the pleasure of visiting Belan and getting together with their relatives, friends, as well as former and current colleagues.

Some put a stronger emphasis on religion, without claiming an exclusive Christian or Muslim origin. A wife and a husband, both of them retired villagers of Muslim origin, have cooked for *kurban* and coordinated the preparation of food since 1992. They were among the initiators. The woman, a former agricultural worker at the collective and later a cleaning woman at the school, born in 1945, told me: "This is already a tradition. We got used to it." When I inquired about the reason of having created this tradition, she said: "The old people understood it like this, that when you make *kurban,* the Lord (*Gospod*) simply protects you against everything, the plants against hail, against everything." Then she cited a Christian woman who had passed away a couple of years earlier: "There was this woman who lived up there, the wife of the hunter, you know, she passed away, may God forgive her. She used to say: 'Our village is prosperous, because we make our *kurban.* We make our *kurban* and the Lord takes care of us,' she used to say." Despite invocations of the elderly, the village *kurban* is not referred to in terms of heritage or traditional cultural value, nor are there struggles over authenticity. Its most usual meaning is a sacrificial get-together that brings prosperity (*bereket*—this is a term of Turkish origin broadly used in colloquial Bulgarian). Muslims may speak of protection from "Allah" and the "Lord"; Christians would refer to the "Lord" and "God." A common practice of Muslims and Christians is to refer to "the one who is above" or to "the one up there." No one asserts *kurban* to be either Muslim or Christian. However, on the Friday morning before *kurban* in May 2010, about twenty elderly men gathered in the mosque for a prayer, without publicizing the event. As usual, there was no gathering in the church before or after *kurban*. This different involvement of the two religions shows that a Muslim connotation is more noticeable. But no official Muslim authority takes part and the ritual is not the subject of claims over correct religious practice (see Ghodsee 2010).

This bridging of the two religions is common in Bulgaria. What attracts attention is that at the key moment of the ritual meal neither religion is given prominence. On the contrary, in the preliminary phase Islam is noticeable but not publicized. This serves to soften the religious connotation, which is important in a region where the presocialist and socialist governments repressed Islam. Harsh policies obliged people to change Muslim names to Christian and punished Islamic practices more visibly than equivalent Christian practices (Gruev 2008). Thus, *kurban* is a statement of unity and community in relation to this violent past and state-promoted divisions.

Muslim Bulgarians remained a majority in Belan despite out-migration to Turkey after 1912, when this region became part of independent Bulgaria. At this time, Bulgarian Christians represented around one-fifth of the population of the village (Uzunov 1993: 33). Shortly after the establishment of socialism, both Muslims and Christians left the village to work in industrial plants, in mines, on construction sites, in the administration, and in education. In 2010 the majority was by far Muslim. In the nineteenth and the early twentieth centuries Muslims tended to live from agriculture and raise animals, producing to sustain themselves, while Christians were craftspeople, shepherds, or masons and had more access to the monetized economy (Brunnbauer 2002: 331–333). Today, however, there are no substantial differences in the domestic economy according to religious affiliation. An elderly Christian man, in fact a committed communist and former mayor, has several sheep, while some Muslims of his generation do not have animals, even though they used to work with animals in the collective farm.

Independently of age, of religious background, of whether or not they own sheep, villagers and their guests readily take part in the village *kurban*. In Belan, this ritual takes place through gifts of money and milk, voluntary work, sharing of food, and the staging of equality. One area of communal sharing is defined by the donations from the villagers. Three employees of the mayor's office collect monetary donations, each of them covering the houses of one area. They bring the collected funds to a bookkeeper who writes the figures in a notebook. In May 2010, 900 leva (450 Euro) were collected, in addition to 800 leva (400 Euro) left from previous years. The bookkeeper, like all villagers, emphasized that no one is expected to give a certain amount, and that people gave from a few cents to 20 leva (10 Euro), and exceptionally there were donations of 100 leva (50 Euro). I inquired if there were higher expectations of businesspeople for example, but no such expectations were explicitly mentioned or evident from the conversations that I heard. In 2010, the village bakery donated bread. As usual, sheep milk was donated from the village flock and from the flock of the large farm. Five sheep, 50 kilos of wheat, and 25 kilos of beans were bought and paid for with the collected money.

Another area of sharing is work for the event; the time and effort are not calculated and there is no return of any kind. Since 1992, every year in the beginning of May the mayor has organized a meeting to decide about practicalities. Ivan, a 73-year-old former professional soldier has been the bookkeeper of the village *kurban* since 2005. Emin, a diligent 80-year-old man, the milker of the village flock, chooses the sheep to be bought and slaughtered for the event. A couple of pensioners cook the meal. Most of the villagers who took over the organizational work in 2010 are of Muslim origin; the bookkeeper and one of the usual helpers, a jobless villager in his late thirties, are Christians. Emin had thirty years' experience as a shepherd at the state-run farm and was known for his expertise with sheep. Ivan does not keep animals; he and his wife say they enjoy freedom and quiet life. The cook said that Ivan, being a friendly person with good education, was the most suitable to act as a bookkeeper: "We invited him [since 2005], he is the most important person in charge [with the organization of *kurban*]." In addition, at least twenty other people share many other tasks.

The village *kurban* takes place on a Saturday. From Thursday on, intense preparation begins. On Thursday, 27 May 2010, in the morning, seven women in their fifties and sixties, all of Muslim origin, gathered in the yard of a centrally located restaurant and cleaned the beans and wheat from little stones and tiny twigs. At the same time, a group of men went to five different houses where there were villagers willing to sell their sheep for *kurban*. Emin selected the animals that two villagers helped transport, one with his truck and the other one with his horse cart, to the meadow situated just behind the school and the mayor's office, where they were slaughtered. Before slaughtering, Ivan the bookkeeper supervised the weighing of the animals and noted the weight and the corresponding amount to be paid to the sheep owners. An elderly man read Muslim prayers just before each sheep was slaughtered; he is the one who usually utters the prayers when the Muslim houses slaughter sheep for the feast of *Kurban Bairam*.[4] Four men helped the butcher skin the animals and clean the giblets. The cleaned animals were taken 20 meters away, to the cold room in the basement of the house of culture (*chitalishte*), which had been equipped as part of an underground bomb shelter in socialist times. The meat stayed there until Friday afternoon when the cooks and other helpers took over.

After the animals were brought to the cold room, the men, supervised by the mayor, erected a temporary shelter from rainproof cloth supported by wooden and metallic girders right behind the house of culture, a few meters away from the mayor's office. The shelter was ready on Friday afternoon. Tables were set up for the meat processing and cauldrons were installed. The cooks, milker, and the bookkeeper took charge of the meat processing. The animals were cut in smaller pieces by joints, according to the Muslim tradition. Six persons stayed there during the entire night.

A third domain of sharing is the gift of milk used to make yogurt for the ritual meal. The village herd and a large-scale farmer offered around 250 liters of sheep milk altogether. Women usually make the yogurt. This is a great responsibility, because the quantity to process is considerable (between 25 and 35 liters per woman) and because the yogurt is offered to all villagers and guests, and with the other foods represents the village during the ritual. On the two days before *kurban*, the sheep milk was brought to eight women in a row. The organizational committee knew without deliberating who should make the yogurt. These were neither very young nor elderly women who were used to the procedure; my hostess was one of them. She received approximately 30 liters of milk in jerry cans. The procedure took her a couple of hours. If one misses the right moment to remove the boiling thick and fat sheep milk from the stove, the yogurt made out of it gets a flavor of burned milk. We knew the result only by the next morning, when the milk had turned into yogurt, on the day of *kurban.* The taste was fine. But if there is any shortcoming in the preparation and the yogurt does not match the standards, there is no way to make it again because of the lack of time and milk, which means that the women who process the milk are not allowed to fail. Sheep yogurt, in addition to *keshkek,* the ritual dish of wheat and mutton, is the traditional food that all locals and guests eat on *kurban.* On the day of *kurban,* some of the cooks and helpers acknowledged having detected a flavor of burned milk in one of the eight pots of yogurt, but none of them tried to know who had made it.

The current *kurban* stages equality. Starting at 11 A.M., a long trickle of local and external guests started arriving at a former café situated on the ground floor of the house of culture where the tables were set up, inside and outside. The café was open only for the event. The wife of the mayor actively participated in serving the tables as she knew this place as one that she had rented formerly. Other helpers were a young jobless villager, two women working for the mayor's office, two other women, and myself. The guests arrived in small groups of relatives, neighbors, and friends. They were all served in the same way, regardless of their social differences: per four guests, there was one large bowl of bean soup, another one of *keshkek,* and one bowl of sheep yogurt. People from nearby villages and the city came, as well as villagers who had moved out a long time ago. A man who belongs to the family running the most successful tourist guesthouse brought a bunch of tourists, young Bulgarians from a distant region. They ate like all the others.

The mayor was accompanied by a politician from the regional council who seemed to be well acquainted with the ritual. The mayor and his guest kept a low profile. Unlike other festive gatherings such as the village fair, during which politicians make speeches, *kurban* is not used as a political arena. People spend time outside before or after the meal, chatting with those whom they have not seen for a long time. But there are no announcements, ceremonial thanks, microphones, or music. The ritual brings the people together in a festive mood, but somewhat quiet and solemn. In contrast, the village fair, taking place later in the summer, involves speeches by politicians, performances of local and guest folkloric groups, loud music, and dances. Sellers of sweets and other foods, toys, and different commodities occupy the square and the central street. The local shop owners set up large barbecues for the sale of food and drinks. They compete with each other and with the incomers for the best place, and conflicts frequently arise.

I argue that the calm atmosphere of the village *kurban* expresses its sacred character. The event is the ritual expression of consensus and egalitarian values; no one's role or status is on display. At the moment of the meal, actual stratification in the village and differentiation between the villagers and wealthier guests, as tourists often happen to be, are downplayed. The symbolism of shared food, the absence of individual plates, and the equal treatment of all guests stress *sameness.* This applies also to the Gypsies who come from the largest of the local villages and who are sometimes discriminated against in everyday life.[5]

Everyone is given food, under the condition that this food is eaten within the company of the others, in the same way. The cooks and the helpers in the improvised kitchen under the shelter criticized demands of persons who asked for food to be poured in small packages for their relatives who could not come. The cooks argued that the food had to be consumed on the place of *kurban,* with the other guests, and not at home, and then, between them, commented that some people wanted to take home as much food as possible. Such criticism was expressed twice, though the commentary did not entail an actual refusal to give food. A few other demands were immediately satisfied, as the cooks knew that some ill persons could not come to the village square. As a general rule, food is to be eaten with the others, according to the specific egalitarian grammar deployed on this occasion.

The preliminary phase of preparation also reveals preoccupation with equity. The decision about whose animals to buy for the ritual was infused with a deep concern on this point. Emin, who selects the animals, knew who among the villagers had an animal to sell. He knew for example that a neighboring house of his own had a ram; the couple who raised it was planning to sell it as a sacrificial animal for *kurban.* The husband had been unemployed for years and the wife was making little money from the small grocery shop she had. Their two sons had left the country a few months earlier and were employed as factory workers in the Czech Republic. For this family *kurban* was a good occasion to make some money. The week before *kurban,* Emin told me that he had already decided not to take the ram of his neighbors, selecting instead the animal of another woman. "This woman went to the mayor, crying, saying she needed money desperately, she wanted me to take her sheep. She has three sheep that she wants to sell. So I'm not taking my neighbors' ram, I have to take hers."

Emin changed his mind during his final visit to the houses willing to sell animals. Realizing that it was not possible to make a decision that would significantly favor one person and disadvantage another, he chose one animal per house among the five "candidate" houses. The ram of the neighbors was purchased, too, but as it was too heavy—75 kilos, that is, twenty kilos above the heaviest of all the other animals—Emin and Ivan the bookkeeper negotiated with the couple. The couple agreed to "step back" with 10 kilos and accept payment only for the remaining 65 kilos. The tariff for all was 4 leva per kilo. During that spring, the price for lamb in usual transactions, not the ones related to *kurban,* varied between 8 and 12 leva per kilo. It was convenient for the sheep owners, who needed money, to sell their animals at a moment when external demand is usually low; even in the late spring and during the summer when this demand reaches a peak it concerns lamb rather than mutton. For *kurban,* the price was set up by the organizers and no bargaining was possible. In this phase of *kurban,* equity was not staged; it was effectively, pragmatically implemented.

Reversal of the Relationship Between Sheep Breeding and *Kurban*

The integrative character of the village *kurban* is a postsocialist novelty, but the ritual builds on an older tradition. If in the nineteenth and early twentieth centuries the ritual was practiced only by groups of sheep-owning families, the event created in 1992 integrates a larger range of participants. Since the wars in the first half of the twentieth century, the importance of sheep breeding has significantly diminished, and did not reattain its earlier level after the fall of socialism. Conversely, the spring *kurban* has become one of the most integrative and popular rituals since 1992. There has been a reversal of the relationship between the sheep economy and the ritual.

Sheep breeding, trade in sheep meat, milk, milk products, wool, skins, and different handicrafts related to wool and skin processing were major resources in the Rhodopes for hundreds of years (Brunnbauer 2003: 189–197; Primovski 1973: 283–287). The number of sheep was the indicator of wealth, in particular for Muslims who sustained themselves more directly from animal breeding and agriculture than Christians, whose men were more often craftsmen and masons. In the nineteenth century the needs of the Ottoman army propelled demand for wool, creating a new source of income for sheep breeders, wool processors, and weavers (Brunnbauer 2002: 331 passim; 2003: 190–191). Belan and Radino are situated in the region that was the last bastion of the Ottoman Empire in Bulgaria; Ottoman rule endured until 1912. After World War I, Bulgaria lost territory to Greece. Sheep herding and its related commerce declined due to the disappearance of the Ottoman markets and because large warmer grazing lands in the winter became more difficult to reach. During the winter the animals had to be kept in stables and feeding them became a serious problem. In the area of Belan, located almost on the border of present-day Greece, the negative effects were limited because the villagers were still able to cross the border and use land on the other side for farming and hay harvesting.[6]

Until World War II, the region was known as backward and poor. Before the establishment of the communist regime in 1944, cows were kept for milk and as draft animals, while "the goat was a small cow for the poor inhabitant of the Rhodope" (Damianov 1972: 56). Although the average size of sheep herds declined after the loss of access to the Aegean Sea, sheep remained the most important animals. The successive wars between 1912 and 1944 (two world wars and two Balkan wars) impoverished even the owners of larger herds and the wealthier craftspeople. Requisitions of food imposed during the wars endangered survival (Damianov 1972). The state maintained an army while food was extremely scarce. Elderly villagers told me how, when they were children before 1944, their parents were always looking for inventive ways of hiding animals and corn from officials who would confiscate them no matter how poor the villagers were. In this context of scarcity, sheep were a crucial source for self-provisioning with food and cash. But the successive wars and the political upheavals that led to the establishment of new borders decisively undermined large-scale sheep breeding (Uzunov 1993: 51–52; Brunnbauer 2002: 332).

Rich evidence attests to the prominence of sheep breeding, milking, and *kurban* up to the first years of socialism.[7] Written data describing the measuring of milk in villages near Belan go back to the end of the nineteenth century (Shishkov 1965: 265–266).[8] The first milking and measuring, called *perdoi* (or *predui*, from the verb *doia*—to milk) took place on the summer dairy farm (*mandra*). The measuring helped determine each one's share from the milk of the flock. The milk from the ewes of every sheep owner was measured in wooden receptacles (Primovski 1969: 177). Usually illiterate shepherds made signs on a stick of wood in order to record the quantities and names, a system of notation abandoned with increasing literacy. An elderly villager told me that he remembered shepherds using the old notation system but he did not know how precisely it worked.

Ethnographic records based on interviews conducted in 1984 among elderly people in a nearby village mention that, at the end of the nineteenth and beginning of the twentieth century, rich men such as local *pasha* or *bei* offered *kurban* in the vicinity of their summer dairy farm on the occasion of the first milking of their flocks; the flock of one such person could be as large as 1,000 ewes. In the same neighboring village, "collective dairy farms" (*saborni mandri*), the most common form, gathered around 400 to 500 ewes.[9] The first milk measuring was celebrated with *kurban* on the meadows surrounding the summer dairy farm.[10] The sheep-owning families and their relatives together ate dishes prepared with lamb and milk. The milk for making yogurt for *kurban* was provided by the flock and the sacrificial sheep were donated by sheep owners or bought collectively for the occasion. The animals were slaughtered in the milking pen or in a clean place on the territory of the dairy farm. A dish made of mutton and wheat (*keshkek*), but also specialties with beans and milk, was prepared by specialized cooks.[11]

In Belan, the first milk measuring, immediately followed by *kurban* on the same day, usually took place in the beginning of June, when the lambs were weaned. Before the completion of collectivization in the 1950s, Belan, like all villages in the region, had several sheep flocks, each formed by the participation of several families, except for those who possessed large flocks of their own. The author of a village monograph reports that, between the middle of the nineteenth century and the 1920s, in Belan and Radino, some people possessed flocks as large as 200 to 800 sheep. During the spring and the summer, the ewes grazed on summer pastures and were kept outside the village, in sheepfolds equipped as dairy farms. According to this monograph, in 1935 in the area of the village (including remote neighborhoods and very small villages) there were six summer dairy farms with a total of 1,045 ewes and 97 goats (Uzunov 1993: 52). Cheese and other milk products were made on each dairy farm.

A Christian villager born in 1918 told me that he had helped in dairy farms since he was fourteen, that is, around 1932. According to him, then Belan had three flocks of 150 to 180 ewes each. Until socialism, his family— he had three siblings—kept around 50 sheep, 10 goats and a cow. But he did not recall having seen *kurban* on the dairy farm. He remembered that the first measuring of the milk every spring was celebrated simply by drinking fresh milk. Another villager, a Muslim born in 1924, said that there was "*kurban* for the sheep" organized on a dairy farm near Belan on the initiative of the Muslim villagers in 1936, 1937, and 1938. There was one sacrificial animal per 40 ewes and about 200 ewes on the summer dairy farm where his family sent theirs. According to him, *kurban* did not attract external guests and had a more pronounced Muslim connotation: "those who knew prayers sang them." He added that with the outbreak of World War II in 1941, the state imposed rationed food provisioning and the re-strictions caused the interruption of *kurban*. He recalled that *kurban* was organized again in Belan in May 1945 or 1946, after the communists had taken over the government. The local inhabitants presented it as a cele-bration of the name day of the communist leader Georgi Dimitrov (Saint George is celebrated on 6 May). He also mentioned that much later, in 1957 or 1958, when collectivization was completed, several villages jointly orga-nized a big *kurban*, but it was already called "village fair" (*selski sabor*) and not *kurban*. The village spring *kurban* created in 1992 inherited features of the presocialist ritual, but it is unprecedented as an integrative village-wide event.

While the economic role of sheep was diminishing, the village *kurban* has grown in popularity. A man, born in 1938, formerly a cowherd at the state-run farm and later a driver, explained that before collectivization there were different *kurban*, but its current form as a village-wide event was the most elaborate and made him feel particularly proud. He also re-lated the newly established tradition to the formation of a village sheep flock: "In addition, we have already our flock of 150 to 200 sheep. We have put them together, they are private, ours, and we have given them to a shep-herd to shepherd them."

By its attendance, popularity, and broadly shared symbolism, *kurban* has proven to be more integrative than the participation in common village pasturing. While, in May 2010, only 43 houses, out of 151 inhabited houses in the village, had ewes in the flock and only they were involved in milk measuring and taking of shares, *kurban* was a village event that attracted around 1,000 participants according to local estimations. The diminished material centrality of sheep has resulted in the creation of one village flock. At the same time, *kurban* became the annual symbolic communal affirma-tion. The ritual gatherings of sheep-owning households on their summer dairies, widespread less than a century earlier, were not revived. Village *kurban* has become a ritual enactment of unity throughout a period of eco-nomic decline and out-migration.

Looking back over the entire century, we can see that the relationship between the economic and symbolic role of sheep at the village level ex-perienced a reversal shortly after the end of socialism. In the presocialist past, those who celebrated *kurban* together in the spring had their sheep pastured and milked together. There is less economic value in sheep now in comparison with before socialism. Economic interest in sheep keeping unites those who participate in the village flock as private shareholders. The spring *kurban* follows the opposite logic; it has been transformed into the most prominent symbolic affirmation of the village community. In contrast with the presocialist practice, the present-day *kurban,* while directly dependent on the village flock for collecting milk for the ritual meal, is not limited to those with animals in the flock. None of the families having their ewes in this flock and thus donating milk claims public acknowledgement of this contribution. Even a large-scale farmer who donates as much milk as the village flock is not granted specific recognition in the frame of the ritual. The symbolism of *kurban* stresses certain community relationships and downplays others. Not only does *kurban* stretch to encompass all villagers, irrespective of keeping animals, but through the ritual this diversified community downplays self-interest, competition, and stratification, and stages equality.

How does this ritual articulate with the economic decline and individualized struggle to make a living? In the following section I outline the major economic transformations under socialism and after its collapse, paying special attention to sheep breeding as this has shifted from being a central component of livelihood to just one economic resource among others in a complex house and market economy.

Sheep in a Complex Commercial and Domestic Economy, Socialist and Postsocialist

Upheavals and ruptures have characterized economic life in Belan, with different political regimes having required villagers to implement different principles of economic and social organization, often with unpredictable effects. The transformations of the economy can be traced by looking at the place of sheep in it. One of the most radical reforms undertaken by the young socialist state was the collectivization of land and animals. The Rhodopes had relatively low productivity in agriculture until socialist collectivization and industrialization. Collectivization was initiated in 1947 and was completed in 1958, with its last phase having become known as "massovization" (Gruev 2009; Migev 1998). In my fieldwork area the process started in 1950 and ended in 1957. The socialist plan imposed collective breeding of cattle and sheep and introduced a larger variety of crops on the collective farm's lands. My informants remembered best the last two decades of socialism; they recalled economic ease and a lively village atmosphere. They emphasized the availability of jobs on the collective farm, in transport, manufacturing, small industries, and administrative and educational institutions. They pointed out that this farm had a large number of animals, that all the available land was cultivated even on the steepest slopes, and that the numerous buses for public transportation were always full. In the 1980s, the two villages of Belan and Radino had a joint population of approximately 1,000 inhabitants. The images that my informants evoked resonate with those typically presented by the communist writers who glorified the success of the Rhodope economy under socialism: its industrialization, urbanization, and the achievements in agriculture and education.[12] Elderly villagers also recalled less happy experiences, especially in the 1950s, when they received little payment in kind and even less in cash. Progressively, the payments were in cash and even payments in advance were proposed. All my elderly informants emphasized their relatively easy adaptation to socialist collectivization, in contrast to other parts of Bulgaria, especially the plains, where the peasants possessed far more land and animals (Gruev 2009).

Socialism typically created small industrial plants; many women in the Rhodopes worked as seamstresses. Many men were employed as drivers in the state-owned transportation company. Schools and kindergartens offered jobs and decisively contributed to raise the educational level. All these employers and the state-run collectives provided salaries.

The regime encouraged domestic agriculture that was supported through the use of equipment borrowed more or less legally from the state cooperative (Creed 1998).[13] The mountain villagers clearly benefited from getting a salary and being able at the same time to produce potatoes, beans, vegetables, meat, and milk for their own needs. This also meant self-exploitation in domestic farming after the workday. Almost all my informants declared that there were between four and five ewes and one to two cows per house, plus usually one calf. The surface of the area that was allowed for hay harvesting, and thus the amount of hay, determined the number of animals each house was able to keep. The sheep and calves were indispensable for feeding the family members, village and town residents alike. It was important to keep a constant stock of animals for ritual purposes too, such as the Muslim holidays and ritual receptions in the houses; part of the meat left was preserved in jars and freezers (see Stamenova 1995 for the eastern Rhodopes). In addition, the collective farm and, since the middle of the 1960s, the meat-processing plant "Rodopa" used to purchase meat and milk at fixed prices. This provided the villagers with savings that they massively invested in house-building and renovation; they also held lavish weddings, soldier send-offs, and high school graduation parties. Despite the official tolerance and later encouragement to produce in the frame of the household, the government always set limits to household production, for instance by determining the legal size of farming land.

The postsocialist period saw the breakdown of the earlier stability of the domestic and village economies. After the collapse of socialism in November 1989, in the very beginning of the 1990s, the collective farm had to implement the new laws by selling the animals and all equipment (see Creed 1998: 219–262). Officially, the collective farm in Belan ceased to exist in 1995; the dismantling started in 1991 and most of its assets were sold by auction by 1992. The sheep and cattle were purchased by external companies. Villagers acquired some of the machines and equipment, and a few bought buildings.[14] Domestic agriculture in Belan lost the state cooperative and the meat-processing plant as the privileged buyers of its produce. The closing of small industries, such as the shirt-making and tractor-making factories, the sharp downsizing of the small wood-processing plant, and the dismantling of the state collective meant the end of regular salaries. Out-migration to the cities and in several cases abroad sharply increased around 2000. Home-produced foodstuffs, both for home consumption and for sale, became of great importance for those who stayed in the village and those who kept commuting to the city. The ways this produce was combined with unreliable and limited income form salaries, wages, and pensions changed.

The dominant political message in the 1990s was that each individual owner would start farming on his own, and that he would sell his produce on the "free market." The vague political discourse assumed that later, some would grow and absorb others, so that the rural areas would eventually reach a state of equilibrium within the new market economy: some would have larger market-oriented farms, others smaller ones, and yet others would give up this activity. This did not happen, at least not in the Rhodopes. Potatoes were the only cash crop that villagers produced on a larger scale. Yet, generally they did not specialize, but kept a diversified mainly domestic agriculture and had a preference for salaried jobs. The inhabitants of Belan and Radino were relatively successful in selling their potatoes until approximately 2008. In the late 1990s and even later, when Bulgarians were struck with a harsh financial crisis, trucks full of commodities such as sunflower oil, cabbage, flour, or washing powder came to barter these goods for local potatoes. Most villagers considered that they made good deals (Cellarius 2000). Potatoes were also sold for cash. When the market was opened to international competition and cheap Polish and Turkish potatoes invaded Bulgarian supermarkets, the interest in Rhodope potatoes declined. Most villagers reduced their production and cultivated only enough to meet their domestic needs. In addition, out-migration of young villagers meant lesser availability of workers. Nonetheless, as the

Rhodope potato has remained a synonym of high quality, some kept good relationships with long-term clients in other parts of the country and still manage to ship their potatoes directly to their customers.

Rural households did not go back to earlier patterns of peasantry. Instead, rural people envisioned themselves as agricultural producers and as part of a larger bureaucratic and political system. Socialism decisively contributed to this worldview (Leonard and Kaneff 2002). Villagers continue to see themselves in this way, despite the neglect and contempt shown to them by the postsocialist political authorities (Creed 1998; Kaneff 2002). The next political signal came when Bulgaria started receiving EU subsidies for agriculture, but their effect is still marginal in the Rhodopes. For the villagers, the demise of the state-run farm has remained the symbolic moment when village prosperity ended. Limited job opportunities and the demographic decline have nourished the feeling of being disregarded by the political power. Tensions and fluctuations characterize the new economic situation.

In Belan, three main modes of using sheep have emerged. The first is the minority breed for the market. The second, the most widespread use of sheep, is as a resource for domestic consumption. The use of lamb and dairy products to feed tourists in house-based tourism is a third, intermediary mode.

Agriculture and animal husbandry, sheep in particular, have uneven commercial success. After 1991, most villagers of Belan did not see sheep as a promising avenue for enrichment. Not only did they lack infrastructure and money to invest in large-scale sheep breeding, but the few adventurous risk-takers preferred to engage in business outside of the village. For none of the villagers is sheep breeding an occupation or a business in its own right, although one large-scale farmer considers sheep to be "an important business" that he pursues in combination with two other activities.[15] Immediately after the collapse of the socialist system, commercial dairy production appeared as a promising entrepreneurial adventure to the mayor of Belan, who acquired the former canteen of the collective farm and turned it into a dairy, buying cow and sheep milk from private owners to make cheese and yogurt. But this business, one of his numerous activities, did not prosper and he abandoned it in the mid 1990s. According to rumors, he made big money from the sale of former state property.

Common Pasturing and the Multiple Facets of the Domestic Economy

The inroads of wider processes and state and international policies have threatened rural livelihoods based on salaries and entailed simultaneously shrinking of stockbreeding. However, sheep breeding still plays a role in Belan. The number of private animals has decreased, but they provide some houses with food and occasional cash. After the completion of collectivization in Belan in 1957, the private ewes—there were up to five per house— were given to the shepherd of the state-run farm during the summer to be shepherded with the farm flock; others formed several small flocks herded by private shepherds. The end of the state-collective flock and that of the services provided by the state-employed shepherd gave rise to the question of how to coordinate the individual households that owned animals. At the same time, the number of privately owned ewes in Belan decreased from 470 in 1989 to 350 in 2009.[16] This decrease resulted in the formation, already in the very beginning of the 1990s, of a unique village flock (one in Belan and one in Radino). Many villagers keep animals for their own needs in food and for ritual purposes, the main of which is the sheep slaughter for *Kurban Bairam.* The houses receiving tourists prefer to slaughter their own animals for their tourists in order to avoid spending money. In addition, they buy from neighbors and from the large-scale herder. The houses that own only a few sheep have established group care for the animals borrowing some organizational patterns from the presocialist and socialist times. A shepherd is now hired by winter's end. The sheep owners organize an assembly to debate and elect one of the candidates. The shepherd receives a salary and food for lunch from those who use his services: one lunch for two sheep, plus 4 leva (around 2 Euro) per sheep per month in 2010.

Why do the villagers need this collective care for the ewes? When I addressed my hostess with this question, she gave the usual explanation:

> We have six ewes. If we milk them twice per day, as it should be, we end up with a bit more than one liter of milk every time. If I want to make cheese, I need the milk to be fresh, almost warm after the milking. It must be processed immediately after milking, during a few hours. If I decide to make cheese every time I milk my six ewes, I will spend hours making cheese every day, twice per day. Every time, from one liter of milk. And how much cheese do I get from one liter? Some grams. Can you imagine spending three months making cheese every single day, a few hours per day, and every time using the whole outfit of wooden frames, cloths for drying, and receptacles in order to end up with a few grams every time? When I take the milk from the common flock three times in a row, I process it and in two days I'm done.

The same rationale applies to yogurt making. Making cheese and yogurt in quantity renders it inconvenient to have a separate small flock. So, the villagers developed a new way to undertake their pastoral activities following an older pattern; they created the village flock. Only a few retired people prefer not to send their sheep to the village flock and still do their own shepherding.

On the one hand, for those who keep sheep, meat, milk, and dairy produce are important components of the self-provisioning scheme of the domestic economy. On the other hand, their significance as market commodities has fluctuated, with seasonal tourism being the main but relatively limited avenue for commercialization. Yet, the coordination of sheep herding and milk measuring are important matters in village life. They are based on collaboration and collective calculation of the inputs and the outputs of every participating house, as in old times. The village flock is made possible through cooperation. The shareholders' objective is not to gain a profit but to use labor efficiently. The flock is also seen as one incarnation of the vitality of the village. Even those who do not keep animals enjoy seeing the sheep crossing the main village road. Village pasturing embellishes this cohesion.

The members of the village flock act as shareholders. Milk measuring and the management of the common flock involve careful calculation of the milk that every house owning sheep may take in relation to the contribution it makes. Collective herding and milking serves the interests of individual houses. When the lambs have been weaned and the ewes have already joined the village flock, the villagers measure their milk two or three times in the period between their arrival at the flock and the moment when they get pregnant again by summer's end. These successive operations of measuring allow recalibration of the quantities that each shareholder is entitled to take home. Since the milk of the ewes starts to diminish in July, there are two or three milking periods. During each of the periods, every house takes a predetermined quantity. Following a list of names, each day a person representing his or her house takes the milk of the whole flock until his or her predefined quantity for the given milking period is reached. When the last person on the list has received milk, a new measuring takes place in order to establish a new list and start a new milking period. During the second period the recalibrated quantity is lower. If enough milk is left at the end of the second period, a third period is set up in the same way.

My hosts in Belan sent six ewes to join the flock in May 2010. They received 80 liters from the first milking period (from three milkings in a row: one morning, one evening, and one the next morning) and made more than 30 kg of cheese; they took 30 liters of milk at the end of June 2010 from the second milking period.[17] In total, there were 127 ewes[18] belonging to 43 houses out of 151 inhabited houses in Belan.[19] Sunday, 9 May was the day of the measuring. The operation took place at the sheepfold in the village, located not far from the houses, on the border with the forest. The shepherd and Emin, the former shepherd of the state-run farm, did the milking. Before this practice, adopted around fifteen years ago, everyone milked his or her own ewes.[20] The villagers say that in order to avoid cheating, this operation is done now by the two men for the entire flock. They alone are allowed into the milking pen.[21] The milk from all the ewes belonging to one house is put together and measured with carafes, as in bars—50 ml, 100 ml, 200 ml, 500 ml, 1 liter.

The former mayor was chosen to write down all names and quantities and to collect money to pay the shepherd. Representatives of almost all participating houses were present. Those who could not come did not take their milk from the first milking. The milk was put in a bucket called "the common" (*obshtoto*), which was also duly recorded in the notebook. This common milk was sold and the money was used to fix the sheepfold. The list of forty-three names started with the name of the representative of the house whose ewes had given the highest quantity and went on down to the one with the lowest quantity. Thus, the quantity of milk of each one determines his position on the list and the order of distribution. One's share is proportional to the quantity given by his ewes at the moment of measuring. The subtlest operation is to decide about the number by which the sample quantity should be multiplied in order to define the share. In 2010 it was 50; if one's ewes gave one liter, then this person takes 50 liters from the first milking period. This decision is taken collectively by those present at the measuring. Several factors are taken into consideration when defining this number: the availability of grass, the number of ewes in the flock, and the number of those still in the barns with their late-born lambs. In other words, the more optimistic the villagers' bet on these factors, the higher the multiplier. Usually milking ends by 10 August and everyone has to take his or her milk before this date.

The collective coordination for the sake of better respect of individual interest and careful calculation of inputs and outputs constitutes the backbone of the operation. The main advantage of collective herding resides in the possibility to take a share of the herd's milk in order to make cheese within a couple of days. Everyone gives a calculated, proportional contribution to the collective management: money and food to the shepherd; milk for the work of the milker (who received 100 liters of milk from the village flock in 2010); milk sold for the maintenance of the sheepfold. Representatives of each house clean the sheepfold several times, depending on the number of their ewes. The bookkeeper is exonerated from paying the shepherd as a reward for his or her work. Milk from the whole flock is also donated for the village *kurban*.

Sheep milk is a source of pride. There is a saying that "the lambs are in Neveno (a neighboring village), but the milk is in Belan," which refers to the fact that in Belan the lambs are weaned earlier and more milk is available for consumption, while in the nearby village the ewes stay longer with their lambs and the lambs grow faster. When milking is finished, the milkers drink a glass of warm milk, praising its high quality. Sheep yogurt and cheese are considered local luxuries. Milking the village flock is a masculine activity, while making yogurt and cheese from it is a feminine one. However, when locals and tourists praise the yogurt, it is rarely presented as "made by the wife." It is presented as "our yogurt, homemade, from our sheep."

Simultaneously, a nostalgic and even apocalyptic narrative dominates the way in which the villagers recount the recent changes. A feeling of material dispossession stems not only from the disestablishment of the state-run farm, but also from the subsequent devaluation of their farming activities. It is expressed by the saying "It is not worth the work you put in it." People constantly speak of their "struggle for life" (*borba za zhivot*), meaning that making a living demands everyday hard toil. The saying also implies that the price to pay for going beyond the baseline of survival is, sometimes, conflict.

Economically successful houses and those worse-off have ewes in the village flock. Not keeping animals is seen sometimes as a source of freedom, for example by retired couples receiving pensions, whose children make a living without the support of their village relatives. For others, sheep occupy an important cluster in the complex configuration of activities and ideas that make up their house economy. This cluster is differently utilized in more or less well-off houses. The family with eight ewes in the village herd in 2010, that together gave the highest sample quantity of milk, is probably the wealthiest family in Belan. They receive two pensions and three salaries and own a grocery store. The family has two houses, the most visited by tourists. Not only do their tourists consume their agricultural produce and home-produced meat and milk, but they often buy sheep milk and lambs from the large-scale farm. In their case, the high number of ewes in the village flock reflects their intense production, a prerequisite for their successful involvement in rural tourism. They do not occupy the top of the local social hierarchy because they have animals. Rather, they have succeeded in using these animals intelligently in combination with other house resources, with the labor of all household members, with income from salaries and pensions, and a grocery store. Moreover, they control certain decisions that give impetus to their tourist business, which is in fact their major money-making activity.

Sheep are important also for families taking in fewer or no tourists and faced with high job instability. My hosts had six ewes in the village flock in 2010. They emphasize that this demands hard work, an ever-lasting value in rural Bulgaria. Moreover, they enjoy consuming their "ecologically pure" foodstuffs (*ekologichno chisto*). But they experience livestock keeping as an attempt to compensate for material weaknesses. Being unable to live from their salaries, the couple, their adult children, and their grandchildren consume much of what they themselves produce. Occasionally they sell potatoes and beans. My hosts also take in tourists, to whom they may offer lamb and dairy products. But they view stockbreeding as a necessity and less as an activity supporting money-yielding tourism. Thus, in Belan, lamb and milk products are consumed within the house, sold to tourists within the frame of house-based tourism, and occasionally traded beyond the village. Social differentiation does not directly derive from more or less involvement in sheep breeding, and it did not under socialism. After socialism, sheep have been used to sustain the household; only in a few cases have they been instrumental in facilitating upward economic mobility. Such mobility has occurred when animals have been successfully marketed in combination with other domestic goods and services, as part of a cycle from the domestic economy to the market and back to the house as money return (see Gudeman and Rivera 1990: 66–72). Over the last ten years, economic success has been determined by the skillful marketing of the domestic economy in the frame of house-based tourism, with sheep as one of the important assets of this domestic economy. Thus sheep have played an unexpected role in the process of social stratification. And sheep have become the basic material and symbolic stuff of the village *kurban*.

Conclusion

For the inhabitants of Belan, the end of socialism meant freedom to circulate and receive guests in this formerly strictly controlled border area. It also meant constant economic instability. The village *kurban* created in 1992 has become a form of communal hospitality. The ritual points to the exact opposite of the tense and sharp stratification that has shaped the political and economic hierarchies of Bulgarian society. The model this *kurban* suggests is a radical departure from both leader-making elective democracy and wealth-based social differentiation. The current ritual is a model of an egalitarian community. No one is celebrated as a leader, including those who do more for the village or for the event. No hierarchy is recognized in *kurban*, though its organization relies on several hierarchical relationships; the latter are thoroughly downplayed at the moment of the public food distribution, and to a large extent before and after. Belan's villagers experience social fracturing and uneven access to resources, but in the village *kurban*, integration is central and social differentiation is denied. Everyone is welcome and fed.

Whereas the economy creates social disjuncture, notably differentiation according to wealth, unemployment, job instability, and low-paid work, the ritual includes all villagers and guests. Its anti-utilitarian grammar, expressed in gifting and free work, celebrates sharing of all with all, as opposed to meritocracy and self-interest as expressed in the dominant economic ideology. Whereas the very idea of the free market implies the need to strengthen competition, the village *kurban* avoids elements smacking of intracommunity competition. (Of course, Belan villagers can and do claim proudly that attendance at their *kurban* outnumbers that of the other villages.) No one makes a profit, except those who sell their sheep for the ritual slaughter. Even these villagers refrain from haggling: the same price applies to all and equity dictates that none of the "candidate" vendors should be left empty-handed.

State-administered religious divisions and violent name-change campaigns against Muslims have marked the presocialist and socialist past of this region. Given this history, a new ritual might have been expected to feature strong religious elements and perhaps to stress an exclusively Muslim identity. Instead, the postsocialist village *kurban* softens the public religious elements in the course of its comprehensive symbolic erasure of divisions. In this way, the ritual not only fosters cohesion between Muslims and Christians; it also integrates those numerous participants who do not define it in religious terms at all.

Although the postsocialist village *kurban* draws on an older pattern of religious sacrifice, it adapts this older pattern to address contemporary concerns. It builds partly on an earlier model of ritual togetherness, but does not really replicate the presocialist spring *kurban* of sheep-owning families. It practically and symbolically transcends the families, as well as all religious and social divisions. The ritual transforms economy in a noninstrumental direction that contributes to the wider making of sociality. The consensus around *kurban* organization is striking. Sociality, rather than competitive self-promotion, makes the event possible and allows the ritual to instill a unique sense of togetherness. Once a year, these potentialities are accomplished in ritual practice.

Notes

1. I worked in two neighboring villages, Belan and Radino (all village and personal names are pseudonyms). This chapter deals primarily with Belan, the larger one. Situated in the very southern part of the central Rhodope mountains, together they have around 500 inhabitants divided into 227 households (official figures). Fieldwork was carried out in 2009–2010, in the framework of the Economy and Ritual group. I owe much to the attentive reading and suggestions of Deema Kaneff, Gerald Creed, Ilia Iliev, and members of the Economy and Ritual group. The archival research was made possible by the kind and efficient support of Tanya Mareva and Katya Sulinadjieva from the Regional Historical Museum, Smolian, and Ana Luleva and Milena Benovska-Sabkova from the Ethnographic Institute and Museum, Sofia. Vihra Barova has provided outstanding local expertise. I thank them all.
2. According to the mayor's office. These data tend to count more households than a

count based on domestic groups that share at least part of their budget, housing, food, and productive assets and activities. For example, a domestic group formed by an elderly couple and their two married sons with their wives and children are considered to be three separate households by the mayor's office, although their livelihoods are related at many levels: they may have a family business together, own animals together, work together in farming, and share meals every day. In this case the members define their domestic group as "we," "our house," or "our family," though they distinguish between the nuclear families inside.

3. I conducted a survey in spring 2010 among twenty-five households (defined as units sharing housing and production assets, and having their meals together) living in Belan and Radino, as part of a standardized group questionnaire. Two of the questions were about what was perceived as the household's most important source of income and what kind of agricultural resources they had. The survey revealed that none of the twenty-five households placed animal breeding and agriculture in general as a main source of income. Out of the twenty-five households, eight cited salaries, seven pensions, five salaries and pensions, and five private businesses (two of them in tourism). When asked about the animals they had, twenty-two out of the twenty-five had animals: seven had sheep, eleven had cattle and sheep, four had only cattle.

4. This man was trained by local *hodjas* and has no institutional affiliation with any official Muslim authority, although he has gone to the mosque since the 1990s. He was the first to join the state-run farm in 1950. He has a reputation for always voting for the socialist (ex-communist) party.

5. The local Gypsies are more integrated than in other parts of Bulgaria where the relationships with the rest of the population are hostile and exclusionary. Yet, the local peaceful relationships with Gypsies, described by non-Gypsies as "our Gypsies," "good ones," and "not like the other Gypsies," follow a pattern of relative inclusion widespread in Eastern Europe.

6. The village played a role in trans-border relations. After 1912, a custom house was erected in Belan, which was transformed first into a guesthouse of the school, then into an administrative building of the collective farm. Today it is being transformed into a private hotel.

7. Massive ethnographic expeditions of the Bulgarian Academy of Sciences took place in the 1970s and 1980s, collecting narratives from elderly villagers about the ways of life in the past. The notes available in the archives contain multiple indications of personal memories narrated by the interviewees. I am aware of the political bias of these expeditions, as they aimed to show a common Bulgarian Christian origin of the Muslim and Christian inhabitants of the Rhodopes and a generalized fading of religion. However, I take the archives as a valuable source of information about some aspects of the ritual and economic past of the population. Later studies of *kurban* (e.g., Blagoev 2004 on *kurban* rituals among the Muslims in Bulgaria) largely draw on the materials generated by these expeditions.

8. Archives of the Regional Historical Museum in Smolian. National program "Rhodopes" 1975 and 1981–1985. The funds used for this section are: National program "Rhodopes" 1975: VI-20, village of Mugla, and VI-21, region of Devin; National program "Rhodopes" 1981–1985: VI-130 from 1981, villages of Mogil-

itsa, Borikovo, Bukata, Chereshovo; VI-130/3 from 1981, villages of Mogilitsa, Borikovo, Bukovo, Uhlovitsa; VI-34-130/1 from 1981, villages of Mogilitsa and Borikovo; VI-126/4 from 1984, village of Smilian; VI-126/6 from 1984, village of Smilian; VI-188 from 1984, village of Smilian.

9. Archives of the Regional Historical Museum in Smolian, VI.126/4. National program 'Rhodopes' 1981–1985. Animal breeding, village of Smilian, region of Smolian. Valentin Lazarov, notes taken in June 1984: 26–27.

10. Archives of the Regional Historical Museum in Smolian, VI.126/6. National program "Rhodopes" 1981–1985. Food and consumption habits, village of Smilian, region of Smolian. Lilia Radeva, notes taken in June 1984: 15.

11. Archives of the Regional Historical Museum in Smolian, VI. 188. National program "Rhodopes" 1981–1985. Traditional spiritual culture, village of Smilian, region of Smolian. Liliana Dimitrova, notes taken in May 1984: 111–112.

12. A prominent figure among those writers was Tsviatko Monov (1985; see also *Rodopski sbornik* 1983).

13. Salaries from small industries and collective farms were continuously supplemented by products from household farming, namely, "land for personal use": plots of about 1 decare (one tenth of a hectare) per family were allowed since the beginning of collectivization. The size of the authorized plot increased in 1957 to 3 decares. This early-revised form of rural socialism became deliberate state policies of "self-satisfying" (*samozadovoliavane*) in the last socialist decade. The processes in the south-central Rhodopes were part of a national policy. The size of the land for "personal use" fluctuated according to various political trends but the principle remained unquestioned until the demise of socialism. Criteria such as the number of household members, their status and gender (retired/working, men/women), and their productivity in the collective farm determined the acreage given to each household (see Creed 1998: 94–96). In 1988, 32 percent of the arable land belonging to the village of Belan was in the hands of "personal holders," 407 families using an average of 3.9 decares each; there were 560 animals in the collective farm and 518 in the personal stables (State Archives Smolian, Fund 503/2/6). Nevertheless, the collective farm was still the main supplier of the official markets: on the eve of democracy in 1989, the state purchased 785,000 liters of milk from the collective farm, whereas the personal holders sold 379,000 liters. The figures for meat (31,000 kg against 18,000 kg) and potatoes (1,198,000 kg against 26,000 kg) confirm this prevalence (State Archives Smolian, Fund 503/2/5). However, at the meetings of the economic council of the collective farm between 1988 and 1990, household production from the exploitation of state-owned land, known as the *akord* system, according to which villagers had to produce for the collective farm (see also Creed 1998: 90–94), was praised for its higher efficiency and lower production cost (State Archives Smolian, Fund 503/2/4). Work on the personal and *akord* plots and care for personal animals demanded efforts during the whole year from all household members, including children. The support on behalf of the collective farm was crucial: it provided machines, seeds, fertilizers, animal food, and other inputs (Creed 1998: 96–101). Relatively high self-provisioning in potatoes, beans and other vegetables, meat, and milk and dairy products characterized the Rhodope mountains in the last two decades of socialism (Stamenova 1995: 194–201).

14. One of the buildings of the former state-run farm was bought by a villager, an engineer, who repairs trucks and machinery, and who acted as the head of the farm's "liquidation commission." Another compound of buildings was first bought by an external company that raised cows. Later it was acquired by a family from Radino that raises around twenty cows in one of the barns. The owners of the compound sublet one of the buildings to the large-scale farmer of Belan who keeps over 200 ewes and their lambs there.

15. This farmer had 214 ewes in spring 2010 and almost the same number of lambs. His "sideline" activities are the cultivation of potatoes for sale and the maintenance of some municipal roads. A few houses give him their ewes to be pastured until the winter. A former veterinary doctor, this 45-year-old man got a job at the collective state farm in the very last years of its existence. In the 1990s, he decided to develop his own agricultural business, because taking care of animals was what he knew best. In recent years, he has been trying to sell dairy products and he was the only producer who counted on making some profit from his cheese in summer 2010. The houses receiving many tourists usually do not produce enough to supply their tourists and buy lambs, milk, and cheese from this farmer. Locals also buy from him. In 2010, this farmer sold more milk products than usual. He told me that the price of the potatoes, his main produce for many years, had dropped dramatically; he could not earn enough from potatoes and road maintenance to cover his investments and to pay salaries to five employees. In previous years, lamb was a major product for him and milk was not. By the end of May 2010, he had already produced 400 kg of cheese. He considered this to be a risk, because he had never produced significant quantities before. However, he felt himself "covered" by the EU subsidies that he had received for the first time in 2010. "My self-esteem is higher now, because I have received something," he said, stressing that the EU subsidies meant recognition of his activity by a political authority, and not only economic support.

16. The figures for 2009 include the herd of the large farm (214 ewes in 2010).

17. The extended family of my hosts has nine members who normally consume the cheese until Christmas, in addition to cow cheese. During the summer, almost all villagers eat sheep yogurt. It is usual to buy extra sheep milk from the largest farm.

18. This does not mean a decrease in the absolute number of ewes. In 2009, the ewes gave birth earlier and could let their lambs alone earlier. There were 196 ewes in the herd, according to the book carefully kept each year. In the beginning, the ewes are not given concentrated fodder, in order to let them show how much milk they are "really able to give" on the day of measuring. What is considered as the "real" quantity of milk is the lowest possible, that is, when the animals have not been fed with concentrated fodder.

19. When the bookkeeper of the collective flock writes the name of a sheep owner, this is the name of the person who, the day of the measuring of the milk, came to represent the whole family. This person represents "us" or "our house," as the villagers say.

20. The sheep have marks, so that everyone can recognize to whom they belong.

21. John Campbell described masculine control over sheep milking *and* cheese making among the Zagore Sarakatsani of northern Greece. There was no sharp prohibition

denying women's right to do these tasks; it was a masculine domain, but not one based on the absolute exclusion of women (Campbell 1964).

References

Blagoev, Goran. 2004. *Kurbanat v Traditsiiata na Balgarite Miusiulmani.* Sofia: Marin Drinov.

Brunnbauer, Ulf. 2002. "Families and Mountains in the Balkans: Christian and Muslim Household Structures in the Rhodopes, 19th-20th Century." *The History of the Family* 7: 327–350.

———. 2003. "Descent or Terrioriality: Inheritance and Family Forms in the Late Ottoman and Early Post-Ottoman Balkans." In *Distinct Inheritances: Property, Family and Community in a Changing Europe,* ed. Hannes Grandits and Patrick Heady, 181–205. Münster: LIT.

Campbell, J. K. 1974 [1964]. *Honour, Family and Patronage.* New York: Oxford University Press.

Cellarius, Barbara A. 2000. "'You Can Buy Almost Everything With Potatoes': An Examination of Barter During Economic Crisis in Bulgaria." *Ethnology* 39, no. 1: 73–92.

Creed, Gerald W. 1998. *Domesticating Revolution: From Socialist Reform to Ambivalent Transition in a Bulgarian Village.* University Park: Pennsylvania State University Press.

———. 2002. "Economic Crisis and Ritual Decline in Eastern Europe." In *Postsocialism: Ideals, Ideologies and Practices in Eurasia,* ed. Chris M. Hann, 57–73. London: Routledge.

———. 2011. *Masquerade and Postsocialism: Ritual and Cultural Dispossession in Bulgaria.* Bloomington: Indiana University Press.

———, ed. 2006. *The Seductions of Community: Emancipations, Oppressions, Quandaries.* Santa Fe: School of American Research Press; Oxford: James Currey.

Damianov, Nikola. 1972. "Sotsialno-Ikonomichesko Polozhenie na Srednorodopskoto Naselenie Prez Vtorata Svetovna Voina." In *Rodopski Sbornik* 3. Sofia: Balgarska Akademia na Naukite: 53–77.

Ganev, Venelin I. 2007. *Preying on the State: The Transformation of Bulgaria after 1989.* Ithaca, NY: Cornell University Press.

Ghodsee, Kristen. 2010. *Muslim Lives in Eastern Europe: Gender, Ethnicity, and the Transformations of Islam in Postsocialist Bulgaria.* Princeton, NJ: Princeton University Press.

Givre Olivier. 2006. *Un Rituel 'Balkanique' ou un Rituel dans les Balkans?* (Ph.D. diss., Université Lumière Lyon 2).

Godelier, Maurice. 1986 [1984]. *The Mental and the Material: Thought, Economy and Society.* London: Verso.

Gruev, Mihail. 2008. "Ot 'Proletarskia Internatsioanlizam' do 'Edinnata Sotsialisticheska Natsia': Politiki kam Balgarite Miusiulmani." In *Vazroditelniat Protses: Miusiulmanskite Obshtnosti i Komunisticheskiat Rezhim,* ed. Mihail Gruev and Aleksei Kalionski. Sofia: Ciela: 13–105.

———. 2009. *Preorani Slogove: Kolektivizatsia i Sotsialna Promiana v Balgarskiia Severozapad 40-te i 50-te na XX Vek.* Sofia: Ciela.

Gudeman, Stephen. 1986. *Economics as Culture: Models and Metaphors of Livelihood.* London: Routledge & Kegan Paul.

Gudeman, Stephen, and Alberto Rivera. 1990. *Conversations in Colombia: The Domestic Economy in Life and Text.* Cambridge: Cambridge University Press.

Hart, Keith, Jean-Louis Laville, and Antonio David Cattani, eds. 2010. *The Human Economy: A Citizen's Guide.* Cambridge: Polity.

Hristov, Petko, and Tsvetana Manova. 2007. "Noviat 'Star' Kurban." *Academica Balkanica 3. 'Zavrashtane' Kam Religioznostta.* Sofia: EIM: 11–30.

Hristov, Petko, and Biljana Sikimić. 2007. *Kurban in the Balkans.* Belgrade: Institut des Etudes Balkaniques.

Iankov, Angel. 2006. "Praznikat na Liaski Vrah: Starodaven Kurban v Chest na Zmeia-Stopan." In *Obrednata Trapeza: Sbornik Dokladi ot XI-ta Natsionalna Konferentsia na Balgarskite Etnografi—Plovdiv,* 2005. Sofia: EIM: 280–286.

Iordanova, Vania. 2006. "Dva Kurbana ot Ustovo." In *Obrednata Trapeza: Sbornik Dokladi ot XI-ta Natsionalna Konferentsia na Balgarskite Etnografi—Plovdiv,* 2005. Sofia: EIM: 301–305.

Kaneff, Deema. 2002. "Work, Identity and Rural-Urban Relations." In *Post-Socialist Peasant? Rural and Urban Constructions of Identity in Eastern Europe, East Asia and the Former Soviet Union,* ed. Pamela Leonard and Deema Kaneff, 180–199. Basingstoke: Palgrave.

Kolev, Nikolai. 2006. "Zhertvoprinoshenie i Obredna Trapeza u Balgari-Hristiiani i Balgari-Miusiulmani." In *Obrednata Trapeza: Sbornik Dokladi ot XI-ta Natsionalna Konferentsia na Balgarskite Etnografi—Plovdiv,* 2005. Sofia: EIM: 292–295.

Leonard, Pamela, and Deema Kaneff, eds. 2002. *Post-Socialist Peasant? Rural and Urban Constructions of Identity in Eastern Europe, East Asia and the Former Soviet Union.* Basingstoke: Palgrave.

Migev, Vladimir. 1998. *Problemi na Agrarnoto Razvitie na Balgaria (1944-1960).* Sofia: K&M.

Monov, Tsviatko. 1983. "Ikonomicheski i Sotsialni Izmenenia v Rodopskiia Krai (1944-1977)." *Rodopski Sbornik 5. Sofia: Balgarska Akademia na Naukite:* 5–40.

———. 1985. *Rodopskiiat Krai: Obnoven i Preuspiavasht.* Sofia: Partizdat.

Polanyi, Karl. 1957. "The Economy as Instituted Process." In *Trade and Market in the Early Empires: Economies in History and Theory,* ed. Karl Polanyi, Conrad M. Arensberg, and Harry W. Pearson, 243–270. Chicago: Gateway, Henry Regnery Company.

Primovski, Anastas. 1969. "Obshtnost na Niakoi Obichai u Rodopskite Balgari." *Narodnostna i Bitova Obshtnost na Rodopskite Balgari.* Sofia: Balgarska Akademia na Naukite: 171–196.

———. 1973. *Bit i Kultura na Rodopskite Balgari—Materialna Kultura. Sbornik za Narodni Umotvorenia i Narodopis 54.* Sofia: Balgarska Akademia na Naukite.

Rodopski Sbornik 5. 1983. Sofia: Balgarska Akademia na Naukite.

Shishkov, Stoiu. 1965. *Izbrani Proizvedenia.* Plovdiv: Hristo G. Danov.

Stamenova, Zhivka. 1995. *Etnosotsialni Aspekti na Bita v Iztochnite Rodopi Prez 70-te i 80-te Godini.* Pernik: Krakra.

Uzunov, Dicho. 1993. *Pri Izvorite na Arda.* Sofia: Jusautor.

5

The Trader's Wedding

Ritual Inflation and Money Gifts in Transylvania

MONICA VASILE

After the collapse of socialism, mountainous rural communities in Transylvania, western Romania, experienced an unprecedented economic boom that was accompanied by spectacularly inflated wedding feasts. Compared to other rural areas in Romania and Europe, the opulence and scale of the "wedding business" (*nunta-afacere*) of this region is unique. A central element of these events is the gifting of large sums of money to the new couple by all guests at their banquet. The cash-gifts involve the community at large, a community that is not understood territorially (although it sometimes overlaps with a village) but as a large pool of relatives, friends, acquaintances, and neighbors.

The anthropological literature on marriage payments has devoted considerable attention to the establishment of a "conjugal fund" through direct and indirect dowry (Goody 1973, 1976), and to the ways in which these transfers transform social relationships (Rheubottom 1980). However, little attention has been paid to communal endowment of the new couple, despite the importance of such transfers in many regions of Europe. In this chapter, I explore the changing significance of communal gifts of cash (*dar, cinste*) in the course of rapid postsocialist economic transformations. I shall show how economy and ritual are conflated in social events.

Wedding outlays in rural Romania have been expanding gradually over the last 100 years under the influence of increased commercialization, modernization, and industrialization (Kligman 1988; Beck 1979; Kideckel 1993). Based on the anthropological literature and my ethnographic observations in various communities, a major increase occurred during the economic boom of the late 1960s and 1970s when most people became employed in state factories and received cash salaries. Work-based collegiality augmented social networks, and improved roads and transportation made it possible for people to more easily travel outside their home villages and regions. Changes occurred in the sizes of weddings and in the kind of gifts offered. An enquiry into ethnographic data collected in Transylvania during the late 1970s by the Constantin Brăiloiu Institute of Ethnography and Folklore shows a shift from traditional gifts in kind to money-gifts.[1] In fifty-four localities (out of fifty-seven), wedding guests gave money, alongside smaller gifts such as clothes, bed linens, rugs, and food and drinks; in a lesser number of cases (18 percent), money was given in addition to livestock, such as sheep or calves. The data also indicates, however, that in twenty-seven localities (47 percent), some people had started to give only money as wedding gifts, setting a trend that was going to last up to the present time.[2]

In the community of Urşi, located in the Apuseni Mountains[3], wedding feasts started to become larger in the 1970s, as elsewhere in Romania. The most important watershed occurred at the end of socialism with the opening of markets, expansion in the construction sector, and the demise of legal structures that had previously restricted private timber cutting in Romania's forests. The village of Urşi is heavily involved in producing and selling timber and forest products, and weddings have followed an economic trend of personal accumulation by channeling funds from the community to the household.[4] Gifts of cash are much discussed but blatant strategies of investment are disguised due to moral tensions. The situation is fluid. Linking the size of weddings to the money-gifts offered by guests, local people say that "people had money in the beginning of the 1990s, and they wanted to get more money at their weddings, plus they wanted to show they have money by making large gifts!" However, others, especially younger people with experience of urban life, see such practices as indicative of a "backward peasant mentality" (*mentalitate de ţărani înapoiaţi*). Criticism is directed specifically at the guests' "showing off" (*a se lăuda, a se da mare*), but the new couple and their families may be targeted if it is felt that they are trying to make a profit at any price. The perception that money has a corrupting influence and has no place in friendship, kinship, or life-cycle events, conceived of as a ritual of affectivity and social bonding, is prevalent in public discourse about weddings among young Romanians throughout the country.

Such tensions between money and morality have been addressed by numerous social scientists. Georg Simmel (1900) explained the inappropriateness of money as a gift: money, with its rigid impersonality, can never become an acceptable mediator of social relationships because a gift given in the form of money distances and estranges the gift from the giver. Money, he concluded, is appropriate only for the impersonal exchanges of the market. Mary Douglas and Baron Isherwood (1978) described the necessity of keeping a boundary between gifts and cash, while Stephen Gudeman

(2008) developed a dialectical approach to this tension. Parry and Bloch (1989) argued that the inappropriateness of money as a gift is a peculiarity of Western culture. Elsewhere, they argue that "where the economy is embedded in society and subject to its moral laws, monetary relations are rather unlikely to be represented as an antithesis of bonds of kinship and friendship, and there is consequently nothing inappropriate about making gifts of money to cement such bonds." (1989: 9). Similar tensions have been noted in anthropological studies of socialism, e.g., when Romanian villagers condemned money-gifts as morally dubious "gypsy practices" (Kligman 1988: 56), or their Hungarian counterparts asserted that to practice a profit orientation in weddings was a betrayal of tradition (Sárkány 1983).

In the light of this literature, it is instructive to observe that harsh haggling over gifts is a conspicuous feature at wedding ceremonies in the Apuseni Mountains. However, the potential destruction of social relationships is averted through particular forms of ritualization.[5] The ritual words that introduce the money offerings during a wedding, although mocking and cajoling, at the same time emphasize the giver's generosity and promise that his gifts will be repaid by God as a form of divine recognition of good deeds. It would be misleading, however, to conclude that weddings only involve the misrecognition or mystification of social conflict (Bourdieu 1990), or that wedding gifts involve a collective self-deception (Bourdieu 1997), and that the ideology of gift, generosity, and sociality veils a bare exchange of cash. One can perceive a rupture at times between what is expressed and what is practiced, but I argue, again following Bourdieu (1997), for a less blunt interpretation of the wedding gift practice, and for the ambiguity and "dual truth" of giving. I suggest that self-interest and solidarity coexist and are intermingled. The ritual feast of the wedding entails both sociality and the exchange of money-gifts. Money-raising is constituted as a ritual, just as the ritual is a form of raising money. Weddings are concomitantly an occasion for people to gather for commensality and dancing, for the newlyweds to raise a conjugal fund, and for guests to secure future returns on their money-gifts. While first observations suggest that the dream of generosity hides the obligation to reciprocate gifts given at Romanian weddings, how hidden is this obligation if it is present in everybody's thinking and on everybody's lips before, during, and after the weddings?

Weddings in Presocialism, Socialism, and Postsocialism: From Boots to Cars

In the village of Urşi, weddings involve a threefold ceremony: the religious celebration in the church (*cununia religioasă*), the civil celebration in the

municipal administrative offices (*cununia civilă*), and a community celebration in the form of a feast held at a restaurant or wedding hall (*nunta*).
The central moment of a wedding is the community celebration, specifically the feast, to which numerous people are invited.

The wedding is a sign of status and a means to create status. Studies
from interwar Romania show the importance of a "proper" wedding in
rural society; the financial inability to carry out a big wedding was shame-
ful. A study from southern Transylvania (Țara Oltului), which presents
data from 1940 (Bernea 1967), shows an interesting practice of nocturnal
weddings. All weddings that did not conform to community norms—for
example those contracted between people who had not attained the legal
age of marriage (eighteen), those involving widows or widowers, or those
among people too poor to afford a big feast—were carried out at night,
away from the eyes of the community. Over a period of five years, the sociologist Ernest Bernea observed twenty-eight nocturnal weddings, out of
which sixteen were carried out during the night because of the poverty of
the newlyweds, who could not afford a daylight procession. These weddings
had only twenty-five guests and were not preceded or followed by a church
ceremony. Not being able to mount a proper feast implied that no religious
ceremony could be carried out. A few "moralist" people in the community
condemned night weddings, because they implied the absence of religious
service and thus were considered to be devilish and to promote fornication
and prostitution (Bernea 1967: 129). Even before the socialist period, a
proper wedding feast was necessarily big and costly, and weddings conducted without a large feast, even due to a real lack of material resources,
created shame and the perception of immoral conduct.

Several studies from other areas in Romania and nearby countries suggest interconnections between the development of weddings and local
economies during the socialist and postsocialist periods, showing that
where economy is thriving, weddings are thriving too. Gail Kligman's *The
Wedding of the Dead* is a fine-grained description of wedding practices
in Maramureș, a region in northwestern Romania. Kligman makes little reference to gifts, money, or other economic aspects, suggesting that
weddings focused less on money-offerings and more on sociality and the
proper performance of the rite. She noticed, however, a paradox with respect to the pecuniary aspects of weddings. Although people considered
financial contributions from guests at weddings to be a Gypsy practice (as
Gypsies are seen to ask shamelessly for money), thus banning them from a
moral point of view, a maximization of material benefits had increasingly
come into ceremonial play (Kligman 1988: 269). Prior to Kligman's fieldwork, the total money-gifts given at a wedding nearly equaled the price of
a pair of boots, but around 1980 it became enough money to buy a TV set,

and at the time of her fieldwork, money-gifts were enough to finance the purchase of a car.

David Kideckel (1993: 195) also reports that Romanian weddings during the last decades of socialism became larger and that they reflected an increased instrumentality of social relations and the differentiation of village households. He notes that an important turning point occurred between 1974 and 1979, as the money-gifts offered at weddings doubled during that period (Kideckel 1993: 198). However, although the couple could receive the equivalent of as much as $4,200 as money-gifts, "this sum could still fall short of the amount the parents had spent for the wedding" (1993: 199). Thus, even as weddings became more lavish in the 1970s, they were not necessarily aimed at profit-making.

In another part of Transylvania, in the mountain communities located along the southeastern border with the region of Wallachia, Sam Beck reports that in the 1970s, a total communal gift was enough to cover half the cost of an automobile or the construction of a modest home (Beck 1979: 244). He depicts an increase in the total amount of money-gifts from previous generations because of increasing prosperity (1979: 243), and describes the communal gift as a "rotating fund," from which outstanding debts accrued in arranging the wedding feast can be repaid and household domestic life can be initiated. Because of the obligation of reciprocity, this system can be viewed as a form of savings that are made by a person while contributing to others' weddings, and that mature when the person or the person's children marry. This interpretation might seem too calculative and crafted by the members as a rotating fund, while it is not purposefully meant as such. In addition to the rotating fund, Beck mentions large endowments on the part of both sets of parents. In this part of Transylvania, communities were better off than elsewhere in the region, and families strived to give equal shares of land, money, and animals to their offspring.

During the 1970s, the villagers that Beck studied were more prosperous than the villagers of the Apuseni Mountains. Therefore, these southern Transylvanians did not experience such a radical change after the fall of socialism as the Apuseni dwellers. The turning point in Beck's case was modernization and industrialization of the nearby towns, which brought prosperity, while in the Apuseni Mountains the turning point was the economic boom of the early postsocialist transition.

Analyzing the late socialist period in rural Hungary, where hundreds of guests were invited to weddings and substantial cash donations were made, Mihály Sárkány (1983) and Chris Hann (2014) discuss the "ritual efflorescence" and "financial inflation" of weddings, which should be seen in relation to economic transformations. Both authors argue for the primacy of sociality over a narrow interpretation of economy. Cash donations to newlyweds served to redistribute wealth and to endow even poor couples with a minimum to set up their households.

These studies suggest that there is a strong correlation between the general rate of prosperity in a community and the grandeur of weddings and, at the micro level, a correlation between the economic standing of a household and the size of weddings. The mechanisms through which such correlations appear are both economic and social. The more prosperous a household is the larger the pool of resources to be invested in a feast, and, the larger the feast, the larger the money-gifts received. In addition, the richer a family is, the larger the pool of acquaintances it can bring together to attend such an occasion, and the larger the pool of friends and relatives that offer to help with the necessary work for preparations. The same trends of reverting to conspicuous exchanges of gifts and sums of cash between all relatives, and lavish feasts, after the fall of socialism were reported by Cynthia Werner for rural Kazakhstan (1997, 1999). However, such inflation occurs in contexts of economic shrinkage. In a similar vein, in the Polish Carpathians, because of the great value placed on weddings, people perceive a continuity of abundance displayed through weddings, even in socialist years of shortage (Pine 2004: 111). Werner's explanation for inflating wedding feasts in conditions of economic decrease is that through ritual people try to secure connections that will eventually serve them economically. Thus, the poorer the family is, the more it needs valuable connections and the more it will invest in getting them. Arguing for the increase in wedding lavishness because of the need for social cohesion, Robert Pichler (2009) depicts the case of an Albanian village in western Macedonia where migrants held lavish ceremonies during times of ethnic conflict in order to maintain a localized sense of social order.

My data suggest that today the Apuseni people hold big weddings, but try to maintain moderate expenses. However, they give and receive high-value gifts that enable the couple to make a gain. I do not suggest, as do several of the studies described above, that the large size of weddings is aimed at social cohesion, or at an increase in social capital or prestige. Rather, I argue that economic calculation is very much at stake in people's ways of reasoning. However, the economic calculations cannot be separated in the case of weddings from the aspects of sociality, such as commensality, display of prestige, or social effervescence. I suggest that norms of mutual support and reciprocity, as well as economic transformations and the increased commercialization that permeates social values, all contribute to ritual inflation. I describe these economic trends in the following pages and then address the long-term transformations in the celebration of weddings and the conjugal fund.

Local Economy: Poor Traders, Rich Traders

The village of Urşi is located on the upper Arieş Valley, a densely forested area. It is famous for sawn wood and the trade of wooden planks. The regional capital, the town of Câmpeni, is 30 kilometers away. The houses are built on steep slopes at an altitude of 1,100 meters. The entire area is renowned for woodworking, woodcutting, and petty commerce. Villages in the northern Apuseni Mountains used to be a Romanian Orthodox enclave in the Habsburg Empire. Hungary shared responsibilities for running the Empire after 1867, but these villagers always resisted Hungarian rule and cultural influence.[6] During the eighteenth and the nineteenth centuries the peasants from the Urşi area were serfs on the fiscal domain of the Empire (*domeniul fiscal*), yet they retained use rights to the forests. As far back as 1796, documents mention massive commercial woodcutting practiced by peasants in the region (Csucsuja 1998: 29). In the beginning of the nineteenth century, petty commerce started to be heavily taxed by the Empire, and forest guards violently enforced new legal regulations, so that at the end of the nineteenth century, the mountain dwellers of the Apuseni were completely impoverished (idem: 39).

Starting in the beginning of the twentieth century, books and articles about the region have frequently depicted starvation and endemic health problems (Suciu 1929; Ciomac 1933). Frequent walking up and down the high mountain slopes, hard work in the forest, long trips for trade, and very meager diets apparently made for an exhausted and poor population. It was also difficult for families to accumulate wealth due to the available technology for exploiting this ecological niche, a demographic pattern of families with seven to nine children, remote markets, and poor soil.

The beginning of the communist regime in 1944 was very hard on people in the Apuseni Mountains. Villages were not collectivized, but until 1956 they were forced to provide the socialist state with quotas of meat and dairy production, which drew severely on the houses' material base.[7] Toward the second half of the socialist period, mostly in the 1970s, the economic situation improved. People earned money as employees of the state-forestry brigades and from illegal petty trade. Food was available for purchase in local shops and people kept a few animals, such as cows and pigs, for home consumption. Electricity and asphalt roads were introduced in the village in the same period. Toward the end of the socialist epoch in the 1980s, when the ruling Communist Party decided to pay off the entire external debt of the country, centrally planned frugality translated into hardships for communities in the Apuseni Mountains because they could not produce adequate food and had to exchange timber for food. In those years, food was apportioned and allotted by vouchers (*cartele*), which were exchangeable in the socialist shops in certain locations and at certain times, subject to arbitrary availability. While traveling, timber traders were often unable to procure food in shops on their route. As the prices for cereals and other food products increased, the relative value of timber in relation to food decreased, and communities that relied on trading timber for their food supply were sharply disadvantaged.

After the fall of socialism, such hardships disappeared in the mountains as the local economy improved spectacularly. The timber market of the region of Transylvania opened up in relation to the European construction market. Fiscal and environmental regulation was also very weak in the 1990s, favoring illegal operations. The postsocialist period also introduced several new property forms that affected the local timber trade. The previously state-owned forests largely remained state forests, but small portions became private forests under a variety of property regimes with multiple and fuzzy regulations. Forests were devolved to individuals only in very small allotments—about 65 percent of the population in Urşi received up to 1 hectare per family.[8] A larger portion of forest, 1,516 hectares, was returned to the administrative commune in a hybrid form combining public and private ownership, called the communal forest (*pădure comunală*), in which villagers have use rights. In addition, 824 hectares became community-based forest, officially governed by an association of proprietors, the *composesorat*. There are 800 proprietors who own shares in this community forest, but in practice, it is ruled by the same municipal office that rules the communal forest.

The village currently counts 504 inhabitants who live in 124 households. It experienced an exodus to urban areas during the socialist period; however, out-migration diminished in the period following the end of socialism.[9] Urşi now looks quite well-off, and the thriving house-based production of timber, although illegal, is strikingly visible all across the village. An asphalt road traverses the hills, which locals say is a fortunate circumstance for development and commerce. The coniferous forests, rich in berries, mushrooms, and medicinal plants, that surround Urşi and the neighboring villages lend a "natural beauty" to the region and are taken as a symbol of the resourcefulness of the local people.

Situated in a favorable market context, the people in the village used their existing networks of trade and skills to bolster their timber commerce. Gains were large and fast. The young villagers in the high Transylvanian communities proved to be entrepreneurial and colonized the whole market for wooden boards in the western part of Romania, reaching also the southern Romanian markets in the town of Craiova. By the time the first generation of postsocialist youth married, their businesses were flourishing and they were circulating a lot of money. These entrepreneurs were called the "Las Vegas generation" based on people's images of Las Vegas acquired from movies such as Casino (1995), full of glitter and bright colors, because the young villagers displayed lavishness in consumption.

A simple picture of livelihood today in the village shows a house economy combined with trade, and, in a few cases, with state sources, primarily pension payments. Most of the families log trees and produce timber; they augment this income by picking mushrooms and berries in the summer, which they sell in well-developed markets and with the help of various networks of intermediaries, dealers, and transporters, based either in their village or in neighboring ones. These small-scale private enterprises, usually illegal, are combined with small-scale animal husbandry for home consumption. Families from Urşi are generally very independent, people who do not work for others as employees even on a temporary basis. Young families do not live with parents, nor do parents and adult children consider themselves to constitute a single economic unit. During my fieldwork in 2009–2010, people had money and circulated a lot of cash. From data collected in a questionnaire survey (see Appendix to this volume), I calculated that an average family makes approximately 700 Euros per month, which is a lot for an Eastern European village family. Economic prosperity and possibilities of gain are visible in the pattern of endowments. Young people at the age of marriage already earn their own money, and have assets and savings of their own. I will give one example. A well-off family in the village has three unmarried children, a daughter, Ana (twenty-two), and two sons, Costea (twenty-four) and Sandu (twenty-five).[10] All three children have plans to get married soon. Their endowment is already accumulated. The daughter Ana and the middle son Costea are going to inherit the tourist guesthouse and bar business, half each. In addition, Costea owns an expensive car and is going to inherit his parents' house. The oldest son will move to the city of Oradea, two hours' drive from the village, where he already owns an apartment and a car. This pattern is fairly common in the village.

The Past: Little Weddings in Little Houses

As far back as informants can recall, couples married young. Women usually married between the ages of fifteen and nineteen, while men married slightly later, between the ages of nineteen and twenty-three. Boys worked from a young age, usually twelve, either in the forest or as servants for richer families in the neighboring villages. It was desirable to break with the family of origin, which meant to unburden it from a mouth to feed with the precious cereals acquired by trade. Thus, to marry meant establishing an independent house with very little endowment from the parents. Only the very few richer families with fewer children endowed their offspring with money to buy land and build a house. After choosing a wife, the man had to work for one year or more to assemble a small amount of money to be able to start a house and buy productive assets such as a horse and cart.

Although the practice of bestowing a dowry was historically widespread across Romanian territory, its importance in contracting the marriage varied regionally and according to class.[11] In Urşi, women were not endowed with the typical "Romanian" dowry, described by folklorists, even for the Apuseni region, as consisting of numerous embroidered bed linens and nightgowns, hand-woven blankets, and stunning tablecloths (Frâncu and Candrea 1888; Meiţoiu 1969). On the contrary, most dowries in Urşi were small and produced by the young women themselves shortly before or after their wedding. The women that I spoke with often told me that their mothers did not give them anything. The bride usually went to the house of the groom with a dowry carried in two bags on horseback as her entire "fortune" (Frâncu and Candrea 1888; Sărbători şi Obiceiuri 2003). Negotiations about or references to the quality and quantity of dowry were entirely absent from the premarital agreements and arrangements between the groom and the family of the bride. There are references to the qualities of the bride, such as her beauty, tidiness, and diligence, but nothing about her endowment, which suggests that material endowment was not an issue.

Marriage in general meant that a couple started building a new house together, as opposed to practices in other areas of Romania where the groom already had a house as part of his endowment. New couples in Urşi began building with a small amount of money that the groom had earned prior to his marriage, and the couple also borrowed money from a few closer kin, neighbors, or godparents as a small starting capital. The first house a couple built was usually a very poor accommodation, which they improved over time. Historically, few couples received money at their wedding.

My data on wedding feasts go back to the 1940s.[12] People's accounts from that period attest that in the 1940s, as now, wedding celebrations in the village were differentiated according to the economic status of the persons involved. In 1948, a man coming from a highly placed family that owned a water-activated sawmill (*firez*) had approximately eighty people invited for his wedding party, and this was regarded as a remarkably big wedding. They celebrated in the house of the groom's parents, in two rooms, with drinks and music. In contrast, families of average means had much smaller parties to which only parents, siblings, and godparents were invited, while poorer families usually did not have a wedding party at all.

In the 1960s, wedding celebrations changed. Not only did the practice of giving money-gifts enter wedding celebrations, but food preparations also intensified. But the number of marriages with money-gifts and banquets was small, limited to the families of above-average means. For example, at one wedding in 1962, sixty to seventy people were invited; they ate and danced together in a room of 30 square meters, "in such a mess that they could not understand anything." The hosts served *sarmale* (cabbage leaves stuffed with meat), *supă cu tăiței* (chicken noodle soup), and sandwiches with cheese. The guests gave money-gifts that were, according to my calculations, ten to twelve times less valuable than current gifts. A more significant difference between the early money-gifts and those that I observed is that godparents in the 1960s gave a considerably higher gift than the average guest, up to eight times more, whereas today the godparents give a gift that is only two to four times more valuable than that of the average guest. The importance of the godfather in the economy of the wedding and in general was far higher than it is today, which is probably linked to sharper status contrasts.[13]

In short, during the 1940s, the 1950s, and the 1960s, most weddings did not yield any money and average people did not have big weddings at all. As one of my informants, an 82-year-old lady, put it—they were "little weddings in little houses." In the 1970s, when there was a relative improvement in living conditions, weddings increased to an average of 130 guests; during the food shortage of the 1980s, this average was maintained. In order to host such large weddings, however, heavy debts had to be secured with local "patrons" (*patroni*), namely, the local shopkeeper, who was the "absolute" broker of food and drinks. For wedding feasts, people slaughtered pigs and calves from their own production—a practice that was officially forbidden. Such regulations were often infringed with the help of the shopkeeper and the local police, who had to be kept silent with bribes or invitations to them to serve as godparents. Although people depended on such practices of indebtedness, they hated them and tried to reduce their obligations and dependence to the minimum, as they continue to do today.

In those times of shortage, reciprocal help with food was very important for wedding feasts. Relatives and neighbors, almost half of the guests, contributed something for the banquet, according to what he or she had available. Eggs, butter, cream, cabbage, meat, and bread were all donated in large quantities to compensate for the relative scarcity of the host family's resources and for the difficulty of buying surplus quantities in the socialist shops. These "gifts" were part of a logic of reciprocity. They were recorded carefully in wedding notebooks, and were later reciprocated with the same products if possible. Compared to other areas of Romania where wedding celebrations of the 1970s were lavish (Kideckel 1993; Beck 1979), weddings in the Apuseni area were relatively modest due to the severe shortages of food and other resources. In the 1980s, when accumulation started to be more frequent for households in the mountains, money-gifts for wedding banquets were already a fashion and the lump sums raised were larger, yet compared to neighboring Romanian areas, they looked modest. Usually, the parents organized the weddings according to their financial power. They either left the entire lump sum raised as money-gifts for the newly-weds or took back the costs of the wedding and left the couple with a modest sum.

The wedding of Eugenia and Dimitri in the early 1980s reflects the growing importance of money-gifts to young couples. Like her mother before her, Eugenia was a single child, so her family was rather well-off. Dimitri came from a respected family, but it was less wealthy. After they were officially married, Eugenia (sixteen) and Dimitri (twenty) wanted to move in together, but they had no land for a house. Eugenia had inherited some land, but Dimitri was too proud to build their house on this land. Eugenia did not want to move in with Dimitri's parents because she was young, wanted "her own thing" (*lucrul ei*), and feared trouble with her mother-in-law. Thus, they decided to build their house on "neutral" ground. They bought a small piece of land and built a house with money borrowed from a few relatives and godparents. After half a year, her parents organized a wedding banquet for them and they raised some money with this occasion. Against the custom of the time, when parents took back the sums they invested in their children's weddings, her parents left them the entire sum of the wedding gifts, and additionally gave them a big money-gift, with which Eugenia and Dimitri managed to buy a better and larger piece of land and moved their house there. Thus, they had a very good start in life, much better than other fellow villagers. As they recount today, the wedding banquet contributed significantly to this good start. It was also a way to tame Dimitri's male pride and to make it seem that the young couple was the one who had "earned" that money, although Eugenia's father was entitled to take back more than half of the respective amount.

The most important asset for a young couple to acquire at the beginning of their marriage was a house to serve as the foundation of the new family. In the case of Eugenia and Dimitri, the money for building the house was mostly contributed by the couple's parents, but in cases of larger families with many siblings, such parental endowment was nearly impossible. In the absence of material possibilities, the wedding banquet proved to be a good opportunity to gain cash for building the house, through the communal money-gift.

The terms used to designate the parental endowment do not differ significantly from terms used to designate gifts received from other people. In contrast to marriage payments that occur in societies with a strong emphasis on the descent-group and intergenerational endowment, in the Apuseni

Mountains the parents give only a "gift." Sometimes they contribute with a significant amount of money, as in the case of Eugenia and Dimitri, but the parental contribution is not differentiated from any other gifts, monetary or otherwise, that the couple receives. It is called a gift (*dar, cadou*). The linguistic expression of the endowment by Eugenia's parents as a gift among other gifts and the indirect way in which the larger sum is given as a sponsorship of the wedding feast suggests that such practices are veiled in ritual occasions as generosity.

But this case in which the parents had a major role in endowing the couple was not typical. Usually, the couple needed sponsorship for starting their new life together from the larger community, and especially from its better-off members, whose support they tried to attract by asking them to serve as marital godparents. Data suggest that the majority of newlyweds needed to borrow money from five to six sources in order to start their life together. Because cash and goods were scarce, the effort to borrow money could easily lead to social embarrassment because nobody was willing to lend. Thus, marriage represented both an occasion to ask for a loan from better-off acquaintances and a way to form profitable alliances with godparents, carefully chosen from among the richer covillagers. After the wedding, the groom often turned first to his godfathers to request a needed loan.

Thus, the initial necessary capital of the young couple consisted of loans, and was raised from the group of better-off relatives, ritual relatives (godparents), and benevolent neighbors. Loans were considered a big favor; but they were not an endowment. They represented capital, which had to be repaid in one or two years. As a few of my informants said, the only real endowment that a newlywed couple actually had was the anticipation of hard work in the future for repaying debts. Couples usually started out as indebted persons who had to prove themselves worthy of becoming independent and self-supporting. This model of beginning marriage without an endowment and of relying on short-term loans began to change in the 1980s, as the money-gifts at weddings became a kind of endowment from the larger community that was expected to be repaid over a lifetime, and deepened in the 1990s when weddings started to become a "profitable business" (*afacere profitabilă*).

Contemporary Weddings: Village Grandeur

The Apuseni wedding has now reached well beyond the level of grandeur that other areas of Romania displayed before the fall of communism. By the year 2000, the number of guests had increased to an average of 350, and the biggest wedding in the area of recent years had 1,200 guests.

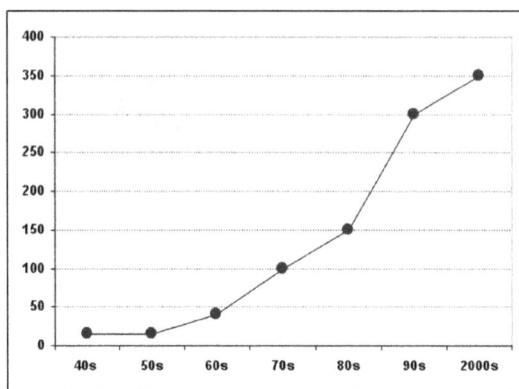

Figure 5.1. Average number of guests at village weddings, 1940–2008, based on a set of forty-five cases

Figure 5.1 shows that wedding feasts exploded in the 1990s with the opening of timber markets after the fall of socialism.[14] Because of this boom, the location of the wedding changed; private houses did not provide enough space for the increasingly large number of guests. At the beginning of the 1990s, weddings were held in a temporary wooden shelter with wooden tables and benches, and everything was destroyed after the wedding. The work for each such construction took substantial time and resources, so people decided to donate money to the village for the construction of a House of Culture (*cămin cultural*) in the center of the village where they could hold weddings and occasionally other festive meals. Most villages in Romania have a House of Culture, which includes a kitchen, a main room, a terrace, and in some cases secondary rooms or even internal balconies.[15] The quality of houses of culture varies between villages; some are bigger and nicer, suitable for more fancy weddings, while others are more modest. The House of Culture in the village of Urși does not suit the villagers' aspirations, and they prefer to hold weddings in fancy local restaurants or in the House of Culture located in the center of the commune—which is decorated with sculpted wooden walls and ceiling that are described as reflecting the area's "wood civilization'" (*civilizația lemnului*), and a floor of black-and-white checker tiles that is suitable for dancing.

In contrast to the past, everyone can now afford a fancy wedding and every wedding yields a cash surplus for the newlyweds. Money-gifts make it possible for even poorer couples to have a lavish wedding because the total money-gift usually amounts to more than the banquet cost. Even when parents cannot afford to endow the couple, this system permits the couple to pay for their own wedding banquet and to have a surplus, which is seen as capital by the young couple to have a good start, and is very often used to buy or furnish a house. The cash surplus from each wedding is bigger or smaller according to a variety of factors, as will become clear below.

The couple and the parents start thinking about the wedding feast far in advance. They book a large restaurant or a wedding hall usually one year or more ahead of time and invite kin, friends, and acquaintances with written invitations or by word of mouth. Friends of friends, or acquaintances of acquaintances, are mostly welcomed too because a large number of guests is the key to a successful wedding. Guests are seated according to their relationship to the bride and groom, and in rural areas there are "important tables" for state and local officials, including the policemen, the mayor, and the forestry guard.

Usually a wedding feast starts at 8 in the evening and lasts through the night into the morning. During the party, people eat, chat, and dance, accompanied by one or two local bands playing popular folk music. Dancing is very vivid, usually in pairs, and sometimes also in large circles (*horă*); people dance holding each other's hands or by grasping the other tightly around the waist or neck. Professional entertainers are hired to tell jokes and witty words about the bride and groom. Female guests, beginning with girls as young as fourteen, pay special attention to their looks; they often wear expensive and fancy dresses and go to the hairdresser in town to get curly, stiff, glittery hairdos.

People put a great deal of effort into the wedding meals. They pay two semi-professional cooks and an additional four to six women from among the family's close relatives and friends to help prepare and serve the food. A mixture of homemade and supermarket products is served, with an emphasis on good quality and presentation. Across Romania, wedding feasts commonly involve five courses. In Urşi, many of the dishes are similar to those that appear elsewhere in the country. The first course is called *aperitive* (hors d'oeuvres), and is composed of an assortment of meat specialties, salamis, fresh vegetables, and cheese. The second course (specific to Transylvania) consists of *supă cu tăiței*, a chicken noodle soup with homemade noodles. The third course is *sarmale*, cabbage leaves stuffed with meat, accompanied by *mămăligă* (polenta); and the fourth course includes roasted pork or beef with boiled potatoes or rice. At the end of the feast, cookies and the bride's cake (*tortul miresei*) are served. Inexpensive white wine and good quality homemade apple or plum brandy (*vinars*), sometimes mixed with water to form a drink called *crampă*, are served throughout the wedding, and half a liter of homemade brandy is also given as a small gift to each guest to take home.

Money-gifts are given to the couple at the end of the wedding. This moment can be variously organized. It can be done in a discrete manner, by offering money in an envelope offered at the end of the banquet. It can be done in a public ceremony, when the couple organizes a public announcement of gifts (*strigarea darului*), marked by jokes referring to the status and wealth of the guests, as I will detail in the next section of the chapter. This ritual entails many subtleties that increase the total amount that is given to the couple. In urban areas, and to a lesser extent in rural areas, the public announcement of gifts is generally considered a sign of "backward-ness" (*înapoiere*) because money is offered so bluntly and without elegance. Young urbanites often say with contempt that because of money-gifts, wed-dings have turned into pure business. Moral overtones can be heard when talking about spending for luxurious items displayed at weddings, but also when talking about the absolute obligation to take a lot of money from one's pocket for such an occasion. The public spectacle of gifting appears for the moralists as the peak of shamelessness in displaying the ultimate end of a wedding: money. Those who choose to perform it at their wedding consider that it is much fun and "money is still money, either inside the envelope or front-staged."

Couples keep a detailed accounting of the wedding, of who came and who gave or did what to help them, in a "wedding notebook." They or their children, irrespective of gender, bear a debt or duty (*datorie*) to participate in the future weddings of all their guests and helpers, or those of their children. Sometimes, these debts are very heavy and seen as a burden. One often hears complaints by young people that they have to attend weddings the following year that will severely draw on their finances. However, par-ticipating in weddings is also seen as building wedding capital for one's own future wedding or for one's children's weddings. Sometimes the reciprocity is severely imbalanced because of an uneven number of siblings between indebted families and because of increasing geographical mobility, which makes it difficult to attend all the weddings of persons to whom one holds obligations. Young people in Urși usually attend four to five weddings a year, and of those, one or two weddings are more than 100 km away from the village.

Money-Gifts 1: Ritual Rhymes, Giving, and Divine Rewards

The highlight of the wedding is the ceremony of bestowing gifts (*dar*) on the couple.[16] The gift-giving ceremony is most spectacular when there is a public announcement (*strigare*) of the gifts. Toward the end of the wed-ding, around 4 in the morning, the local entertainer (*vornic*) takes a con-tainer and collects cash from every guest; as the *vornic* receives the money, he holds it up and announces the amount. The rhymes recited by the enter-tainer are revealing of the logic of the custom. When the ceremony starts, the *vornic* invites the guests to give their gifts generously and to reciprocate the feast they have received.[17] He then intones,

> *Respected and honest guests*
> *As you have already seen*
> *The bride and the groom*

Together with their in-laws
Bothered to serve us
With many kinds of dishes
Well prepared and well served.
An old story goes like this
That good dishes
Have to be paid for.
Give as much as you want
A sheep or a calf,
Money, as much as you want.
We take also small amounts,
And do not get scared of big amounts
We're ready to count them.[18]

The little poem emphasizes the free character of the gift, "*give as much as you want,*" and its variability, suggested by referring to big offerings and small offerings, but also of the obligatory nature of the gifts. In fact, the size of the gift is set and nonvariable. The *vornic* reminds the guests of the costly foods and organization of the feast, which has to be repaid. The gift is seen as a repayment for the feast offered, bringing the meal and the idea of commensality and hospitality symbolically to the core of the wedding ritual. But this hospitality does not invite further relationships. The meal and the gift create community and solidarity on one hand and gain on the other hand.

Then, as the *strigarea darului* proceeds, the entertainer says in rhymes that the young groom gives advance thanks for the gifts, mentioning his relatives, friends, and neighbors, and then the *vornic* calls for a prayer (*Tatăl Nostru, Pater Noster*) to be said aloud by all the guests. The prayer is meant to put a good omen on the ceremony and the newlyweds, and for everybody else to be satisfied, as suggested by two verses that introduce the gifting ceremony as related to God's grace.

May God spill his grace,
To multiply the gift.[19]

Further verses also reveal the connection between God's grace and the gift. God acts upon people's attitude and makes them generous:

God,
Sweeten their soul,
To come up with the gift,
Make their heart good
And their hand free
To be able to give.[20]

The *vornic* keeps asking for largesse, saying that the godparents, who are the first to give the gift, ate well and entertained themselves, and because of that they should not be sorry for remaining with empty pockets, implying again the idea of repaying the offered feast.

The *vornic* suggests that the guests should think before giving a gift, search their pockets, and give what they "have," implying that everybody can afford a different sum. The *vornic's* polite words suggest that people should give whatever they have in their pockets, but often the *vornic*, or other guests who chime in as the *vornic* circulates through the room, prompt a guest to give more by alluding to his stinginess. Gifting is a proof of status, and as a guest gives his gift, the *vornic* suggests with more rhymed words that everyone now knows how respectable the donor is. The godparents are the first to bestow, then the parents and closer relatives. The godparents and the parents usually lie when they announce their gifts, announcing double or triple the sum that they actually give. The *vornic* describes these sums as "money worthy of an emperor" (*bani demni de un împărat*). Higher amounts are announced because the godfather's gift raises the bar, or "lifts the table" (*ridică masa*), and exerts pressure on the other guests to increase the amount that they give. Although everyone knows that the announced sum is inflated, they still adjust their sums according to it. I was told, for example, about cases when godparents did not want to lie and people removed money from the gifts that they had already prepared. Gifts given by the parents and close relatives also exert pressure on other guests to give proportionately. As he collects the money-gifts, the *vornic* continues his rhyming commentary: the gift-givers, he says, will receive the amounts they gave multiplied by God on other occasions; their money will return to them. The *vornic* also translates the sums of the money-gifts into goods that the young couple can buy: a pig, a bed, and so on—making the whole gifting ceremony appear as a joyful building-up of a small fortune for the new house.

The ritual words and acts are meant to smooth the process of giving money and to stimulate the guests' generosity, by couching the act of giving in terms of showing off status, kindness worthy of an "emperor," and the promise of supernatural returns by God's grace. We also see the gift couched in terms of thankfulness, or as repayment for the costs and labor involved in mounting the feast. The gift is suggested to be the result of the interplay between how much people want to give and how much they can give.

Money-Gifts 2: Haggling, Facts and Figures

At weddings in 2009–2010, a pair of guests paid a money-gift of 120 to 150 Euros. If we count the higher gifts offered by the godparents, the parents, and the close relatives, the money-gifts at an average wedding yielded nearly 14,000 Euros.[21] Weddings at the upper limit of 500 guests netted around 33,000 Euros. In 2011, one of the richest girls in the village married. She had 800 guests at her wedding and the minimum gift was 150 Euros. I calculated the total gift amount at 60,000 Euros, without considering the higher amounts given by relatives and godparents. Given these figures, the value of the money-gift for a "good" wedding increased by a multiplier of approximately twelve since 1980.[22] This was roughly proportionate to the increasing wealth of the population. People belonging to the Las Vegas generation were very proud to describe how they had exceptionally big weddings "for their times" with 500 invited guests. They were described by other villagers as having a special taste for big parties and for "breaking" (*a sparge*) large sums of money. They embodied an effervescence of consumption relative to personal accumulation at a young age. The guests at the Las Vegas generation's weddings were enchanted with this grandeur and opened their purses generously to newlyweds. Generosity was not a problem for the guests of the period because everyone in the area was making big, fast money.

The story of two brothers, Cornel and Sivu, who became enemies after their weddings, provides an example of the elaborate haggling and the tension between relationships and wealth that surround the practice of money-gifting. Cornel, the younger brother of a well-off family of average standing, decided to get married. His parents offered to pay for the majority of the wedding expenses because they could afford it, and because they wanted their son to have a good start in life. Hearing his parents' offer, the older brother, Sivu, became angry and envious. Invoking his seniority, he claimed that his younger brother should not get married before him. In Urşi, there is no custom regarding which siblings should marry first, so it was clear to all that Sivu was envious and wanted a share of his parents' wealth. A few years before these events, Sivu had agreed with his parents to inherit his grandparents' land and house at the time of his marriage. At the moment of his brother's wedding, however, he evidently realized that this was a bad deal compared to what his brother stood to gain, as land and old houses were no longer in fashion. Sivu also had another reason to be envious. Because people repay wedding attendance debts to the family and not to individuals, by marrying first, Cornel stood to have a greater number of guests at his wedding than Sivu would at a later marriage, and the money-gifts received by each would be disproportionate. Sivu got so angry that he started avoiding his parents and brother in public.

Sivu anticipated correctly. His brother's wedding was a success; many guests came and he gained a lot of money. The parents paid for the entire wedding and did not take back anything; they left the money for their son, "because it is right to do so." Cornel's parents even lent money to the less well-off bride's parents, a fairly large amount (1,200 Euros), to be given as a wedding gift (*cinste*) to the new couple so that the bride's parents could appear honorable in the eyes of the community. The large sums of gift-money were not only expressions of generosity. The loan ultimately caused some conflict between the two sets of parents because the bride and groom chose to have money-gifts given in the more urban and discrete use of envelopes. Because Cornel's parents did not see the bride's parents give the full sum of 1,200 Euros, they suspected that the bride's parents gave only a portion of the money they had given them. The gifts given by the two godfathers were also intensely negotiated before the wedding. One of the godfathers, a timber businessman who emigrated from the village to a city ten years ago, insisted on giving his normal gift of 500 Euros and leaving the entire sum with the couple. The other godfather, a guard at the touristic complex in the neighboring village, wanted to give a lower sum of 250 Euros combined with the gift of a washing machine.

One year later, Sivu, the older brother, "out of stubbornness and pride," as his mother says, decided to borrow money and to organize his own wedding without help from his parents. In this case, money-giving was riddled with conflict, mistrust, and disappointment on all sides. After the religious ceremony, the parents of the bride and groom negotiated the money-gifts among themselves, in private, in the backyard of the village church. First the bride's parents, who were less well-off, suggested a gift of 500 Euros. In response, the groom's parents offered 500 Euros too, but they added, "not only for the public 500 Euros, we really intend to leave that money with our son for real" because they wanted the bride's parents to commit to leaving the same amount. Although they both committed to give 500 Euros, Sivu's parents did not trust the bride's parents, and asked Sivu "what do you know from Vali [the bride], how much will your parents-in-law give you?" Sivu answered cautiously that they said 500 Euros, but he knew that they did not have money at the moment. Sivu's mother describes the haggling as bad-spirited and anxious, "with a potential for gossip and mistrust." At the end of the day, Sivu's mother still did not trust the bride's parents to respect the deal.

Sivu also got a worse deal than his brother with the money-gifts from his godparents. In contrast to Cornel, who received money-gifts in envelopes, Sivu opted for a public gift giving ceremony, *cu strigare.* Each godfather announced a gift of 750 Euros but actually gave only one-sixth of the amount (125 Euros). While the younger brother gained a lot at the wedding and his wedding was called a success, the angry older brother barely managed to cover his expenses.

People are not open about their business dealings and about money. Even when they buy a car, they find it slightly inappropriate to be questioned about how much it cost. Cornel's mother, however, talked rather openly with me about the money involved in the weddings of her sons. I estimate that Cornel made approximately 13,000 to 14,000 Euros from his wedding. With this money, he bought timber and sold it again at a higher price, increasing his investment by approximately 10 to 15 percent. Cornel then converted most of his wedding money into capital, which he invested in his business with the purchase of a special truck for carrying timber; the remainder of his wedding money was used to improve his house.

The other brother, Sivu, struck a bad deal with his parents from the very beginning by deciding to take over their old house as part of his endowment. Later, when he realized that a large amount of money was to be given by his parents to his brother, he was angered that this sum would be much greater than what he had received. Driven by anger and hasty to take revenge, Sivu did not gain anything at his wedding, and people say he barely paid back his debts. Being unhappy about this result, Sivu took the family tractor, which had been purchased by his parents and brother, and began to use it heavily. Sivu did not ask for permission to take the tractor, nor did he make any other arrangement with his family for sharing it. Sivu's relatives were unhappy with this situation, but they tacitly accepted it as a small compensation for what everyone regarded as a failed wedding.

Are Weddings All About Money?

In Urşi, people do not shy away from recognizing that the wedding is more about money than anything else, as far as the principal characters are concerned. We have seen in the story of Cornel and Sivu that parents do not give automatically large gifts, but may have to be prompted, urged, and coaxed—especially by the other set of parents. Parents balance their generosity against the cost of mistrust and discomfort with their future in-laws. Guests also have to be persuaded to open their purses generously by the performance of the couple's closer relatives during the wedding. Because there are no set rules about how much parents and godparents should give, decisions concerning who receives, who gives, and what is given depend on the negotiation skills of the parties involved. Hence, people very often openly defend their best financial interest; they do not lower their voices or try to be polite when negotiating with people who theoretically are due affection and respect, such as their parents, their future godparents, or their future in-laws. People in other Romanian areas often use alternative strategies for bargaining to avoid disrupting social relations among people who are or will become close relatives, by using for example the institution of the matchmaker (*peţitor*). In those areas, the matchmaker has the authority to be as shameless as necessary to organize the bargaining of the gifts and the dowry in the most acceptable way. In the case of Urşi, by doing all the negotiations themselves, family members risk embittering relationships. The harsh bargaining and potential for resentment that reside in the wedding money dealings show how much the wedding ritual is imbued with an economic logic that can lead to the detriment of social relations. In addition, the high sums that a wedding can yield shows how much the economic life of a household can be influenced by a successful wedding ritual. A successful wedding has good entertainment, music, dance, and food, but most importantly yields a large amount of money. Failed weddings also occur not as an automatic result of the newlyweds' position in local hierarchy, but as a result of individual faults. Thus, the outcome of a wedding can be regarded as a matter of skill, of negotiation, and of securing the right deal. In advancing the model of lavish weddings, young folks from the Las Vegas generation not only made fortunes out of their wedding, but also marked their status as successful entrepreneurs and persons of distinction. These opulent feasts also came to mark the difference between the socialist period of shortage and the postsocialist period of prosperity.

Conclusion

In this study of an Apuseni village, I have focused on the absence of elaborate weddings in the past and on the explosion of lavish weddings that has taken place in recent years. The village is an extreme case, economically and ritually. Wedding ritualization is related to a specific form of livelihood. Before the 1970s, in the high villages of Apuseni weddings, and marriage more generally, meant legitimacy for engaging "productive" exchange relations, especially those related to money-borrowing (*împrumuturi*). In poor areas, both endowments from parents and gifts at the wedding were small and so the couple had to rely on loans from better-off relatives, neighbors, and godparents to start a house. The small community temporarily endowed the couple in the form of loans. Later, during the flourishing socialist years of the 1970s, the highland villages became more prosperous and reverted to the model of communal marriage payments that could be called the community endowment. Goods became largely available, people were more mobile, and community buildings were available to accommodate large feasts. For these reasons, the weddings "opened up" and the communal endowment became more visible and permanent, taking the form of money-gifts instead of loans. Instead of borrowing money to buy a house, the newlyweds borrowed money and food to organize large feasts and received substantial money-gifts from all the participants, but especially from parents, better-off relatives, and godparents. From the money-gifts, they repaid their debts and had a significant surplus. In the course of their lifetime they gave back to the community by offering gifts at the weddings held by their guests or those of their guests' children. This mechanism of communal endowment was perfected after the fall of socialism. When personal accumulation increased, so did the wedding expenses and gifts, which allowed for a very large gain for a newlywed couple.

Inspired by life stories of the Las Vegas generation, I have suggested that weddings are a ritual way to engage in personal accumulation. The young generation that became rich during the economic boom and adopted patterns of conspicuous consumption at a young age set the trend for wedding banquets. A familiarity with the risky nature of the timber trade, a skilled "eye" for windfall profits, and the habit of circulating cash were common among the men of this generation. In the context of such lifestyle changes and given the almost exclusive say of the newlyweds regarding the wedding, as opposed to more conservative areas where the parents control the marriage and the wedding, the young "skilled eyes" saw the possibility of increasing gain. Given the resources that became available after the fall of socialism, the young couples of the Las Vegas generation opted to hold big weddings and implicitly demand generous gifts. The wedding banquets became a legitimate and easy way to secure cash that otherwise would have required more risky business.

The weddings kept inflating even when market opportunities diminished during the economic crisis that started in 2008. Even though the younger generation (now in their middle and late twenties) did not earn as much money as the generation before it, the weddings have remained at the same level, partly because the "wedding business" is still profitable and the reciprocity chain continues. The increase in ritual elaboration, and individual economic outputs, affect economy in a circular fashion. Ritual becomes a means for redistribution from the community to the newly established family. The larger the ritual, the larger the community involved, and the larger the amounts distributed as gifts for the conjugal fund.

Sometimes the pragmatic attitude and harsh bargaining occasioned by marriages disrupt social relations. The stories I collected often point to sharp calculations and even stinginess, as suggested by the story of the two brothers. However, the analysis of ritual words recited during the money-gifting ceremony suggests that generosity is a much-praised value, displayed and asked for at weddings. Previous animosities and uneasiness about giving money are veiled in ritual performances and turned symbolically into generosity. Moreover, the person who gives is assured that his or her gift will be repaid, if not in the mundane world, then in the spiritual realm. The situations described involve reciprocity at different levels: guests whose wedding was attended by the family of the newlyweds are repaying their debts, while other guests indebt the newlyweds with their attendance and gifts. The feast is also repaid with money-gifts; which, if generous, will be repaid in turn by God in material and spiritual forms in the future. Some of these exchanges involve economic calculations, and some are based on beliefs. Such reciprocities are not hidden but outspoken.

Contrary to Bourdieu, for whom the generous and altruistic gift is a fake, a dream without foundation in practice, or a misrecognition, the society of the Apuseni highlands tells a story of truthfulness. Despite scattered voices denouncing "peasant mentalities" and viewing money-gifts as an inappropriate practice, the purpose and circulation of money-gifts are openly presented, as well as the articulations of repayment obligations. Another mark of the truthfulness of wedding gifts in the Apuseni is that what is shown to the world as ritual and what people live in their daily lives are in relative correspondence; during the poverty of the past, weddings were an underdeveloped ritual with few gifts, but with the sharp increases in wealth during the postsocialist period, weddings have become opulent. I have explained that one powerful dream of this society is not generosity but accumulation, whereas generosity in gift giving is an expression of accumulation as well as a promise (from God) that it will sooner or later come to pass. The dream of this society is well served by the coin that is asked for and announced loudly. The significance and implications of the gift might be ambiguous and dual, yet the gift follows closely the process of accumulation. There is no collective hypocrisy of disinterestedness but an open pursuit of gain through the wedding gifts from the part of the newlyweds and also an open pursuit of the givers to make the others indebted and God benevolent.

We might go further and ask whether such wedding-enabled accumulation is not only the short-term order of things, as Parry and Bloch (1989) would have it, but if weddings and money-gifts also serve long-term purposes, such as the reproduction of community through rituals of togetherness. In Urși, as throughout all rural Romania, villagers consider out-migration to be the greatest threat for the existence of community, and they claim that out-migration is motivated primarily because of the lack of possibilities for personal accumulation in rural areas. Thus, the short-run purposes of personal accumulation in a wedding also serve the overarching reproduction of community. Weddings reproduce community in a physical, as well as a symbolic sense, by creating personal bonds to the territory, building houses, and affirming social ties in the form of future social obligations.

Acknowledgments

I thank my informants in Urși, who granted me their trust and their stories. For the preparation of this chapter, I am grateful to Adriana, Sorin, Costel, and priest Ilie Grecu, who facilitated my access to local weddings, to Jena, my invaluable host, and to Jenica and tata Petru, whose wedding stories inspired much of this essay. Many thanks go also to colleagues in the Economy and Ritual group and to Gonçalo Santos for a productive sharing of ideas.

Notes

1. This data was collected with the purpose of creating an ethnographic atlas, mapping all Romanian areas. Thus, information is very succinct, taking the shape of questionnaire responses. However, it illuminates in a quantitative manner the spread of various practices. The data that I used was published as a collection of concise interview citations regarding wedding practices, in the volume dedicated to the region of Transylvania (Sărbători și obiceiuri: Transilvania, 2003). In order to give the numbers that reflect trends in social practices, I have chosen fifty-seven responses that I consider to be comprehensive and reliable, representing fifty-seven localities.

2. One of the Romanian terms for wedding gifts either in kind or in cash is *cinste*; the act of giving is *a cinsti,* to give the *cinste. Cinste* can also mean honesty, correctness or respect, honor, virtue; *Cinste* as a gift is directly related to the idea of hospitality with food and drink on a special occasion; see Cash, this volume.

3. Urși (a pseudonym) is located in the upper Arieș valley in the Apuseni Mountains. Fieldwork was undertaken in 2009–2010 in the framework of the Economy and Ritual Project.

4. Money does not feature as prominently in other life-cycle events. Small cash-gifts are offered at baptisms, and nothing is transferred at funerals (although guests are invited to a feast, the *parastas*).

5. For the uses of ritual and ritualization in conflict situations see Edelman 1969, and for a wider discussion of ritualization see Bell 1992.

6. Population in the area is called a special name, *Moți,* which stands for the Romanians as the embodiment of romantic heroism and national resistance. According to interwar authors (Ciomac and Popa-Neacșa 1936), for the Hungarians, the *Moți* are considered barbarian and violent Romanians; a derivative of the name is found in *Dezsasmocz,* the Hungarian name given to the figure of a vagabond merchant of wooden barrels, who goes from door to door selling his wares and scaring little children.

7. In Romania, beginning in 1946, severe food requisitions were imposed on peasants as a consequence of urban food needs, war reparations, drought, and famine (Kligman and Verdery 2011: 109). Each region and household was assigned a quota for each of several grains and vegetables, dairy products, wool, and meat, calculated on surface area adjusted to soil fertility (idem: 109–110). In Urși, people mostly remember having to give away pigs.

8. Urşi has 66 hectares of privately owned forest.
9. According to the statistics of the commune (in which another fourteen villages are incorporated), the population decreased drastically between 1941 and the 1970s and 1980s, however, it has been relatively stable since 1992. The population of the commune in 1941 was 4,138 inhabitants, in 1992 it was 2,336 inhabitants, and in 2002 it was 2,371 inhabitants.
10. All names are pseudonyms.
11. Romanian historians show that dowry (*zestre*) was very widespread across both urban and rural areas in the Romanian Principalities (Wallachia and Moldova) and in Transylvania (Jianu 2009; Vintilă-Ghiţulescu 2007). Dowries of wealthy daughters in the eighteenth and nineteenth centuries consisted of precious silk dresses and fur coats, embroidered with rubies and emeralds, jewelry, necklaces with three rows of golden coins, entire villages, and gypsy slaves. Less well-off fathers in rural areas gave their daughters land, one or two cows or pigs, and necessary clothing, bed linen, rugs, and carpets (Sărbători şi Obiceiuri 2003; Peteanu 2008). Poorer families with more than five children usually did not give anything as dowry.
12. My data come from a questionnaire survey of twenty-five cases, in which I asked informants about the number of guests, location, money-gifts, number and status of godparents, and menu at their own wedding and at the weddings of their children. I supplemented this survey with additional interview data to cover roughly 30 percent of all village households, accounting for information on weddings over the span of seven decades.
13. Godparents for marriage fulfill a similar role to godparents at baptism. Through the holy sacrament performed by the priest in the church, they are supposed to become the newlyweds' spiritual parents, a bond customarily highly valued and respected and imbued with reciprocal obligations. Godparents thus become ritual relatives of the newlyweds, which theoretically implies the incest taboo. The godfather usually has a ceremonial role in the wedding, but also a practical role of financially assisting the young couple. In this village, godparenthood relationships tended to be vertical; only richer villagers were traditionally asked to be godfathers. In this way, young couples secured the possibility of money loans and additional services, such as free milling or access to a horse and cart owned by the godfather. For more details on godparenthood practices see Vasile 2012.
14. The forty-five cases reported derive from interviews and questionnaires. In all forty-five cases I collected information about past and present weddings along with life-histories. However, not all interviews contain the same amount of detail about wedding strategies, negotiations, attendance, or expenses. In 2009–2010, I attended three weddings in the village and was able to analyze in detail another five weddings that took place shortly before my fieldwork began.
15. The uses of the House of Culture, an institution to be found in almost each village of Romania, changed in time. Taking off in the interwar period, as a state-driven policy, the house of culture was thought of by the government as a center for educating backward peasant masses. Later on, during socialism, it became a space and an institution for conservation of "authentic," "traditional," peasant culture; the house of culture gathered folkloric groups performing traditional music and dance, dressed up in traditional clothes; houses of culture were also an important element

for socialist propaganda. During the postsocialist period, many such houses of culture simply transformed into ballrooms and wedding halls, to be rented out against small fees payable at the village-hall, most of them losing the explicit educative function or the tradition-oriented characteristics. For more detailed comparative analysis of the House of Culture in socialism and postsocialism, see Donahoe and Habeck 2011.

16. Although it is primarily about sums of cash, the denomination of the cash gift is the same as for a gift in kind, *dar* or *cinste.*

17. The ritual rhymes given in the essay were collected in the area by Cristea (2007); I collected similar rhymes at the weddings I have attended, the form and content of such performances being fairly standard all over the area.

18. The intoned verses in Romanian are:
Cinstiți meseni,
După cum ați văzut,
Cinstiții tineri
Cu socri dimpreună
S-au sculat și ne-au servit
Cu mai multe feluri de bucate,
Bine pregătite și bine servite.
Este o poveste veche
Că bucatele bine pregătite
Trăbuiesc și plătite.
Fiecare, ceea ce va vrea,
Câte-o mia, câte o vițea,
Bani câți va vrea.
Și puțini luăm
Dar nici de mulți nu ne spăriem
Cât timp avem, stăm și-i numărăm.

19. Dumnezeu sa-si verse harul
Sa le inmiiasca darul.

20. Lor îndulcește-le sufletul
Ca să vie cu darul,
Îmbună-le inima
Și le sloboade mâna
Să poată nașii cinsti

21. Approximate amounts can be easily calculated because money-gifts are usually standard.

22. In order to grasp the change, we can think in terms of the cost of a car (Dacia, the premier Romanian brand); in 2011, the couple could afford six cars from the money-gift, compared with only half a car of the same brand in 1980.

References

Beck, Sam. 1979. *Transylvania: The Political Economy of a Frontier* (Ph.D. diss., University of Massachusetts Amherst).

Bell, Catherine. 1992. *Ritual Theory, Ritual Practice.* Oxford: Oxford University Press.

Bernea, Ernest. 1967. Nunta în Țara Oltului. Încercare de sociologie românească, in Vol. colectiv *Studii de folclor și literatură,* București: EP.

Bourdieu, Pierre. 1990. *The Logic of Practice.* Stanford, CA: Stanford University Press.

———. 1997. "Marginalia—Some Additional Notes on the Issue of the Gift." In *The Logic of the Gift: Toward an Ethic of Generosity,* ed. Alan D Schrift, 231–244. London: Routledge.

Chelcea, Ion. 1932. Câteva constatări asupa caracterului psihologic al moților, *Societatea de mâine, revistă socială economică* 9, no. 6: 77–79.

Ciomac, Ion Luca. 1933. *Probleme economice din Munții Apuseni și ai Maramureșului.* Cluj: Tipografia Națională.

Ciomac, Ion Luca, and Valeriu Popa-Neacșa. 1936. *Cercetări asupra stărilor economice din Munții Apuseni.* București: Editura Universul.

Cristea, Avram. 2007. *Obiceiuri și datini din județul Alba—schiță monografică.* Alba Iulia: Unirea.

Csucsuja, Istvan. 1998. *Istoria pădurilor din Transilvania. 1848–1914.* Cluj: Presa Universitară Clujeană.

Donahoe, Brian, and Joachim Otto Habeck, eds. 2011. *Reconstructing the House of Culture: Community, Self, and the Makings of Culture in Russia and Beyond.* New York: Berghahn Books.

Douglas, Mary, and Baron Isherwood. 1978. *The World of Goods: Towards an Anthropology of Consumption.* New York: Routledge.

Edelman, Murray. 1969. "Escalation and Ritualization of Political Conflict", *American Behavioral Scientist* 13(2): 231–246.

Frâncu, Teofil, and Gheorghe Candrea. 1888. *Românii din Munții Apuseni (Moții).* București: Luis.

Goody, Jack. 1973. "Bridewealth and Dowry in Africa and Eurasia." In *Bridewealth and Dowry,* Jack Goody and Stanley J. Tambiah, 1–58. Cambridge: Cambridge University Press.

———. 1976. *Production and Reproduction: A Comparative Study of the Domestic Domain.* Cambridge: Cambridge University Press.

Gudeman, Stephen 2008. *Economy's Tension.* New York: Berghahn Books.

Hann, Chris. 2014. "The Economistic Fallacy Under and After Socialism." *Economy and Society* 43(4): 626–649.

Jianu, Angela. 2009. "Women, Dowries, and Patrimonial Law in Old Regime Romania (c. 1750–1830)." *Journal of Family History* 34, no. 2: 189–205.

Kideckel, David. 1993. *The Solitude of Collectivism: Romanian Villagers to the Revolution and Beyond.* Ithaca, NY: Cornell University Press.

Kligman, Gail. 1988. *The Wedding of the Dead: Ritual, Poetics, and Popular Culture in Transylvania.* Berkeley: University of California Press.

Kligman, Gail, and Katherine Verdery. 2011. *Peasants under Siege: The Collectivization of Romanian Agriculture, 1949–1962.* Princeton, NJ: Princeton University Press.

Meițoiu, Ioan. 1969. *Spectacolul nunților—monografie folclorică.* București: Comitetul de Stat pentru Cultură și Artă.

Parry, Jonathan, and Bloch, Maurice. 1989. "Introduction: Money and the Morality of Exchange." In *Money and the Morality of Exchange*, ed. Jonathan Parry and Maurice Bloch, 1–32. Cambridge: Cambridge University Press.

Peteanu, Claudia S. 2008. "Setting the Dowry in the Land of Năsăud in the Second Half of the Nineteenth Century." *Romanian Journal of Population Studies* 2, no. 2: 61–71.

Pichler, Robert. 2009. "Migration, Ritual and Ethnic Conflict: A Study of Wedding Ceremonies of Albanian Transmigrants from the Republic of Macedonia." *Ethnologia Balkanica* 13: 211–229.

Pine, Frances, and Haldis Haukanes. 2004. "Ritual and Everyday Consumption Practices in the Czech and Polish Countryside: Conceiving Modernity Through Changing Food Regimes." *Anthropological Journal on European Culture* 12: 103–130.

Rheubottom, David. 1980. "Dowry and Wedding Celebrations in Yugoslav Macedonia." In *The Meaning of Marriage Payments*, ed. John L. Comaroff. London: Academic Press.

Sărbători şi Obiceiuri. Transilvania. Vol. 3. 2003. Academia Română. Institutul de Etnografie si Folclor C. Brăiloiu. Bucureşti: Editura Enciclopedică.

Sárkány, Mihály. 1983. "A lakodalom funkciójának megváltozása falun." *Ethnographia* 94: 279–285.

Simmel, Georg. 1978 [1900]. *The Philosophy of Money*. London: Routledge & Kegan Paul.

Suciu, Petru. 1929. *Tara Moţilor. Regiunea industrei lemnului*. Cluj: Editura de ziare.

Vasile, Monica. 2012. "A Typology of Godkinship Practices." *Annuaire Roumain d'Anthropologie* 49.

Vintilă-Ghiţulescu, Constanţa. 2007. "'The Father and His Daughter': Marriage Strategies and Issues in Romanian Society (18th Century)." *Romanian Journal of Population Studies* 1 (1–2): 56–67.

Werner, Cynthia. 1997. "Marriage, Markets and Merchants: Changes in Wedding Feasts and Household Consumption Patterns in Rural Kazakhstan." *Culture and Agriculture* 19 (1/2): 6–13.

———. 1999. "The Dynamics of *Feasting* and Gift Exchange in Rural Kazakstan." In *Contemporary Kazaks: Cultural and Social Perspectives*, ed. Ingvar Svanberg, 47–72. London: Curzon.

6

"We don't have work.
We just grow a little tobacco."

Household Economy and Ritual Effervescence in a Macedonian Town

MILADINA MONOVA

This chapter explores changes within the household economy in the post-socialist, post-Yugoslav town of Prilep, and the way in which these transformations mirror changes in social and ritual relationships.[1] Specifically, I examine the production of tobacco and the *slava* ritual, which here refers to the celebration of the household patron saint.[2] I juxtapose the household-based "tobacco-growing configuration" with the "*slava* feasting configuration" and find them to be almost perfectly congruent. In a context of economic hardship, former factory workers holding casual jobs, often within the grey economy, retreat into the household economy, and therefore rely more on kinship and friendship relationships than they ever did during socialism. When I asked families "Who comes to your *slava*?" and "Who works tobacco with you?" the answer I invariably received was: "The closest" (*najbliski*). Close relatives (*rodnini*), friends (*drugari*), and neighbors (*komsi*) are typically amalgamated in this category.

The celebration of the household patron saint is called "house *slava*" (*kukjna slava*) and the home-grown and home-processed tobacco is called "home tobacco" (*domasen tutun*). Both are indoor activities in opposition to outdoor ones that do not involve exclusively "the closest." Tobacco green leaf cultivation is a market-oriented, contractual activity, belonging to the sphere of "private work" (*rabota na privatno*) in opposition to "state work" (*rabota na drzavno*), or "outdoor work" (*rabota nadvor*). These terms reveal the specificity of Yugoslav socialism, which left some room for small-scale private business. Tobacco growing is a labor-intensive activity that brings together all members of the household, including children, and mobilizes all those relatives, neighbors, and friends who "care for" (*se grizi*) the members of the household, potentially if not necessarily in reality. The same cast of actors is drawn together for the *slava* ritual. The household (generally a married couple, i.e., the head of the household and his wife) is at the core of both the tobacco-growing configuration and the *slava* feasting configuration, which comprise friends and neighbors as well as kin.

Through an examination of the tobacco-growing configuration and the *slava* feasting configuration of several households, I also draw attention to inequalities, conflicts, and cleavages at multiple levels of Macedonian society, some inherited from the socialist past, others rather newly constituted. Today's increasing social differentiation and postsocialist dispossession are new, but they have been shaped by older divisions rooted partly in the industrialization of the socialist city and partly in the domestic group and village community of the preindustrial era. In the past, rituals enabled villagers, families, and kin to restore peaceful relationships and perform openness (Rheubottom 1976: 23) and to balance social and gender inequalities (Obrębski 2001a, 2001b, 2002). In the present, in the urban context, with much smaller households, ritual activity has become more diverse and innovative, centering on the relationships that ensure household viability and exemplifying what Gudeman (2008) calls "economy's tension."

I begin by tracing the rural-urban migration process that remodeled the city of Prilep during socialism, focusing on the inhabitants of one suburb who were among the last to leave their villages at the beginning of the 1970s. This period of migration was a defining moment that has shaped the status of these migrants and their descendants down to the present day. Each wave of migration has to be considered in relation to the cycles of growth and recession that marked socialist industrialization. The villagers who moved to Prilep from the region of Borovo between 1970 and 1973 found a city that was already suffocating with growing unemployment and no housing facilities.[3] The newcomer *Borovtsi* settled in the northern district of the city by building illegal houses and resisted attempts by the municipality to send them back to their villages. Earlier peasant migrants (especially those arriving in the first wave after 1944) had obtained jobs in newly built factories or in public administration, and had been offered cheap housing and private agricultural land (Monova 2001, 2002). Those who arrived after 1970 had no such possibilities and were forced to rely more upon their household economy.

"In Prilep, there is tobacco since there is God!" I was told when I asked for how many generations people had grown tobacco. Tobacco is a two-century-old cash crop for urban dwellers as well as for many farmers in the region. During socialism, many urbanites gradually abandoned tobacco farming in favor of factory work, given the attractions of fixed working hours and a guaranteed salary. From time to time, they grew "just a little tobacco" (*samo malce tutunce*) to fund a daughter's wedding or to build another story for the house. However, the newcomers from Borovo, who gave this name to their new urban neighborhood, remained dependent upon cash cropping. The tobacco leaf sustained both household economy and ritual life.

In 2009 and 2010 house-based tobacco growing expanded dramatically in Prilep and throughout the region.[4] The government decision to increase the subsidy from 45 denars to 60 denars (1 Euro) per kilo, coupled with experts' predictions of higher prices, provoked a sudden rush into the sector.[5] Households considered it worthwhile to invest their labor in tobacco once again, even though this work had been unpopular in socialist days. My household survey in 2009–2010 revealed an interesting tendency. When asked about their spending patterns, or how their incomes were allocated to different budgets, heads of households systematically placed ritual celebrations among their top priorities. There were bitter complaints about indebtedness, shortage of money, and persisting unemployment.[6] Yet people did not want to reduce the number of such celebrations, which they classified as both "expensive" and "unavoidable." "One could postpone the payment of a bill, but not an important calendar day such as *slava*, Christmas, Easter or Forgiveness," I was told.

I argue that seasonal activity in growing tobacco is more than just a rational response to the cyclical social demand for cash. If more and more families in Prilep combine casual jobs and factory work with house-based tobacco growing, this is also because they need to invest more heavily in rituals, which in turn secure the social relationships that provide access to jobs in the industrial sphere and the wider economy. Kinship and friendship bonds, or "the closest," are drawn ever more intensively into labor relationships—not only on the shop floor of the factory but also inside the house while processing tobacco. In turn, the *slava*—the most important household-based ritual—becomes the celebration of "the closest" and reaffirms and reinvigorates this particular web of relationships. In a context where former peasants have become former workers, for many, the household economy is the last refuge against poverty.

Borovski District: A Socialist Shanty Town

A city of craftspeople and merchants in the late Ottoman Empire, Prilep was transformed during the first half of the twentieth century into a leading tobacco-producing and tobacco-manufacturing center (Bunteski 1998; Koneski 2004).[7] Rural-urban migration intensified under socialism, responding to the demand for labor in the newly constituted industrial fields.[8] Borovski district took shape in the early 1970s as the last neighborhood in Prilep to emerge from this migration. Children and women were the first to leave the remote villages in Borovo. When they followed, the male heads of household struggled to find the connections that would "give a state job" and facilitate the acquisition of land legally designated for agriculture to construct a new house and reunite the family. Most houses remain unregistered and unfinished to this day, "naked" with their unfinished floors and bare walls. In contrast to the solid houses built by earlier migrants in the southern suburbs, in the north, most houses were built with adobe-like material, whitewashed, and randomly erected over what were officially designated as agricultural lands. The municipality initially demolished the illegal flimsy dwellings and attempted to send the Borovtsi back to their villages. Step by step these policies were relaxed, partly for humanitarian reasons and partly because state bureaucrats could line their pockets with bribes. At the time of my fieldwork in 2009–2010, the Borovski district of Prilep consisted of about 300 houses built by families from fourteen villages. The average household comprised two adult generations of unskilled workers, either officially unemployed or combining temporary employment in factories with jobs in the grey economy, tobacco growing, pensions, and support from relatives working abroad.

Although socialist Yugoslavia had the highest rate of registered unemployment in Europe during the 1980s, few Western scholars paid much attention to it.[9] The Yugoslavian "third way," "market socialism," and "self-management" by workers were widely acclaimed, and only a few observers pointed out the country's problems (Ramet 1985). After the dismantling of the state and the explosion of ethnic conflicts, Western analysts suddenly replaced their earlier rosier assessment of Yugoslavia based on its workers' councils with the much less attractive one of ethnic and national strife. The Yugoslav wars were explained with the formulas of a "new exceptionalism" (Woodward 1995: xiv) rooted in ancient ethnic hatreds and a Balkan culture of blood revenge.

Susan Woodward (1995) proposes an alternative framework to explain Yugoslavia's disintegration by highlighting the structural problem of unemployment in the Yugoslav socialist economy and the regional imbalances that were accentuated by decentralization (reinforced by the Constitution of 1974). In a survey conducted in Macedonia in 1981, respondents ranked unequal employment opportunities as "the first and most painful source of social inequality," more important than the problems of housing and education (Kimov, cited by Woodward 1995: 321). Faced with rising industrial unrest, in autumn 1989, the federal governments of Yugoslavia and the United States, together with the International Monetary Fund, negotiated a new financial aid package to address the state's debt problem. The new package stipulated sweeping economic reforms, including a currency devaluation, a wage freeze, sharp cuts in government spending, and the elimination of socially owned, worker-managed companies. This "shock therapy" was implemented in January 1990 and real wages promptly collapsed. State revenues that should have gone as transfer payments to the republics and provinces were redirected to service the foreign debt. Shortly afterward, war brought the rapid end of the Yugoslav federation. For former Yugoslav republics with most of their markets inside the federation, the dismantlement of the state signaled the collapse of their economy.

Tobacco: Between the Factory and the Field

The tobacco industry has been the major source of employment in Prilep for many generations.[10] Together with state timber, mining, and quarrying enterprises, the state tobacco monopoly integrated Borovtsi into the world of waged labor, as it had integrated many others in the past (Monova 2002). Once the heart of the city, by 2009 the "Tutunski Kombinat" was a faint shadow of its former glory. The state had become the principal proprietor of the factory after buying out its debt (110 million Euros in 2006). The state and the municipality together own most of the land around the city, which they rent to landless urban families for their crop production, while others cultivate their own land in villages nearby. The state also owns the irrigation system that supplies the entire region. Until 2002, the factory held a monopoly on the purchase of raw tobacco from small-scale producers. During the late socialist period, there were not more than 12,550 families growing tobacco in the municipality of Prilep.[11] Before 1990, the state-owned processing plants and now-closed cigarette factory employed a combined total of about 3,000 persons. Following restructuring, this figure has fallen to around 680 permanent and seasonal workers. After the liberalization of the sector and by 2009, six new companies opened in competition with the Tutunski Kombinat. Although practically in a state of bankruptcy, Tutunski continues to be the preferred purchaser for many farmers because it gives the highest prices under contract.[12]

Between June and October the city shows a colorful face, from bright green to golden yellow. Outside the historical center, most houses drape their external walls with green garlands of tobacco suspended on wooden frames. When this sun-curing is completed, the leaves are transferred for first airing and humidification, either to the empty upper floor of the house or inside the garage, which is where most families stock the leaves and strip them from the stalk according to their size. Walking on the street is an occasion to take pride in one's skills and compare the quality of one's own tobacco with that of the neighbors. People comment in the manner of art critics that "*the best work*" results from selecting leaves of the same size and successfully aligning them densely, like "*pearls in a necklace.*" These leaves are "*a beauty,*" "like silk" (*smila*) because they have been stripped by hand and not with a machine. They dry to a color that is "*yellow like gold*" and will not turn brown. Further distinctions are drawn between "home tobacco," meaning that which is grown on family or rented land, and "state tobacco," meaning that which is processed through wage-labor in the Kombinat. Producing tobacco at home is considered "more clean work," while factory employment in this sector is spoken of as dirty and dangerous.

Traditionally and even today, the tobacco harvest has served as a unit of measurement in comparing the worth and wealth of different houses built in different periods. Thus a single-story house is worth "two tobaccos," which means two harvests or two seasons of tobacco growing. Each additional floor is formulated as "one tobacco." Most of the best houses in Prilep were built, furnished, and then extended up to three stories between the 1950s and the end of the 1970s. Unskilled industrial workers like the Borovtsi continued to grow tobacco, but irregularly and with diminishing frequency. Since the workday for the majority of white-collar and factory workers ran from 7 A.M. to 2 P.M., most people had the time to pursue an agricultural activity or other private business in the latter part of the day. In the local cultural setting "home-grown tobacco" belongs to the sphere of private/domestic life. It is an "indoor" activity meant to support, to sustain, and to rescue what Gudeman and Rivera (1990) call "the base." On the ritual side, the house *slava* accomplishes the same goal.

Evolution of the Household Structure and *Slava* Relationships

Thanks to the studies of Józef Obrębski and David Rheubottom, we have detailed accounts of rural social structure in Macedonia in the years before socialism, including economy, ritual and kinship ideology.[13] While Obrębski (1932–1933, 1977, 2002) emphasized social and class inequalities at the level of the village community, Rheubottom (1971, 1976) focused on conflicts and cleavages within the domestic group, where agnatic kinship was the fundamental principle. In the traditional multifamily households, sons' wives were under the authority of the *domacinka*, the wife of the patriarchal head, the *domacin*; the youngest daughter-in-law was of inferior status to the eldest daughter-in-law. The tensions and inequalities led ineluctably to separation and partition, for which women generally were blamed (they were accused of sowing discontent and disunion between father, sons, and brothers). Similarly to Obrębski, who pointed out "the individualism of the conjugal family," Rheubottom stressed the intrinsic dichotomy in the joint-family system between the interests of the household of marriage and the household interests within a group governed by the institution of "domacinship" (Rheubottom 1971: 48). Conflicts arising from task and kinship obligations find resolution only when the father and the husband is also the head of the household, or when the wife and the mother is *domacinka* (Rheubottom 1971: 288).

During socialism, wage-labor provided resources in rural districts, but not enough to meet the household budget fully; land was an insurance against unemployment (Rheubottom 1971: 109). This maintained inter-dependencies within the patriarchal family between household members working the land and those in the city, under the rule of the head of the household. Wages are an indicator of a household's nonviability, and in his survey Rheubottom showed that households with low per capita landholding were more likely to have at least one member working in the city for wages. Among wage earners, he captured an emerging feature giving rise to yet another tension within the household—the tendency of the wage-earner toward semi-independence.

Rheubottom distinguished between two types of celebrations among rural Macedonians: events occurring irregularly such as weddings and baptisms, and annual observances such as Christmas, All Souls' Day, and the *slava*. In Prilep today, and particularly among Borovtsi, the house *slava* is said to be the most significant, and its importance for maintaining good relationships with "the closest" is overtly stated. In the past as today, the core of the house *slava* is the conjugal unit composed of the head of the household (*domacin*) and his wife (*domacinka*). Unlike other family celebrations that illustrate a clear patrilateral bias (e.g., on All Souls' Day wives visit the tombs of their husband's deceased parents and only visit those of their own parents if time permits), the house *slava* posits relative equality within the relationship between the *domacin* and *domacinka*, or what is also called "the father's side and the mother's side." Although the *slava* is inherited from the male side and attests to the household's patrifiliation, the ideology of the ritual is overtly bilateral, addressing agnates from both sides. Priority is given to the natal households of both the husband and the wife. Siblings and parents from both sides are the most prominently represented guests. The second most important category of guests comprises uncles, aunts, and cousins (usually with heavier representation from the male side). The third most important is the segment of friends. During socialism, the number of *slava* celebrations observed within a descent group multiplied with urbanizations and household division. People explain these "changes in the tradition" as a result of modernization, full employment, and sons willing to hold their own *slava* feast instead of waiting to inherit the responsibility at their father's death.

Many households in Borovski district were founded by sons who had separated from their father's household, and a *slava* is still typically held to mark this moment of fission (cf. Hammel 1968: 23). In principle, the eldest brother is the legitimate heir of the *slava* of his father. He can initiate a *slava* of his own only if he proceeds to partition, in which case a younger brother will take over the patron saint of the original household. The son who "takes over" (*zemaa*) the father's *slava* is generally the one who will inherit the house and take care of the aging parents. It is an arrangement made between brothers; or between the parents and a married daughter who returns to her natal household with her husband and children. Today it is also very common in Prilep for a married grandchild to move to a grand-parent's house under the agreement that he or she will inherit the "house (in exchange) for care." Once a household's *slava* has been transferred to a younger family member, the former patriarch no longer holds his own feast, but attends those of his sons, sons-in-law, and married grandchil-dren. Today, households headed by younger brothers often celebrate their own *slava*, choosing their own patron saint with or without consulting a priest. Very often the saint comes in a dream giving advice, or directly rec-ommending himself as protector.

When one of the sons has taken over the father's *slava*, the son and his wife become the feast-holding unit for the descent group. The old father is then said to have "his *slava* taken over" (*slavata mu e zemena*). This is said to be "now normal" when the (eldest) son marries, and the senior couple gains the new role of affine (*svat*), or father- and mother-in-law, to the bride. Although the *slava* still celebrates the whole family, this reshuffle affects authority and hierarchy inside the house. The first feasting segment is no longer composed of the old *domacin*'s and *domacinka*'s siblings and parents, but those of the young couple. In practice, from the male side there are not spectacular changes—the son invites his parents as the most im-portant guests, and senior members of the agnatic group still attend, as they did when the elder *domacin* held the feast. However, now the son invites his friends instead of those of his father. The main change in the recruitment of guests is from the female side—now priority is given to the daughter-in-law's siblings, parents, and close relatives instead of those of the elder *domacinka*. In all cases, invitation very much depends on the quality of the relationships between kin, whatever the degree of proximity. In general this taking over of the *slava* means budget autonomy for each household, but not deep changes in property relationships. In most cases, the senior couple retain ownership of the house and most of the land until death.

Household divisions carried out by sons and brothers inside the house are symbolized by modern urban architecture. Each floor is a separate do-mestic space in the house. After marriage, and especially after the birth of the first child, the son's household takes possession of an upper floor, which is almost a replica of the first one built years before by the senior generation. Each apartment contains a kitchen, bathroom, guestroom, sleeping rooms and—if possible—separate outside access. This partition is prepared several years before the son's wedding, and occurs as soon as the younger couple feels capable of making a living for itself. Among poorer families who live in the old one-story houses, household division is represented as it is in the villages—by the construction of a wall that divides the house and by the construction of extensions to add separate rooms, a kitchen and a bathroom (Rheubottom 1971: 34). A fence divides the courtyard into two parts, and a newly built gateway leads to the son's household. Through establishing which among the households living together under the same roof is the *slava*-holding unit, we can find out whether there is household division between father and sons. This information is crucial as it also explains why some of "the closest" participate in the tobacco-growing configuration while others do not.

Compared to the socialist period, another important change concerns the size of the household units. The joint family structure that was still common in the early socialist decades has been replaced by the nuclear family. However, these smaller units celebrate more *slavas* in their natal households, and therefore address more saints than in the past. Households may receive fewer guests at their own *slava*, but overall they take part in more *slava* celebrations than before. Celebrations are generally characterized as a "duty" that "one must respect" or "cannot omit." They are thought of as "expensive," even if the number of guests has declined in recent decades. During socialism it was customary to invite twenty to thirty people for dinner, while these days the average is ten to fifteen people. Only close kin and friends participate in, and, unlike the past (in the village), no one is expected to show up unless they have received an explicit invitation. The general rule is reciprocity: "if I visit him for his *slava* he visits me for mine" ("*komu si bil na slava kje ti dojdi*"). Occasionally, financial considerations lead households to dispense with the celebration of a *slava* and most of the name day celebrations of household members. Some families celebrate the name day (*slava na ime*) of the head of the household, or of a teenage child or grandchild, instead of the house *slava*. In this way, the household reduces its ritual costs but continues to venerate and receive the protection of a saint.

The number of guests is commented upon in the community, and there is an expectation that more prosperous households will invite more guests and spend more cash on food and drinks. As reported by Rheubottom (1976: 21), "the lavishness of the display" is considered to please the saint, and it is of key importance socially. In Prilep, those who can afford the costs should offer guests beer rather than homemade wine; tonic and Coca-Cola rather than homemade fruit syrup; and salt cookies and sweets from the supermarket rather than one's own home-baked cakes. Among Borovtsi, the ritual meal features both purchased and homemade items in a way that highlights the housewife's culinary skills. The effervescence generated during a *slava* day reveals persistence and change. In Prilep, Saint Nicholas (19 December), the protector of waters, is the most celebrated house patron saint.[14] Preparations are demanding, especially for women, who often try to get a day off from work, visit the hairdresser, and buy some new clothes. The day begins early in the morning with a visit from the priest for the ritual blessings and sharing of the special *slava* bread (*kolac*). With some 3,000 households celebrating St. Nicholas and only seven priests to petition the saint, not everyone in Prilep is able to get a priest to come to their home, and some believers prefer to go one day earlier to the church to have their bread blessed. The dinner is the most important meal, the meal of "the closest." However, families offer lunch the day after the feast to guests who could not come for dinner because they were involved in another *slava* of St. Nicholas as guests of the first order of importance. The lunch is also of key importance for the third segment of friends that people prefer to see apart. Guests who come only on the following day are said to be visiting "on crutches."

Work Group and Ritual Group

Having charted changes in the household *slava* as a ritual celebration, let us return to the household as an economic unit. The core of the tobacco-growing configuration is the conjugal unit that sponsors a household *slava*—and vice versa. Among the individuals invited to the *slava* feast, we typically find the external members of the labor group. These are called "the closest," and they include nonkin. There is a tendency to form the same configuration on the shop floor of the factory: when one member gains employment, he or she gradually brings in others from the group. This residential unit hosts external participants when they are needed for productive tasks. They are recruited from a larger group of kin who may or may not have a common budget and common property, and may or may not live under the same roof. It generally includes neighbors and at least one friend who helps. If Ego's household is the core of the configuration, we can map his cooperative links to close kin on both sides—the husband's and the wife's. This group works together in key moments of the household's annual cycle.

As Cohen has shown in his study of tobacco-growing families in Taiwan under a state monopoly, this cash crop has specific consequences for family relations due to its heavy labor demands (Cohen 1976). In Prilep, during socialism, when relatively stable wage-labor employment gradually displaced household tobacco production, households could fission more easily, without regard to labor requirements. Today, tobacco cultivation is rendered more complicated by the dispersed nature of the domestic groups, many of which struggle to combine tobacco growing with factory work. The tobacco-growing configuration is formed for each productive cycle and is dissolved when the season is over and the profits have been divided. If no changes have occurred in the working status of its members, it may be recomposed for the following season, though some changes are likely. For example, if an adult son finds wage-labor employment during the season, he can withdraw from the configuration—either because he considers his new income enough for him and his conjugal unit, or because his new job does not allow him to participate in the successive phases of tobacco processing. Apart from contributing to production directly, members of the tobacco-growing configuration, especially friends and neighbors, may contribute to its performance indirectly, for example by taking care of children, lending money, or helping with housework in order to release another household member for tobacco-related tasks. The configuration functioned similarly under socialism, but tobacco growing has become more important with the general problems of the labor market. The Borovtsi have been familiar with the crop since the 1920s, and in Borovo it was actively promoted as the principal cash crop (in place of opium) by the socialist state. After steadily declining, both in the countryside and in the town, production has increased after the resumption of subsidies, since households see this crop as a low-risk investment to help them compensate for the loss of secure jobs and welfare entitlements.

Tobacco farming is a flexible enterprise. Because little capital investment is needed, it can be treated as an ad hoc arrangement rather than a lifelong commitment. To quote my informants when referring to the positive aspects of tobacco cropping: "the good thing about tobacco is that it does not require continuous care. One year you take it up, the next you drop it, and it is even better for your land to take a rest." In fact my survey showed that tobacco growing was not quite so occasional or temporary as people claimed, but discontinuity was common and it was evidently connected to the developmental cycle of the nuclear family and the variable nature of its external links.

Stefan's Family

The extended tobacco-growing configuration of Stefan exemplifies my argument concerning its congruence with the *slava* feasting configuration (see figure 6.1). His extensive net of *slava* relationships also shows that even as the average number of guests attending each feast has fallen compared to the feasts of the socialist period, the total number of *slavas* attended within a year among kin has considerably increased. The increased number of *slavas* that each house attends reflects the continued pattern of household division in the urban environment. At the same time, the fragmentation of households also leads to a multiplication of ritual celebrations that mobilize the same units within a given descent group. Although households appear to be economically independent, they continue to rely on the support and assistance of kin to ensure adequate income for each family.

I observed the tobacco-growing configuration of Stefan and his wife Maria in 2009–2010 during two tobacco seasons, and was able to gather rich supplementary information about all the houses involved and most of their individual members.

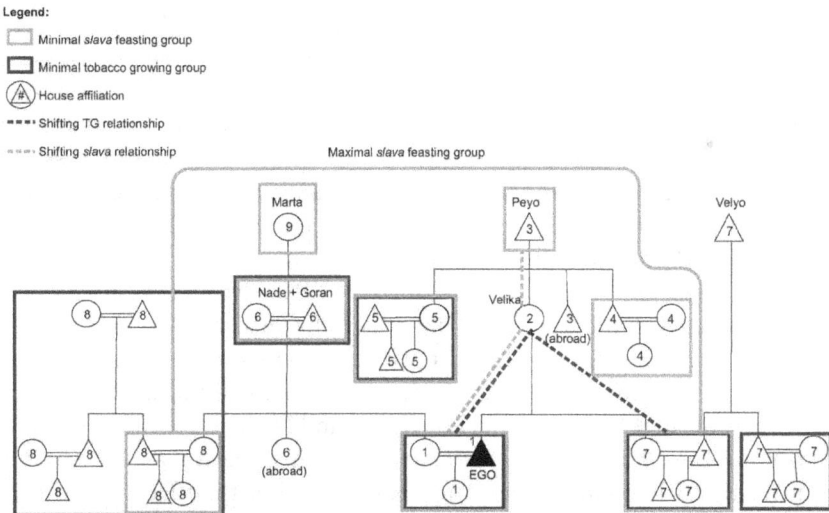

Figure 6.1. *Slava* feasting and tobacco-growing configurations.

The tobacco-growing configuration is drawn from nine houses, four of which comprise nuclear families (houses 1, 4, 5, 6); three are occupied by single people (2, 3, 9), and two contain joint families—the parents, and the nuclear families of their two married sons (7, 8). As a general rule, every house grows its own tobacco, but exceptions occur among individuals living alone and joint families. Among the single individuals, house 2 is in a shifting tobacco-growing relationship with houses 1 and 7; houses 3 and 9 do not grow tobacco. House 6 also presents an anomaly because it still counts an adult daughter who is working abroad as a household member, even though she is not active in either tobacco-growing or *slava* celebrations. House 7 presents the most complex tobacco-growing configuration. This house contains 3 nuclear families: the widowed father Velyo and his two adult sons with their wives and children. Velyo does not grow tobacco or help his sons; the two sons grow separately; and one of the sons gains some assistance from his wife's parents. In contrast, the other house that contains 3 nuclear families (house 8) works together in *zaednica* (cooperation) and therefore constitutes a single tobacco-growing group. In summary: Stefan's economic and ritual configurations are made up from nine houses, which include thirteen to fifteen nuclear families, depending on how individuals who live and work abroad are counted. Of these, five houses or six families are tobacco-growing units.

The diagram also indicates the mutual interdependence of three generations in most cases. The oldest individuals—Marta, Peyo, and Velyo—are in their late sixties to early eighties. They do not grow tobacco, but provide important financial contributions in the form of pensions, individual economic initiatives, and land. The middle generation, in their fifties, were predominantly factory workers during the socialist period, but only two of them succeeded in maintaining jobs during postsocialism. The youngest generation, in their late twenties and early thirties, feels pressure to establish their financial independence, but needs assistance from others to grow tobacco, care for children, and build their houses. In total, Stefan's network of "closest" relatives includes twenty-six adults who live in Prilep, but only seven of them held permanent jobs in 2009–2010. Five were factory workers, one was a hospital nurse, and one was a pharmacist.

Among the houses in Stefan's network, his wife's parents' house (6) is exceptional in its prosperity. Maria's parents originate not in Borovo but in villages located on the rich plain. Goran and Nade moved to the city at the end of the 1950s. Two of their three daughters have married and one is a music teacher. Goran and Nade have been full-time factory workers continuously since socialist times. They have a spacious three-story house that they built in the 1970s in a prestigious suburb. They possess 13 decares (1.3 hectares) of excellent land on the outskirts of the city, where they also have a summer house. In a city where few possess more than five decares, Goran and Nade are wealthy. He does not work shifts and can leave his workplace before 2 P.M. Lacking additional labor resources, he and his wife concentrate on producing fruit and vegetables, both for the market and for the household. They resumed growing small quantities of tobacco with the help of a machine because the increase in the government subsidy justified the significant investment.

In addition to controlling land and other assets, the oldest adults in this sample all received pensions, while remaining economically active. Velyo, in his late sixties, earns a wage as a night watchman in his native village in Borovo, where he also collects and processes mushrooms that he sells dried in the Prilep market. Peyo, in his early eighties, is an officially registered beekeeper and honey producer, who benefits from a new European Union subsidy for this activity (formally registered in the name of his son). From her late husband, Marta inherited the equipment and the skills needed for distilling alcohol from grapes, which allows her to supplement her pension with payments in cash or kind. These three pensioners still own land and houses, even though in Peyo's case his sons have divided as far as their cash incomes are concerned. It follows that the senior generation is able to provide support to the increasingly impoverished younger generations.[15] For example, Peyo, Stefan's maternal grandfather, regularly gives cash to Stefan's mother and less regularly to his grandchildren; he allows Stefan and some of his other grandchildren (house 7) to farm his land; and he supplies all of his children and grandchildren with firewood. Peyo also recently presented one of his sons (house 4), who is more than fifty years old and who partitioned some twenty years ago, with a car, hoping to benefit from being driven back to his village during the honey season.

Thus Stefan's household receives land, money, and other resources from his maternal grandfather. From the wealthier parents of his wife, they receive beans, meat, and brandy, plus cash from the distillery business of her maternal grandmother, Marta. In addition, the social relationships that stem from Maria's native household are vital in disposing of the tobacco harvest at the best market conditions. Nonetheless, this household, too, is vulnerable. Two salaries and supplementary income from farming are insufficient to cover the medical expenses for Maria's mother, Nade, who has recently been afflicted by an "expensive disease."

Kinship Networks and *Slava* Relationships

The nine houses of Stefan's tobacco-growing configuration hold eight house *slavas* (see figure 6.2). Six of the *slavas* were inherited, and only two are new. The new *slavas* are St. George, celebrated by Stefan and Maria, and St. Michael, celebrated by Stefan's uncle in house 4. Of the six inherited celebrations, four are still being hosted by the eldest or middle generations, while two have been "taken over" by a married son of the youngest generation in the two houses with joint families. In house 8, the oldest son now celebrates the *slava*, while in house 7 it has passed to the youngest son. In both cases, the other families in the house attend the *slava* of the hosting family, and are counted as members of this family by the priest during his blessing ceremony.

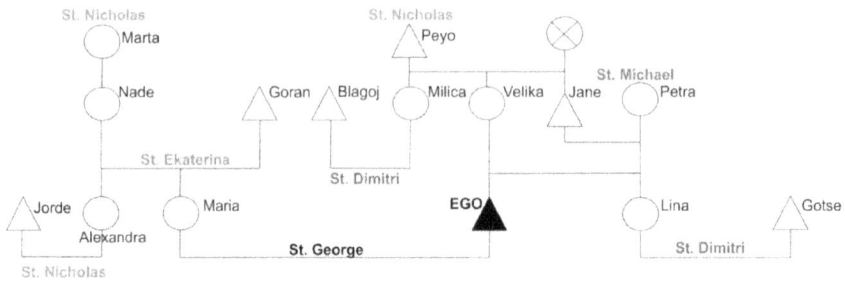

Figure 6.2. Household *slava* relationships.

Stefan and Maria attend seven *slavas* each year—four in his family (3, 4, 7) and three in hers (6, 8, 9). Stefan does not have any close relatives on his father's side. His widowed mother Velika (house 2) does not hold a *slava* in her house, but she is in a shifting *slava* relationship with her father and son. Velika presides over her father's *slava*, playing the role of the *domacinka*; she prepares all the meals for the feast and organizes the priest's visit. While Maria is the *domacinka* for Stefan's *slava*, Velika also helps substantially with the preparation of food and other arrangements. These arrangements are not only practical, but reflect traditional patterns whereby widows "return" to their father's houses, and in which mothers' labor and loyalty "belong" to their sons.

Like most other Borovitsi, Stefan and Maria face potential conflicts in deciding how to meet their social obligations of attending the *slavas* of their "closest." Three of the *slava* in which Stefan participates have St. Nicholas for their patron and two have St. Dimitri. On the day of St. Nicholas, Stefan and Maria should celebrate *slava* with Stefan's maternal grandfather (Peyo), Maria's maternal grandmother (Marta), and Maria's sister (Alexandra). On St. Dimitri, the couple should celebrate with Stefan's sister (Lina) and his maternal aunt (Milica).

On St. Nicholas the couple is therefore expected at three *slavas* where they are guests of the first order of importance. They resolve the potential conflict between their overlapping commitments by alternating the order of attendance each year between dinner on the first day and lunch on the second day at Peyo's and Alexandra's *slavas*; even though their relation to Marta is equally close, they always visit her during the first day of slava for coffee and sweets. The arrangements for the St. Dimitri *slavas* are a little simpler: Stefan and Maria always attend his sister's feast first because she is a relative of first importance, and visit his aunt for lunch the day after because, in this case, they are guests of secondary importance.

Other individuals resolve the overlap differently. For example, Peyo has four children, seven grandchildren (two of whom are married), and four great-grandchildren. He attends four *slavas* per year—those of two children and two grandchildren. He has two children who do not have a *slava*: Velika, already mentioned, and a son who lives abroad; Peyo's grandchildren and great-grandchildren through this son are not part of the local *slava* or tobacco configurations. Since his wife passed away, Peyo no longer visits the *slavas* of his wife's agnates. Nevertheless, though he has lost some connections at the level of his generation, he has gained new *slava* occasions among grandchildren who have married and hold feasts of their own. Consequently, each year Peyo hears the priest petition a saint for him on five occasions, including his own *slava*. Four different patron saints are petitioned: St. Nicholas, St. Archangel Michael, St. George, and St. Dimitri (the last is the patron of the household of his oldest daughter and that of his only married granddaughter). Although he has the same overlapping house *slava* invitations for St. Dimitri as his grandson Stefan, Peyo prioritizes the dinner party of his daughter's household and visits his granddaughter for lunch the next day.

Velyo, the widowed father-in-law of Stefan's sister, lives under the same roof as his two married sons and their children. He has given his *slava* to his youngest son's household, which occupies the second floor of a shared house, while his oldest son, whose family occupies the first floor of the house, does not want to have a *slava*. Now in his late sixties, Velyo attends only two *slavas* per year—those held by his sister and his younger son. It is possible that, when male or female grandchildren marry and move out, he will attend more *slavas* like Maria's grandmother, Marta. Marta attends six *slavas* per year—those held by her two daughters and four married granddaughters. These examples reveal the importance of the domestic cycle and household structure, but actual outcomes are determined by many further contingencies. Younger people are generally more likely than are their parents or grandparents to issue and receive invitations to the *slavas* of nonkin (neighbors and friends). As shown in the following example, invitations to the *slavas* of nonkin are not based on friendship alone, but reflect the key roles played by those who are invited in a household's tobacco-growing configuration.

One Tobacco Season with Stefan

Within the large tobacco-growing configuration described above, let us now look more closely at Stefan's tobacco-growing configuration and the three persons who formed the core of its activities in 2010: Stefan, his wife Maria, and his mother Velika, a widow who lives alone in her own house. Stefan and Maria do not live in Borovski district, but close to the city center. They did not grow tobacco until 2010, although since childhood they had periodically helped their parents and relatives to pick and string leaves. They had not anticipated working with tobacco in the first years of their marriage but came under financial pressure when they took a bank loan to buy a house and had a baby. "That's how we got stuck in here," Stefan told me. He worked abroad for one year (as a cleaner on a cruise liner for 600 Euros per month), giving up a "good place" in the administration of a textile mill, where he had earned almost 200 Euros per month.[16] Maria is a worker on the shop floor at the same factory and earns 100 Euros per month, the basic wage for an unskilled worker in the textile industry. A combined income of 300 Euros is insufficient, but the maritime work was not a long-term solution for a young couple with a baby. When Stefan returned to Prilep he had to wait six months before friends in his former factory found a vacant position for him "down there on the shop floor," at the bottom of the hierarchy. It was a humiliating situation, he says, in part because it meant working at the level of those he had formerly recruited, including his wife and his brother-in-law.

As a result of these difficulties, in the winter of 2009–2010, following the example of many other urban families, Maria and Stefan decided they would grow tobacco in the 2010 season. Experts had predicted on television that the demand for raw tobacco on the world market would increase, so Maria and Stefan calculated that the investment, especially with the increased government subsidy, was sure to pay off. They knew they would not "make a profit" (*napraim profit*), but at least they would get "a coin or more" for themselves.[17] For the necessary land and labor, they turned first to Stefan's mother, Velika.

At the time that Stefan and Maria decided to try tobacco growing, Velika was working in an illegal sewing workshop (which was officially bankrupt), and had not been paid for the last seven months. The only reason she had not dropped this job was her anxiety that, if she did so, she would lose her last chance of recovering what she was due.

Velika really wanted to find legal employment to see her through to the age of retirement and to cover her health insurance. She had eighteen years of work experience with the Tutunski Kombinat as a contract seasonal worker, and six years full-time experience as a cleaner at a state-owned textile factory that closed down in 2006. After 2006, she worked in five different textile workshops "sometimes with, sometimes without a contract." According to Velika's experience, employers seldom offer contracts to middle-aged women like herself on the grounds that these women have husbands and children to support them and will not "die from starvation." To make ends meet, she relied mainly on support from her elderly father

Peyo, whom she helped with washing, cooking, and cleaning, and on money sent by her youngest brother, who worked in Germany.

The 2009 season was considered to be the best since socialist times, stimulating even more urban households to invest in tobacco for the coming season of 2010. Velika decided to drop her unpaid job in the workshop and followed her son's suggestion to grow tobacco with him on land that she had previously worked with her daughter. She had been helping her daughter on a small scale, but in 2010 the income derived from more intense cultivation would help to support Stefan's family. Patriarchal ideology lay behind Velika's decision: "Because my son decided to start growing, and a mother belongs to the family of her son. My daughter—she has her own mother-in-law and her own family" (see figure 6.3).

The land that Velika had cultivated with her daughter in 2009 belonged to her father Peyo, who agreed that in 2010 priority should be given to Stefan, the male child.[18] Maria and Stefan had initially tried to find another piece of land that was accessible by foot (while pushing a cart) from their house, but they could not afford to rent a plot of the necessary quality. Maria's parents were also unable to help the couple due to medical bills and the educational expenses of Maria's youngest sister. Thus they decided to use Peyo's land despite the additional complications posed by its distance from their house and the negotiations that were necessary with other family members. In 2010, Stefan's sister continued to grow tobacco, but on rented land further away from her house. Although mildly inconvenient, the rent was affordable and the shifting arrangements caused little tension or disagreement between the siblings. The greater source of tension every season

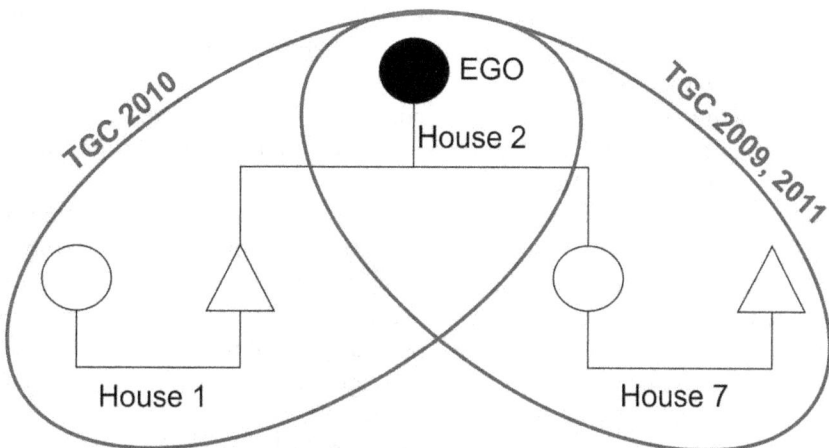

Figure 6.3. Changes in a tobacco-growing configuration over three years.

occurs in the official negotiations that must be undertaken with Velika's brother (house 4) who will inherit the land from Peyo and therefore has the right to refuse to let his niece and nephew work the land, even though he does not want to grow tobacco there himself.

Stefan and Maria faced another problem related to their lack of land at the beginning of the growing season. Urban families that produce tobacco on a modest scale generally avoid purchasing seedlings from specialist farmers, and instead make their own seedbeds in the garden of their house or a patch of wasteland. Neither Stefan's nor Velika's garden, however, had enough space for the required quantity of seedlings. Velika eventually planted her seedlings in an abandoned courtyard of a neighbor's house. Seedlings require sixty days of care, and when one has sown in an illegal place, this is a period of great anxiety.

At the beginning of June, before the start of the harvest season, Maria was extremely concerned as to how they would manage to combine full-time factory work with the urgent tasks of the harvest and looking after their little girl, who was ordinarily cared for by the neighbors. In the past, some socialist factories had paid no heed to workers' absenteeism at harvest time, but the tasks have been radically affected by increased discipline in the factories and a decline in the size of the family labor force. Maria's shifts changed every week, and only Velika was fully committed to tobacco farming. The family's ability to balance factory work, tobacco-growing, and childcare was complicated by an additional factor: Stefan's and Maria's house was undergoing urgent renovation (carried out free of charge by Stefan's closest friend), and tobacco-processing tasks had to be concentrated at Velika's house. Stefan, Maria, and Velika had to manage all of the work on their own because members of the larger configuration could stop by to offer their help only rarely, as they were themselves growing tobacco or working away from Prilep.

To make matters more complicated, Velika was unexpectedly offered a job in September, and she had to begin immediately. Some of the tobacco-growing tasks, including some of the stringing, had to be relocated to Stefan's house after all, and this contributed to a further fragmentation of the core working group and a heavier burden of work for each member. Meanwhile Maria needed to spend more time at her own house to prepare her daughter for school. During the weeks when Maria worked night and afternoon shifts, the daily harvest work was divided between the house of her mother-in-law and her own, even though the latter meant an additional thirty minutes for the labor of pushing the cart.

Velika's new job was not easy. She was hired (thanks to the connections of her son) as a seamstress to work on a heavy textile-weaving machine and had only a one-month probationary period to prove that she was capable of sewing seventy pieces per day. This month corresponded with the "fifth hand" of the tobacco harvest, when the tobacco of the finest quality is picked. Since this harvest fetches the highest price in the market, no grower can afford to reduce inputs at this stage. Maria and Velika were able to schedule nonoverlapping shifts, which was crucial for their ability to continue processing with a core group of just three persons. While stringing can be postponed until darkness and continued under the light of a lamp, the leaves in the field cannot wait. Similarly, stripping has to follow the harvest within a day: the green leaves will rot if they stay piled up for too long.

Stefan was aware of the problems that his mother's job would entail, but the opportunity was nonetheless too good to pass by. Then, unanticipated sources of stress appeared. After Stefan was hired in 2004, he had found positions for his wife (2006) and brother-in-law (2007). Velika's acceptance of the new job thus brought four close relatives working together in the same plant, and relations were not harmonious. Conflicts on the shop floor were quick to continue in the house. Velika stopped talking to her son for a more than a week, after he reprimanded her for "talking too much on the shop floor" and behaving "as if she were at home." (Yet the potential for conflict did not offset the benefits of finding work for other family members; in 2011 Stefan also found a job for his sister). The frenetic work rhythms continued until mid October, with exceptionally good weather creating a need for almost "seven hands" instead of the usual five. Velika stated at one point: "Honestly, in the morning I am praying God to send us frost, to relieve me of all this." When the last tobacco garlands were hung out for curing the three core members of this configuration were finally able to return to a more normal routine, each in his or her own house and giving priority to factory work. The last stage of processing takes place in November when the leaves are "ironed" and assembled into bails.

The quality of the dried tobacco is assessed by the tobacco processing company on the basis of a contract fixing the quantity of raw tobacco that the company will purchase from the primary producer, and stipulating an average price. Sometimes, buyers from private companies do not respect this written agreement and offer prices lower than those in the contract. In 2010, demand was not so high and prices were lower, the result being that the best price to be found was that of the state owned tobacco-processing company. Stefan and Maria were one of the lucky households to have contracted with the Kombinat, a deal that they owed to Maria's father, an old employee of the processing factory who had signed a contract for his daughter. Thanks to his good connections, the entire crop was labeled as the highest quality, so between January and March, Velika, Maria, and Stefan were able to dispose of their tobacco and receive the full subsidy. After paying back debts for the investments they had made and covering all cash outgoings, their profit was 600 Euros, which they divided into three equal parts. Stefan and Maria were disappointed by the final outcome, and the couple decided not to engage in growing the next year. Velika, in contrast, decided that she could not afford to withdraw: "200 Euros is 200 Euros, I cannot refuse." In 2011 she resumed work with the tobacco-growing configuration of her daughter.

Conclusion

In this chapter I have tried to show how changes in economy reflect both changes in labor and ritual relationships. In his study of conflict and cleavages in a Macedonian village during the early 1960s, David Rheubottom convincingly demonstrated how the family of marriage "emerges as a locus of primary loyalty" (Rheubottom 1971: 181). The same conclusion holds a few decades later in the urban context, where it is strongly reinforced. However, the indicators of household viability are reversed in the contemporary, postindustrial urban context. In the 1960s, Rheubottom found that the incidence of wage-labor in the city implied the nonviability of the household, which then lacked the labor it needed (1971: 237). Today in Prilep, household viability is indicated by the degree of involvement in tobacco growing. The less a household is involved in wage-labor, the more it is obliged to have recourse to small-scale family farming.

The emphasis on the house *slava* reflects the dependence on kinship relationships in house-based tobacco growing and processing. In fact, people draw on a much larger set of relationships than with those who contribute directly with their labor and attend the house *slava.* These persons may include a relative abroad who sends cash, or a friend at home who carries out skilled work for the household without charge. Without this wider circle, the inner core of the tobacco-growing configuration would not suffice. But the house *slava* only recognizes and celebrates the contributions of "the closest" to a house's existence.

The dynamics within the tobacco-growing configuration reflect inequalities and power relationships between household members, in terms of status, gender, and generation. By contrast, the *slava* allows the staging of equality and solidarity, continuity and peace. In a sense, it validates the entrenched inequalities of the wider tobacco-growing configuration, even as it acknowledges the participation of all those who support the house that organizes the ritual. The transformations of the ritual reflect the fact that households have become smaller and more fragmented. The *slava* has come to reaffirm the strength of the few relations that really matter. It offers ritual compensation to those who do not directly profit from the redistribution of material wealth and reaffirms hierarchical positions within what people call "the closest." Its closed nature and the diminishing number of guests testify to a fragile consensus and the ever-present threat of losing control over relationships that can no longer be taken for granted. These relations need to be reinforced, yet it is not only because people have less money that they invite fewer people but also because their basic relationships have become less cohesive than before.

In a long-term historical context, "home-grown tobacco" in Prilep represents a divergence from the standard narrative of the rise of industrial work and waged labor, as told in classical social theory. Under socialism the pattern was basically the familiar one: peasants became wage-workers. They were increasingly disdainful of agricultural work, which they gradually abandoned, even if the break was not radical and elements of the old kinship ideology persisted among the smaller households of the city. Over the last twenty years, however, Prilep has seen a significant expansion of petty agricultural production based in the household. Like so many small-scale farmers elsewhere, money is their scarcest resource. Tobacco is grown to bring in the additional "coin" needed to pay debts and to survive. In order to produce and commercialize their cash crop, these urban households have to absorb part of their costs "at home" or "internalize" them, just like rural smallholders (Ortiz 1979). Through self-exploitation, facilitated by the persistence of house-based ritual that I have described in this chapter, urban families can participate in both wage-labor and agriculture. The two sectors are mutually dependent and subsidize each other, but they also deplete each other and reproduce long-term impoverishment.[19]

Notes

1. Field research took place in 2009–2010 in the context of the Economy and Ritual group. I am extremely grateful to Ljubco Risteski, Assistant Professor of Ethnology in the Ss. Cyril and Methodius University in Skopje and Sonja Zogovic, researcher at the Institute for Old-Slavic Culture in Prilep. I would not have been able to understand the complexity of the issues without my friends Dejan, Monica, and Milka Ilovi in Prilep. In addition to colleagues within the Economy and Ritual group, James Carrier, Gerald Creed, and Patrick Heady have provided helpful comments on drafts of this chapter. I thank them all.

2. The *slava* (the word literally means "glory" or "fame") can be celebrated at other levels but that of the house is by far the most important. This was already the case before the demise of socialism, at least in urban contexts. For classification and analysis of other subtypes of *slava* in more traditional contexts, see Rheubottom 1976: 21.

3. According to Yugoslav statistics, in 1978 there were 521,677 demands for new housing unfulfilled throughout the country (Cichock 1985: 214). In a sociological

study of the "housing problem" in socialist Hungary (late sixties), *Szelényi* (1983) argues that socialist policies on housing promoted a "new pattern of urban inequalities." Unlike what socialist propaganda claimed, the state-sponsored new housing was systematically allocated to the "middle class"—educated bureaucrats, intellectuals, and white-collar workers—and not to the "new proletarians" coming from villages. He draws on data collected by Yugoslav sociologists and economists in pointing out similar developments in Yugoslavia, referring to an existing "housing crisis."

4. The questionnaire instrument devised by the Economy and Ritual group was applied in the early months of 2010.

5. The production and manufacturing of the small-leaf oriental aromatic tobacco is the leading agriculture subsector in the Republic of Macedonia. From over 80,000 applications for agricultural subsidies submitted to the Ministry of Agriculture by 20 February 2009, referring to autumn crops, fruit trees, and cattle, around 26,000 were from tobacco-farming households. From those, more than half (17,000) were from the region of Prilep (*Macedonian Business Monthly,* February 2009). Production of raw tobacco increased considerably—from 16,200 tons in 2007 to 23,000 in 2009. The purchase of tobacco in 2009 was carried out by six registered tobacco companies under contracts with farmers (registered as households) and in accordance with the Law on Tobacco and Tobacco products (*Macedonian Business Monthly,* January 2011). For that season the highest average buyout price per kilo was of 200 denars (around 3 Euros before subsidy). The Union of Tobacco Producers' Associations estimated that for the 2009 season in Prilep between 1,000 and 2,000 women were engaged as daily laborers remunerated at 100 denars (around 1.70 Euros) per hour (Macedonian Information Agency, 18.09.2009).

6. In 2009 the unemployment in Macedonia stood at 32.2 percent (State Statistical Office). With its 39 percent unemployment rate, Prilep leads the country. The vast majority of the unemployed (82.5 percent) are between fifteen and twenty-five years old (Macedonian Information Agency, 14.01.2008).

7. After the collapse of the Ottoman Empire, Vardar Macedonia became a part of the Kingdom of Serbs, Croats, and Slovenes (1918), later called the Kingdom of Yugoslavia.

8. The urban population rose from 24,816 in 1948 to 60,474 in 1973 and 73,351 in the census of 2002.

9. The official national figure of around 15 percent concealed enormous regional variation. In 1984, registered unemployment in Macedonia was 21.1 percent, while in Slovenia it was a mere 1.5 percent.

10. In 1873 the *Régie Ottomane* des *Tabacs* based in Salonic opened the first warehouse in Prilep for the purchase and processing of tobacco. In 1925, during the "old Yugoslavia," the Tobacco Research Institute was founded, and it is still the main distributor of seeds for growers of the region. In 1949, the factory was nationalized and the tobacco industry diversified with a cigarette factory and new processing plants (Bunteski 1998).

11. The total number of households (*domacinstva*) growing irrigated and nonirrigated tobacco in Prilep's district dropped, between 1975 and 1980, from 12,550 to 9,447 (Koneski 2004: 64).

12. According to an expert's personal estimation, some 15,000 jobs throughout the city of Prilep depend in one way or another on the existence of the Kombinat. It is thought that if the government stopped maintaining the Kombinat artificially, the entire city would die out. Moreover, given that in the Tutunski most of the employees are husbands and wives, closing down would leave entire families without incomes. At the moment, Tutunski works as an intermediary by purchasing raw tobacco for the Swiss giant Sokotab, based in the city of Bitola where the primary processing takes place. Fermented tobacco is then transported to Greece where cigarettes are produced.

13. Józef Obrębski's monographs and articles on Macedonia, based on fieldwork undertaken in 1932–1933, are not translated into English (with the exception of one draft essay). I draw on materials in Macedonian (articles and field notes) translated from original materials in the "J. Obrębski special collection," University of Massachusetts, last accessed online at http://www.library.umass.edu/spcoll/umarmot/?p=204. Rheubottom worked in another region a generation later. He was unaware of Obrębski's work, and yet there are some striking resemblances in his analysis, as well as significant differences.

14. It is certainly not a coincidence that in 2006 Prilep municipality was the first in Macedonia to "invent" a new community ritual called "Town *slava*," with St. Nicholas as town saint protector. Since then five other towns have followed this example. The municipality chose St. Nicholas "because he is the most celebrated house patron saint in the region." Every year on 19 December a local industrial leader or businessman sponsors a large party in the town center, which includes free food and a public liturgy by a representative of the Macedonian Orthodox Church.

15. This is not to imply that "horizontal" transfers play no role at all; for example, a migrant worker in Germany may well send remittances to support a sibling.

16. More than 300 Prilep inhabitants were recruited for maritime work by the same foreign agency, leading to the quip "Prilep, city of sailors!" (Macedonia is a landlocked country.)

17. Respondents often said, "We don't earn money but it's worth doing the effort" (*nema pecalba, ama se isplakja*) when referring to calculations of monetary income minus all cash spent on production during the season. They make a clear distinction between "making a coin or more" (*da zemem nekoj denar*) and the concept of "profitability" (*profit*) or "money-making" (*pecalba*), which are used as synonyms (Monova 2013).

18. Part of the land legally belonged to Velika's brother, who had separated from his father's household decades before. Each year the brother delayed in giving his consent for relatives to use his plot, causing Velika to bemoan the fact that she, as a daughter, was not eligible to inherit land according to customary law.

19. A third component in the postsocialist equation in Prilep, which I cannot explore further in this chapter, is the mushrooming of highly exploitative textile workshops, controlled by managers who can disregard the law thanks to their close relations with local politicians. The infrastructure inherited from the socialist era has made Prilep an attractive location for the global garment industry, a development supported by the postsocialist state.

References

Cichock, Marc A. 1985. "Reevaluating a Development Strategy: Policy Implications for Yugoslavia." *Comparative Politics* 17, no. 2: 211–228.

Cohen, Myron. 1976. *House United, House Divided: The Chinese Family in Taiwan.* New York: Columbia University Press.

Gudeman, Stephen. 2008. *Economy's Tension: The Dialectics of Market and Economy.* New York and Oxford: Berghahn Books.

Gudeman, Stephen, and Alberto Rivera. 1990. *Conversations in Columbia: The Domestic Economy in Life and Text.* Cambridge: Cambridge University Press.

Halpern, Joel. 1967. *A Serbian Village: Social and Cultural Change in a Yugoslav Community.* New York: Harper.

Hammel, Eugene. 1968. *Alternative Social Structures and Ritual Relations in the Balkans.* Prentice-Hall, Inc., Englewood Cliffs, NJ: *Macedonian Business Monthly.* February 2009; January 2011.

Macedonian Information Agency, 14.01.2008; 19.09.2009.

Monova, Miladina. 2001. "De l'historicité à l'ethnicité: Les Égéens ou ces autres Macédonien," *Balkanologie* 5, no. 1–2: 179–197. In *Homelands in Question: Paradoxes of Memory and Exile in South-Eastern Europe,* ed. K. Brown. Paris, AFEBalk.

———. 2002. "De la logique de retour à la logique d'établissement: le cas des réfugiés de la Guerre civile grecque en République de Macédoine." *Études Balkaniques: Cahiers Pierre Belon* no. 9: 73–92, Paris.

———. 2013. "'We Are All Chasing after the Euro': Labour, Calculations and Ideas of Well-being among Tobacco Growers in a Macedonian Town." In *Social Practices and Local Configurations in the Balkans,* ed. N. Bardhoshi, G. de Rapper, P. Sintès. Actes de colloque, Tirana, UET Press: 115–129.

Obrębski, Józef. 1934. "Czarna Magja w Macedonii." In *Kurier Literacko—Naykowy,* dodatek do No. 111, "Ilustrowanego Kuriera Codziennego," 23.04.1934, s. VI-VIII.

———. 1936. "System relygijny macedonskiego," cz. 1–5. In *Kurier Literacko—Naykowy,* dodatek do No. 111 "Ilustrowanego Kuriera Codziennego," No. 24, 15.06.1936, s. XIII-XIV, nr 26, 29.06.1936, s. XIII.

———. 1977. "*Ritual and Social Structure in a Macedonian Village.*" In *Research Report* No. 16, ed. Barbara Kerewski Halpern and Joel M. Halpern, Department of Anthropology, Program in Soviet and East European Studies, University of Massachusetts at Amherst.

———. 2001a [1932, 1934, 1936]. *Фолклорни и етнографски материјали од Порече,* Кн. I. Ред: Т. Вражиновски, С. Јовановска, В. Караџоски, Институт за старословенска култура, Матица Македонска, Скопје—Прилеп (*Folkorni i etnografski materiali od Porece,* Tome 1., ed. T. Vrazinovski, S. Jovanovska, V. Karadzoski, Institut za Staroslovenska Kultura, Matica Makedonska, Skopje/Prilep).

———. 2001b [1932, 1934, 1936]. *Етносоциолошки студии,* Кн. II, Редакција и превод од полски јазик Т. Вражиновски, Матица Македонска, Скопје (*Etnosotsiolozki studii,* ed. and trans. T. Vrazinovski, Matica Makedonska, Skopje).

———. 2002 [1932, 1934, 1936]. *Етносоциолошки студии,* Кн. III, Редакција и превод од полски јазикТ. Вражиновски, Соработник и превод од англиски јазик

Л. Гушевска, Институт за старословенска култура—Матица Македонска, Скопје-Прилеп 2002. *Etnosotsiolozki studii,* (ed. and trans. from Polish T. Vrazinovski; trans. from English L. Gusevska), Institut za Staroslovenska Kultura, Matica Makedonska, Skopje/Prilep.

Ortiz, Sutti. 1979. "Expectations and Forecasts in the Face of Uncertainty." *Man* 14, no. 1: 64–80.

Ramet, Sabrina. P. 1985. *Yugoslavia in the 1980s.* Boulder and London: Westview.

Republic of Macedonia, State Statistical Office, Labor Force Survey, *News Release* No. 2.1.10.07.

Rheubottom, David. 1984 [1971]. *A Structural Analysis of Conflict and Cleavage in Macedonian Domestic Groups* (Ph.D. diss. University of Rochester), Ann Arbor, MI: University Microfilms.

———. 1976. "The Saint's Feast and Skopska Crna Goran Social Structure." *Man* 1: 18–34.

State Statistical Office, Labor Force Survey, *News Release* No: 2.1.10.07.

Szelényi, Ivan. 1983. *Urban Inequalities under State Socialism.* Oxford: Oxford University Press.

Woodward, Susan. 1995. *Unemployment: The Political Economy of Yugoslavia, 1945–1990.* Princeton, NJ: Princeton University Press.

Бунтески, Ристе. 1998. *Мателиалната положба на населението во Прилеп и Прилепско, 1870-1940,* Прилеп 1998 (Bunteski R., *Materialnata polozba na naselenieto vo Prilep i Prilepsko* (1870–1940)).

Конески, Методи. 2004. *Економски и општествен развој на Прилеп и Прилепско по ослободувањето: 1944-1990.* Друштво за наука и уметност, Прилеп (Koneski M., 2004. *Ekonomski i opstestven razvoj na Prilep i Prilepsko po osloboduvanjeto:* (1944–1990), Drustvo za nauka i umetnost).

▼ Appendix

The "Economy and Ritual" Project and the Field Questionnaire

The project ran officially from March 2009 to March 2012. We worked together at the Max Planck Institute for Social Anthropology in Halle (Germany) from March to July 2009, when the researchers began their field studies. Gudeman made field visits to Bulgaria, Kyrgyzstan, and Hungary, and the group met again in Macedonia in January 2010. The team members spent differing amounts of time in the field, as they describe, but all returned to Halle by autumn 2010. The writing up was sometimes punctuated by our eight different understandings of the ethnographies, but that enriched the results. Versions of the book chapters were presented to various audiences, in Halle and elsewhere.

The project's core theme was not the only topic covered during the field research. Apart from individual subprojects, several members encountered widespread use (or desuetude in the case of the village where Vidacs worked) of the godparenthood complex, which has drawn relatively less attention in European than in Latin American anthropology. To develop this part of the research, which is not reported in this book, we met in September 2011 at the Max Planck Institute to present papers and discuss the topic of "Contemporary Ritual Kinship." A number of scholars from parts of Europe joined us to present their findings as well. A selection of these essays is being prepared for publication as a Special Issue of the *Journal of Family History*, edited by Monica Vasile.

As a result of our initial theoretical work together and the ethnographic findings, the entire team became interested in the different ways that models of "self-sufficiency" are enacted in the house, broader communities, and nation-states where the researchers worked. In November 2011 the group offered a session in Montreal entitled "Between Autonomy and Connection: Changing Ideas and Practices of Self-sufficiency in Postsocialist Eurasia." Revised versions of these essays will be published shortly as the second volume in this series under the title *Oikos and Market: Explorations of Self-Sufficiency after Socialism*.

From the beginning of our work together in Halle we gave considerable attention to devising common and comparative questions and a field questionnaire. During our meeting in Macedonia in January 2010, we developed the following questionnaire that everyone subsequently used:

Household #			Date of Interview	
Members of Household	1 (Respondent)	2	3	4
Age				
Gender				
Marital Status				
Currently resident?				

Instructions:
1) Household means people living under one roof. If this is inapplicable, redefine as most appropriate.
2) Sample should be random selection.
3) Interview head of household.
4) Add additional columns and rows in all charts (including above) as necessary.

SECTION I: ECONOMIC OVERVIEW

A. SOURCES OF SUPPORT FOR HOUSEHOLD

What are the different sources of support for you and your family?

1. What are the different **sources of money** for you and your household? (Yes/No; quantify and identify type of activity if possible)

	Yes/No	Identify type of activity and quantify if possible
Wages or salaries (cash income for labor; including irregular work)		
Pensions (work and medical)		
Unemployment benefits		
Other social benefits		
Income from other sources (farming, selling things grown or made, business, tourists)		
Other		

1A. Which of these is most important for your household?

2. What other ways do you provide for the needs of your household? (**non-money**) Do you:

	Yes/No	Identify type of activity and quantify if possible
Raise animals for home use		
Grow food for home use		
Make things for home use (sew, carpentry, repairs)		
Collect things for home use (fruits, wood, mushrooms, herbs)		
Hunt, fish		
Barter		

3. How do other people help you to provide the needs for your household? Do you:

	Yes/No	Identify type of activity and quantify if possible
Hire people (incl. for day labor)		
Engage in labor exchange (i.e. receive help from others)		
Share "cooperative" care of animals, land, etc.		
Other		

4. Do other people give you or your household:

	Yes/No	Identify type of activity and quantify if possible
"Gifts"		
Food		
Assistance		
Lend tools or equipment		

5. Have you ever taken a loan in money?
   If yes,

	when	for what	amount	from whom
Ex. 1				
Ex. 2				

6. Have you ever made a loan in money?
   If yes,

	when	for what	amount	from whom
Ex. 1				
Ex. 2				

7. What kinds of things do you usually borrow from other people?

8. Is there anything you would not loan to another person?

9. Do you have savings in money? If not, did you have savings in money in the past?

10. Do you put money together with other members of the household? Do you have a common purse?

B. MARKETS

1. What things (e.g. among your personal/household possessions) would you not sell? (Prompt: something you sold but did not want to, or now regret)

2. What should the community (village) not sell? (Prompt: an example of things that were sold, but should not have been)

3. What should the state not sell? (Prompt: an example of things that were sold, but should not have been; feelings about privatization)

C. CELEBRATIONS AND RITUALS

1. Participation of members of your household in celebrations/rituals/events in the **past year**?

Celebrations/ Rituals/Events (to be listed)	What happened?	Did you organize?	Did you attend? (organized by someone else)	Was it expensive (for your household)? (y/n)	Did the occasion involve gifts? (y/n)

2. If respondent is or was married, when was your wedding? How many people attended?

D. MANAGING ECONOMIC LIFE

1. Do you have a reserve of:

	Yes/No	Additional Details (type, quantity)
Food		
Drink		
Animal food		
Fuel/Firewood		
Other (incl purchased goods)		

2. What was the most expensive purchase you made last year?

3. How much do you pay for: (make sure to indicate whether monthly, yearly, etc.)

Electric	Gas	Water	Phone	Mobile	TV	Internet	Garbage Collection	Other	Other

4. In the past year, how much did your household spend on health, medicine, and doctors?

5. Does your household purchase insurance of any kind? If not, would you like to?

6. Does your household keep financial records of any kind?

7. In the past year, did your household spend money on holidays, restaurants, bars, concerts? (Prompt: ask about House of Culture events, trips to the city)
8. Have you ever donated money?

E. If you suddenly got (price of a 2 room apartment in the capital) what would you do with it?

F. Questions Specific to Ethnographer

SECTION II: OTHER TOPICS TO FOLLOW UP INFORMALLY

A. Sharing

B. Gifts

C. Comparative information about socialist period, transition years, and present

Contributors

Jennifer Cash received her Ph.D. in Anthropology from Indiana University. Before joining the Economy and Ritual project she held teaching positions at Indiana University, Franklin College, the University of Pittsburgh, and University College London. She is the author of *Villages on Stage: Folklore and Nationalism in the Republic of Moldova* (2011).

Stephen Gudeman, Professor of Anthropology at the University of Minnesota, has undertaken fieldwork in several countries of Latin America. During 2008–2012 he was co-Director of the Economy and Ritual project at the Max Planck Institute for Social Anthropology in Halle (Germany). Gudeman has published extensively in journals and written or edited eight books, the most recent of which are *Economy's Tension* (2008) and *Economic Persuasions* (2009).

Chris Hann is a Founding Director of the Max Planck Institute for Social Anthropology at Halle. He formerly taught anthropology at the Universities of Cambridge and Kent (Canterbury). Hann has published extensively on Eastern Europe, both before and after the collapse of socialism. He is co-author of *Economic Anthropology: History, Ethnography, Critique* (2011) and co-editor of *Market and Society: The Great Transformation Today* (2009) (both with Keith Hart).

Nathan Light, currently a guest researcher in the Department of Linguistics and Philology at Uppsala University, Sweden, received his Ph.D. in Folklore from Indiana University. He has taught widely in history, folklore, anthropology, and sociology at the University of Toledo, American University-Central Asia, and elsewhere. His publications include the volume *Intimate Heritage: Creating Uyghur Muqam Song in Xinjiang* (2008) and numerous articles on Central Asian society, culture, and history.

Miladina Monova holds a Ph.D. in Social Anthropology from the École des Hautes Études en Sciences Sociales, Paris, based on a study of Greek refugees in Yugoslav Macedonia. She has taught anthropology at the University of Lille 1, and held Fellowships at Collegium Budapest, the École Française d'Athènes, and the Center of Advanced Studies in Sofia. She has published extensively in the fields of refugee studies and ethnicity and nationalism in the Balkans.

Detelina Tocheva received her Ph.D. in Social Anthropology from the École des Hautes Études en Sciences Sociales with a study of child protection in Estonia. Her first postdoctoral project, also based at the Max Planck Institute for Social Anthropology, concerned post-Soviet Russian Orthodoxy in northwestern Russia. She has published numerous papers on these subjects in journals such as *Anthropological Quarterly* and *European Journal of Sociology*.

Monica Vasile, currently a Research Fellow at the Integrative Research Institute on Human-Environment Systems, Humboldt University, Berlin, holds a Ph.D. in Sociology from the University of Bucharest. Her first postdoctoral position was at the Max Planck Institute for the Study of Societies, Cologne. She has published numerous articles in books and scholarly journals, on topics related to forest commons, property relations, corruption, and environmental conservation.

Bea Vidacs, currently a Senior Researcher in the East-West Research Center on the Ethnology of Religion at the University of Pécs, Hungary, was educated in Budapest and London and holds a doctorate in Anthropology from the City University of New York. She has carried out field research in Cameroon and Hungary and taught anthropology in the United States and in Hungary. She is the author of *Visions of a Better World: Football in the Cameroonian Social Imagination* (2010).

Index